Lust & Philosophy. A novel

The Exact Unknown and Other Tales of Modern China

Massage and the Writer: Essays on Asian Massage

At the Teahouse Café: Essays on the Middle Kingdom

American Rococo: Essays on the Edge

The Kitchens of Canton. A novel

Confucius and Opium: China Book Reviews

The Mustachioed Woman of Shanghai. A novel

SEXUAL FASCISM

ESSAYS

BY

ISHAM COOK

Magic Theater Books

ISBN-13: 9781732277465
ISBN-10: 173227746X

Cover design by Wang Chen

All photos by Isham Cook unless otherwise indicated

Printed in the United States
Magic Theater Books

www.ishamcook.com

DEDICATED TO

THE VICTIMS OF SEXUAL FASCISM

CONTENTS

Introduction 1

1 Sexual Surveillance in the Age of Covid-19 11

2 The Sewage System, or What Is Fascism? 31

3 The State of Rage: The American Sexual Dystopia . . . 69

4 An American Talisman 84

5 Toilet Terror 92

6 American Massage 113

7 Massage diary: Laos, Thailand, Cambodia, Vietnam . . 130

8 The Breasts of Bali: An Update 150

9 A Modest Proposal Regarding Sex Work:
Why All Sex Should Be Paid For 173

10 Transgressions: From Porn to Polyamory 192

Bibliography 225

1. Free distribution of contraceptives to those who could not obtain them through normal channels; massive propaganda for birth control.
2. Abolition of laws against abortion. Provision for free abortions at public clinics; financial and medical safeguards for pregnant and nursing mothers.
3. Abolition of any legal distinctions between the married and the unmarried. Freedom of divorce. Elimination of prostitution though economic and sex-economic changes to eradicate its causes.
4. Elimination of venereal diseases by full sexual education.
5. Avoidance of neuroses and sexual problems by a life-affirmative education. Study of principles of sexual pedagogy. Establishment of therapeutic clinics.
6. Training of doctors, teachers, social workers, and so on, in all relevant matters of sexual hygiene.
7. Treatment rather than punishment for sexual offenses. Protection of children and adolescents against adult seduction.

Wilhelm Reich's Seven-Point Program, First Congress of the German Association for Proletarian Sex-Politics, Düsseldorf, 1931. (cited in Sharaf)

INTRODUCTION

GIVEN THE AMBIGUITY of the phrase "sexual fascism," I'd like to start off by stating what I do *not* mean by it. This book is not an investigation into what's sexy about fascism, nor is it a toolkit for employing sex, or repressing it, in the service of fascism; those drawn to my title in this frame of mind need not read further. I resolutely support sexual equality and freedom, and I am not a fascist in any way, shape, or form. My book would qualify for book burning if the practice ever came back. It's been a while, but oh yes, we had them. The last major book burning was carried out by Food and Drug Administration agents on August 23, 1956, *six tons* of Wilhelm Reich's books tossed into the Gansevoort public incinerator in New York.

Sexual fascism can be defined as sexual repression with fascist characteristics. To unpack this a bit, it is how the fascist state employs sexuality to extend its control over the population. One might demand to know which "state" I'm referring to, as there is no longer any overt, full-blown fascist state on the model of WWII-era Germany, Italy, and Japan. As an historical phenomenon fascism may seem of little relevance to sexual politics in today's world. But this view hinges on a narrow definition of the term, one that identifies fascism only with its triumphant outcome, when fascists succeed in taking over a nation and coming into unchecked power. Of course, in the decades since the mid-last century there have been no shortage of brutal, totalitarian dictatorships—North Korea being the preeminent dystopian exemplar. The difference is that they don't call themselves "fascist" anymore. Post-WWII realpolitik has shorn the word of its former appeal, and "ethno-nationalism" serves as the current euphemism.

An alternative is to view fascism as a process, that of *fascist politics*, an expandable platform employed by rightwing extremists for leveraging ever-greater influence and ultimately total power over the population, as well as the fate of perceived antagonists domestic and foreign. With Trump's America in mind, Jason Stanley has provided in *How Fascism Works* perhaps the most concise definition ever penned: "A distinguishing mark of fascist politics is the targeting of ideological enemies and the freeing of all restraints in combating them." And although Robert O. Paxton's definition in *The Anatomy of Fascism* was meant to characterize the earlier 20th-century prototype, it's not farfetched to assume we came perilously close to seeing its realization had Trump won reelection in 2020:

> [Fascism is] a form of political behavior marked by obsessive preoccupation with community decline, humiliation or victimhood, and by compensatory cults of unity, energy and purity, in which a mass-based party of committed nationalist militants, working in uneasy but effective collaboration with traditional elites, abandons democratic liberties and pursues with redemptive violence and without ethical or legal restraints goals of internal cleansing and external expansion.

Defining *sexual fascism* hinges on whether we treat it as a psycho-political or purely as a political phenomenon. Psychologically speaking, it designates the constrained habits and behavior people display due to cultural and ideological conditioning under the patriarchal state. The study of the unconscious acquisition of sexual strictures through collective indoctrination began with

Wilhelm Reich, notably in *The Mass Psychology of Fascism* (published in 1933). As he wrote, the state reproduces its structure in miniature in the family, with the father deemed the natural head of the household and the mother fulfilling a subservient yet vital role as birth-provider:

> The authoritarian state gains an enormous interest in the authoritarian family: it becomes the factory in which the state's structure and ideology are molded….The suppression of the natural sexuality of children and adolescents serves to mold the human structure in such a way that masses of people become willing upholders and reproducers of mechanistic authoritarian civilization….Wholly unconscious of what they are doing, the parents carry out the intentions of authoritarian society.

As Stanley adds, "To boost the nation, fascist movements are obsessed with reversing declining birthrates; large families raised by dedicated homemakers are the goal." Hence the constant nostalgia among the conservative right for a return to the "family values" of motherhood, fertility, and Christian piety (what Reich termed "mystical contagion"). Feminism, conversely, is held to be the single greatest threat to the family, as even conservatism's upholders understand that "sexually awakened women, affirmed and recognized as such, would mean the complete collapse of the authoritarian ideology…To define freedom is to define sexual health. But no one wants to state it openly" (Reich).

Politically speaking, sexual fascism proceeds from the ensemble of judicial and carceral measures employed by the state to discipline the population in the most intimate aspects of their lives. While freedom of sexual choice and expression has in the modern democracies steadily increased over the past one hundred years, the United States, as will be examined in the chapters that follow, presents a contradictory phenomenon, retreating in as many ways as it has advanced. How far we are from genuine erotic liberation was strikingly articulated by the American feminist Shulamith Firestone in *The Dialectic of Sex* (1970). Her mapping out of the future post-bourgeois family remains as relevant today as it was half a century ago, though it is as radically removed from the patriarchy of her—and our—era as Friedrich Engels' *Origin of the Family, Private Property and the State* (1884) was from his. As Firestone imagined it, children would have an independent legal and sexual status far beyond what even the most progressive thinkers would dare envision today, above all with her rejection of the age of consent:

> The concept of childhood has been abolished, children having full political, economic, and sexual rights, their educational/work activities no different from those of adults. During the few years of their infancy we have replaced the psychologically destructive genetic "parenthood" of one or two arbitrary adults with a diffusion of the responsibility for physical welfare over a larger number of people. The child would still form intimate love relationships, but instead of developing close ties with a decreed "mother" and "father," the child might now form those ties with people of his own choosing, of whatever age or sex. Thus all adult-child relationships will have been mutually chosen—equal, intimate relationships free of material dependencies. Correspondingly, though children would be fewer, they would not be monopolized, but would mingle freely throughout the society to the benefit of all.

Her era's idealism, one might say naivete, allowed Firestone to push a rhetoric of gender liberation to a logical extreme, one that, ironically, returns full circle to pre-1880s America, when children were indeed treated as little adults and regarded as wholly capable of giving their consent in marriage as young as ten or twelve (seven in Delaware). Since that time, the legal age of consent has risen across the board from ten to twelve to fourteen to sixteen in most of Europe and sixteen to eighteen in the Anglo countries, including the U.S. Yet it is in exactly these countries, in spite of or because of their strict sex offense laws, that teenage sexuality seems hardest to control. It is doubly ironic that in the most punitive of lands, the USA, teenagers as old as seventeen are legally defined as children incapable of sexual consent, but when it comes to their own infractions, teenagers are considered to be fully aware of what they are doing and are punished as adults. Long before they reach legal age or have any conception of what the sex offender registry is, they find themselves on it; seven states place children as young as seven or eight on the registry (Stillman, "The List").[1]

Sexual fascism becomes sexual terror when its impact permeates society to the degree that it merges with other forms of terror to deepen and intensify society's collective fear. As pro-sex feminist Gayle Rubin wrote in her prescient 1982 essay, "Thinking sex: Notes for a radical theory of the politics of sexuality,"

> [U.S.] sex law is harsh. The penalties for violating sex statutes are universally out of proportion to any social or individual harm....The law is especially ferocious in maintaining the boundary between childhood "innocence" and "adult" sexuality. Rather than recognizing the sexuality of the young and attempting to provide for it in a caring and responsible manner, our culture denies and punishes erotic interest and activity by anyone under the local age of consent. The amount of law devoted to protecting young people from premature exposure to sexuality is breathtaking.

In the decades since, sex laws have only proliferated, in conse-

---

[1] This cultural schizophrenia goes back to the colonial era when American adolescents were simultaneously encouraged and forbidden to have sex in the bizarre practice of "bundling"—letting teenage couples spend the night together with a board placed between them on the bed.

quence of regular sex panics that seem to spring out of nowhere but from deep within the national psyche, beginning in the late 1980s with alleged Satanic ritual abuse in daycare centers and recently resurrected in fresh guise in QAnoners' accusations of Satanic baby-eating by the Democrat elite. The sex offender registry, a sinister apparatus of state-sponsored grassroots terror George Orwell couldn't have dreamt up, took shape over these decades following the Jacob Wetterling Act of 1994, Megan's Law of 1996, and the Adam Walsh Act of 2006, each named after a high-profile pedophile murder.

Another current of American sexual terror goes back to the Mann Act or White-Slave Traffic Act of 1910 and concerns commercial sex. Originally intended to keep tabs on the brothels and the women allegedly trafficked into them, it expanded into comprehensive police surveillance directed against adulterers and elopers who crossed state lines or traveled anywhere in order to have sex; unmarried couples could be arrested for checking into a hotel room together even without crossing state lines (Rubin). In other words, the term "trafficking" was stretched to mean any form of illicit sex. The Mann Act remains very much alive today, though "trafficking," a classic floating signifier, has once again changed its meaning to suit the designs of self-righteous, opportunistic, power-hungry politicians, evangelicals, and "carceral feminists" (to use Elizabeth Bernstein's term). Properly defined, trafficking refers to the global underground trade in arms, drugs, and humans (the latter including but not limited to sex workers, both the willing and the duped). Now it designates any commercial sexual activity, and "traffickers" any and all customers of sex work, down to porn viewers in the confines of their home, since as consumers they sustain and promote the trade with their purchases, whereas sex workers are supposedly trafficked into the trade against their will and are therefore victims in urgent need of rescue, regardless of whether they entered into sex work of their own accord. There is a clear intent to this Newspeak, for what better way to frighten people off porn if they are made to feel complicit in the enslavement of the performers they are viewing? Once the net is cast so widely as to encompass the entire sex industry, millions of consumers are thus implicated in illicit activity and live under the shadow of suspicion, with potentially punitive consequences. Carceral feminists allied with Christian activists, to cite Bernstein,

> have come to foster an alliance with neoliberal consumer politics and a militarized state apparatus that utilizes claims of a particular white, middle-class model of Western gender and sexual superiority in achieving its goals [of] the postindustrial security state....Sex trafficking and surveillance have in fact become co-constitutive, with sex trafficking reciprocally serving to moralize the extension of new modes of surveillance....Evidence of this increasing institutionalization also exists in the growing numbers of anti-trafficking divisions of police departments and law enforcement-led "anti-trafficking taskforces" that have sprung up around the nation, an institutional arrangement which, like the founding of the Federal Bureau of Investigation during early 20th-century campaigns against white slavery, is likely to prove lasting in its effects.

The USA is well situated to test out hypotheses on sexual fascism because no other developed country in the world is as repressive. If this comes as a surprise, one of the most sophisticated means of advancing sexual fascism in our time is through mass media conditioning which celebrates, precisely, the opposite: sexual freedom. The country is drenched in sexual imagery, much of which functions to indoctrinate children and teenagers in cosmetics regimens and courtship rituals so as to develop their "sex appeal," while providing the rest of the population an illusion of unbridled sexual expression in pornography, both the explicit and the tamer, disguised varieties in film, TV, and the fashion media. Not that this freewheeling deluge is necessarily always a bad thing, but we shouldn't be surprised if it causes people to be more obsessed with sex than they would otherwise be.

To start off the book with the present dystopian state of affairs, Chapter 1 "Sexual surveillance in the age of Covid-19" compares different approaches to social and sexual control in China and the USA and speculates on the future. Chapter 2 "The sewage system, or What is fascism?" looks backward to the early 20th-century and forward into the twenty-first to chart the achievements of fascist violence. Fascist forces in the U.S., long ensconced in Republican states, are brandishing their clout with greater openness and shamelessness, most recently in their coordinated efforts to erode abortion rights. Chapter 3 "The state of rage: The American sexual dystopia," Chapter 4 "Toilet terror," Chapter 5 "An American talisman," and Chapter 6 "American massage" illustrate the ease with which ordinary Americans can get into serious sexual trouble who in almost any other country would be insulated or protected from the same.

One predominant feature of contemporary social reportage is the artificial construct and affected narrative pose of so-called "objectivity," an authorial stance supposedly inoculated against personal bias, as if nobody can be trusted to provide an authentic account of anything without it. Emphatically dangerous territory is firsthand reporting on sexual experience, which is seen to be automatically tainted and the author implicated in pejorative or harmful, possibly exploitative activity, all the more so if he is male. But I've long believed that by avoiding the controversial, authors compromise their integrity. The antidote to this internalized fascism is to remove the barbed wire from the brain and confront the demon head-on. I proudly insert myself into the narrative in Chapter 6 "American massage"; Chapter 7 "Massage diary: Laos, Thailand, Cambodia, Vietnam," four countries which present an instructive contrast to the U.S. in their greater degree of sexual freedoms; Chapter 8 "The breasts of Bali," which looks at historical attitudes to public nudity; and Chapter 9 "A modest proposal regarding sex work: Why all sex should be paid for," a Swiftian satirical take on prostitution, also to be taken at face value as an innovative proposal that will never come to pass yet would be highly illuminating if it did. The situation is not monolithic. There remains indeed much genuine sexual expression in the U.S., all worth fighting for and preserving. Chapter 10 "Transgressions: From porn to polyamory" looks at the trials and tribulations of the current sexual avant-garde in the U.S.

I would like to acknowledge the valuable contributions from people who have helped illumine my path in this pioneer territory: the many sexually liberated women I have known over the years (who always seem to outnumber the men), particularly during my last (going on) three decades in China, the friendly sex workers who have reaffirmed for me the rightness of their profession when practiced on their own terms, and the generous critiques of early readers unintimidated by the title of my book, the authors Arthur Meursault and F. E. Beyer and the video artist Burbex (www.youtube.com/c/burbex).

1

SEXUAL SURVEILLANCE IN THE AGE OF COVID-19

XINJIANG PROVINCE, the world's most advanced security state, provides a window onto what the future holds if the world takes a more dystopian turn. It wasn't always like this. I've been visiting the Chinese province since the 1990s, when it was quite the freewheeling place, more so than the rest of the country.[2] My first visit, in 1995, took me and my then Chinese girlfriend to Urumqi, Turpan, Kashgar, and Kuqa, the latter three cities predominantly Uyghur. The capital Urumqi's population at that time was split between the Muslim Uyghurs and Han Chinese—the latter increasing at the expense of the indigenous Uyghurs throughout the province. It was a strange and fascinating place. Apart from a few air travel routes, sleeper buses outfitted with

---

[2] A colorful account of hashish running in the Xinjiang wild west of the 1980s is provided by Robert H. Davies' *Prisoner 13498: A True Story of Love, Drugs and Jail in Modern China* (Mainstream Publishing, 2002).

narrow bunks and old repurposed school buses were the only means of transportation around the province, at times trudging along the desert floor when blowing sand obscured the roads, as we sat upright on the hard seats, sometimes for overnight hauls, and were served the same stir-fried udon-like noodles with mutton and green peppers in tomato sauce and disks of salty *naan* flatbread for breakfast, lunch, and dinner at makeshift restaurant stops manned by quaint dusty-clothed folk looking right out of the nineteenth-century American West, many of them Caucasian-featured.

Kashgar is in the province's far west and was then a major gateway to Central and South Asia. Buses took backpackers down to Karachi on the scenically spectacular Karakoram Highway and brought Pakistani merchants up to Kashgar. We met all types, including Tilmann Waldthaler, a published travel writer from Germany, who was biking across Asia all the way from Hong Kong. In those days few Western restaurants in China had palatable food, but the banana pancakes at the local backpacker hangout, the open-air John's Cafe across the street from the Seman Hotel where everyone stayed, did the job.

In the decades since, I've made frequent business trips from Beijing to Urumqi. Over these years, Han-Uyghur relations went into a downward spiral in the face of police repression and campaigns to subjugate Uyghur culture, suppress their language, and flatten their ethnicity down to a few anodyne signifiers— costumed dance routines jostling among those of other "minority nationalities" for the amusement of Chinese TV audiences. In the 1990s, Beijing had two lively Uyghur streets, in the Ganjiakou and Weigongcun communities, each with scores of restaurants. They seemed to have brought over whole neighborhoods, baking *naan* loaves in medieval-looking streetside ovens, slaughtering sheep right out on the street (requiring bike riders to maneuver around the pools of blood), and shouting "Hashish! Hashish!"—a staple of Uyghur culture—at any foreigner passing by, since they knew we understood the universal Arabic word and the Chinese didn't. Yet already at that time rumors swirled among the Han that the Uyghurs were poisoning their dishes with marijuana to addict them (the Chinese fearfully regard all illegal drugs as the same; cannabis is not distinguished from heroin or cocaine). If any dishes had been infused with cannabis I would have noticed, as I often ate at their restaurants. Uyghur males could be seen at street corners slicing off pieces of *qiegao* cake from a huge slab on their bicycle carts, made of golden raisins, dates, walnuts, sesame, and the Osmanthus flower, something like an energy bar but richer and thicker, requiring a cleaver to cut through. By the turn of the century, the thousands of Uyghurs in Beijing were booted out and sent back to Xinjiang. Today a few token Uyghur restaurants remain in the major cities, mostly run by the Hui, China's other Muslim group, who have long been pacified by the Han and rendered politically harmless. The Hui have their mosques and strictly avoid pork, but that's about it. Intermarriage with the Han is fairly common, and I've known Hui whom I never realized were Hui until they told me. That's the outcome the Chinese Government intends for the Uyghurs.

Around the time of the Beijing 2008 Olympics, tensions exploded in a series of vicious terrorist attacks on Han civilians by Uyghurs affiliated with the East Turkestan Islamic Movement. The Government's "Strike Hard Campaign" managed to quell further attacks after 2015. In the years since, accounts in Xinjiang have trickled out to form a picture of extreme, North Korean-style repression, the wholesale punishment of an entire ethnic group: at least a million Uyghurs cycled through re-education camps, many kept there indefinitely and tortured, and throughout Xinjiang, males forbidden from growing beards, females forbidden from veiling their face and forcibly sterilized, praying in mosques curtailed, the Uyghur language banished from schools, and passports to travel abroad no longer issued.[3]

---

[3] As bad as the Uyghur repression is, we might instructively compare it to the U.S. Government's method for containing Native Americans. Both

Another casualty of the Campaign has been the province-wide, seemingly permanent implementation of a security state with an unprecedented level of physical and electronic surveillance, affecting the entire population. Uyghurs are singled out for much more comprehensive scrutiny than the Han, but during the post-crackdown period, the internet in Xinjiang was cut off completely, as I discovered on one visit to Urumqi around five years ago. That was eventually lifted; it had to be if the Government wanted to keep encouraging Han migration to Xinjiang. International news and social media sites are blocked in China; it's no longer a question of which sites are blocked but which sites are not blocked. Still, one easily gets around this by a VPN. In Xinjiang, VPNs don't work as well, and stop working altogether during crackdowns. (This establishes that VPNs are only allowed to operate in China at the grace of the Government, which could stamp them out if they so choose but for the present has decided not to alienate domestics and foreigners dependent upon VPNs for international communications.)

On my most recent trip to Urumqi, in early December 2019, the coronavirus was coursing through Wuhan though no one knew it yet. My five-star hotel had airport-like security in the lobby that we had to pass through. After my first day of work to visit the downtown area to find a restaurant and back to my hotel, I encountered three startling sights. They illustrated the new security state so serendipitously it was as if I had been on a guided tour by boastful apparatchiks for my edification. First, to get from my workplace (a university) to the restaurant, I had to pass through six security checkpoints, starting with the entrance to a subway station (subway checks are already routine in Chi-

---

groups comprise about one percent of their national populations, thus small enough not to present a threat (particularly after past extermination drives). Corralling Native Americans into tiny reservations a fraction the size of their original land and pacifying them with a culture of addiction in the form of casinos, alcohol, and opiates does not, to my mind, constitute a substantial improvement over the Chinese approach.

nese cities). Most of the other checkpoints were in intersection underpasses. I couldn't walk across the city unhindered but repeatedly had to open my backpack to a guard's gaze or put it through an X-ray scanner; each checkpoint also required me to pull down my N95 face mask (for air pollution) so that the face-recognition camera could read me. It was the last two checkpoints, however, I found most confounding. The main downtown drag was sectioned off block by block, with tents set up at each intersection which pedestrians had to pass through in order to proceed to the next block, while every department store or shopping center had its own checkpoint upon entering. Nothing remotely like this had been in place on any of my previous trips to Xinjiang.

Next, I decided to walk all the way back to the hotel. It was a long walk, some ten kilometers, my main form of daily exercise. As I was passing through a nondescript residential neighborhood lined with small shops and eateries, a large white van screeched to a halt on the opposite side of the street and police or security guards poured out bearing truncheons. At the same moment, female Uyghur shopkeepers in traditional headscarves emerged bearing poles. It seemed someone was being subdued, but with the van blocking my view (not wanting to get any closer and drawing attention to myself), I couldn't make out what was happening. The disturbance suddenly stopped. The guards lined up at attention and the shopkeepers stood in place still pointing their poles, as the head policeman gave them a speech. I had stumbled upon, I realized, an anti-terrorism drill. Presumably, the shopkeepers had been warned in advance so that they could perform on cue.

Finally, on a street not far from the hotel, I was passing by a small police substation, more of a police box, when a Uyghur officer emerged with an intent expression. Right outside the station stood one of the countless surveillance cameras you see on streets and buildings in China. In Urumqi, they appeared every fifty meters or so and many had multiple lenses for high-

resolution facial recognition. The cop paid me no attention. He
held a large, formal portrait-style photo of a man up in view of
the camera, and thereupon disappeared back into the station. I
tried to figure out what he was doing. They were looking for
someone and the cameras weren't turning up any matches, so the
man's portrait was fed to the camera to better sync the system,
though the question remains why this needed to be done manual-
ly instead of digitally uploading the portrait into the database;
perhaps the cop had just gotten his hands on this particular portrait and didn't have a scanner.

The thought occurred to me, and could not fail to occur to anyone in my place, that this is the future. Don't think it couldn't
happen in the West: in the U.S., face-recognition cameras have
been installed on city streets for years, and all it would take is a
major national disturbance or calamity to bump surveillance
measures up to state-of-emergency mode. Thankfully, the rest of
China at that moment was comparatively relaxed. If face-
recognition surveillance was running in the background and the
technology ever experimented with, upgraded, and perfected, you
wouldn't know it, as long as you stayed out of trouble. And there
was an evident upside to the technology that was enjoying popular support: a reduction in street crime. Yet I wondered, was all
the surveillance in Xinjiang not really, or not just, about the repression of the Uyghurs but rather something else? The unrest
and terrorism provided the authorities with the occasion to turn
the province into a giant laboratory for developing the ultimate
security state. The population's freedom may be curtailed a bit,
but their sacrifice is for the benefit of the nation. It's only a matter of time before this massive surveillance apparatus is rolled
out across the country, inevitably so in the event of a national
emergency.

Even without a national emergency, would any government
really want to subject its people to the same treatment as Xinjiang? The Uyghurs have it bad enough, but more than half of
the province's 25 million consists of Han and other ethnicities, all

of whom must put up with the daily hassles of increasingly omnipresent and omniscient surveillance, their cities partitioned
into multiplying border checkpoints. Even after acclimatizing
oneself to all of this in the interest of getting through the day,
what kind of long-term psychological impact follows from having
to repress the effects of living in an urban environment that feels
like an airport, where you must repeatedly go through X-ray security to cross from one neighborhood or street to another? This
is enforced neurosis on a massive, institutionalized scale, and a
human rights aberration.

From technology's standpoint, what happened next was a
godsend, the green light to expand the surveillance laboratory
nationwide: Covid-19. [4]

THE CASE OF CHINA

If there is such a thing as a politico-sexual Rubicon beyond which
there is no turning back, it's going to be when the state removes
your right to privacy in the last redoubt: public restrooms, changing rooms, hotel rooms, and your own home—places where nakedness occurs and surveillance cameras are normally out of
reach. Up until the Covid-19 outbreak, no state had ever dared
breach this line. It existed only in the realm of fiction, most fa-
mously the 24-hour two-way "telescreen" installed inside every
home in George Orwell's novel *1984*, enabling the government to
peep into citizens' private lives. Because the idea is so repugnant,
even tyrannical dictatorships are loath to cross this line. To
maintain its legitimacy, the state relies on a base of popular sup-

---

[4] Post-publication note: It is indeed happening, and as Chinese author
Murong Xuecun (*Deadly Quiet City*) laments, much faster than anyone
could have realized: "The pandemic did a huge favor to the Chinese
Communist Party, which took the opportunity to expand its power infi-
nitely" (Li Yuan, "Has Shanghai Been Xinjianged?" *The New York
Times*, 6 May 2022).

port, which risks being eroded altogether in the face of a measure
so drastic that no plausible justification for it exists. That's why
Orwell's classic dystopia is regarded as too exaggerated to ever
come to pass in reality, as satire is designed to be.

Recently, a CNN news report revealed police in China's
Jiangsu Province to be engaging in this very measure, installing
surveillance cameras inside people's homes (Gan). They weren't
dissidents under house arrest (who are almost certainly surrounded with such cameras), but ordinary people, coronavirus-
free workers returning to the city of Changzhou after months of
lockdown in their hometowns. In-home cameras were necessary,
the police argued, to monitor their two-week stay-at-home orders
because placing them outside their front door, as some apartment complexes in Chinese cities were doing at the time, subjected them to vandalism.

Local authorities have long reached their tentacles into Chinese people's private lives to an extent scarcely tolerated in the
rest of the world. This is due to a traditional absence of privacy
rights in China, particularly since 1949. Few older Chinese have
experienced "privacy" as Westerners understand it, having only
ever known narrow quarters crammed with extended families,
members of multiple generations occupying the same bedroom
and even the same bed, packed student and worker dormitories,
and other sardine-tin communal arrangements. In recent decades nuclear families have achieved greater privacy as housing
capacity has expanded, but people are otherwise accustomed to
routine encroachments into their personal lives by nosy neighbors, neighborhood committees, and the police. Yet although the
Chinese may have a higher tolerance for privacy intrusion, in-
home video surveillance is clearly overreach. One resident inter-
viewed in the CNN report was "furious." The police had positioned the camera across his apartment toward his front door so
that he was always in its view while in his living room. It "had a
huge impact on me psychologically," he said. "I tried not to make
phone calls, fearing the camera would record my conversations

by any chance. I couldn't stop worrying even when I went to sleep, after I closed the bedroom door." The Changzhou police were put on the defensive and deigned to apologize, promising the cameras would be removed as soon as the self-quarantine period was over (Gan). Apparently, it was only tried out in one Chinese city, or at least that was the only city reported on.

But other intrusive measures have since the Covid outbreak been instituted across the board and are now routine. An outbreak of cases in one's residential complex or community forces it into a "hard" lockdown—residents aren't permitted out of their apartments (Wuhan's lockdown lasted almost three months).[5] A small outbreak in one's district or city may result in a less stringent, partial lockdown, keeping residents inside their complex and working from home, with a different family member allowed out every other day to shop, and only essential workers allowed to go to work. When a lockdown is lifted but there are still local cases outside one's district, people may come and go freely but have to present a pass card upon returning to their complex or scan a QR code; more and more complexes are now using face-recognition scanning to let in their residents. Shopping malls, public buildings, many food establishments, and in some cities, buses and subways require the scanning of a QR code linked to one's identification through a downloaded government app, confirming on the spot you've been in the city (but not to any outbreak district) for the requisite two weeks.

If the Chinese are putting up with these annoyances, it's because they appreciate the importance of tracking down carriers of the virus. The more places you've shown your code, the more

---

[5] A colleague who happened merely to drive through one such community in Ningbo in late 2021 was contacted by the authorities after arriving home and forced to home-quarantine; they had scanned the license plate of every car passing through. Another colleague was suddenly locked down at his five-star hotel in Shijiazhuang during an outbreak there in 2021; he was stuck there for two weeks, free to wander but not exit the hotel.

complete is the log of your movements and those you've inter-
sected with. This is valuable information when it comes to de-
termining the source of an outbreak and contact tracing all the
people affected. There are indeed benefits to China's zero-Covid
approach. In no other country is the wearing of face masks in
public a matter of etiquette alone; the masks and constant scanning of QR codes are a hassle, to be sure, but almost one-fifth of
the world's population can relax in the knowledge that their possibility of catching the virus is still statistically nil. It's a load off
their mind—in stark contrast to the rest of the world. China's
economy was only moderately affected before returning to normal
activity a few months after the outbreak, and their medical system was only momentarily taxed, buying time to develop vaccines and medicines and spruce up the health infrastructure, as
it prepares for the inevitable arrival of the virus when the nation
reopens its borders, as it must eventually.

The dark side of this lockstep conformity, of course, is that
top-down public health measures can easily shade into political
and symbolic dictates merely aimed at testing the public's obedience. Over the past two years of the pandemic in China, numerous reports have surfaced of horrendous behavior by local governments after instituting Wuhan-style hard lockdowns—locking
people in their apartments with limited access to food and denying ambulance service for non-Covid-related emergencies. Complaints that people can't even be let outside to walk their dogs
might seem petty when lives are being saved, but the mass cull-
ing in some Chinese cities of people's pets on alleged disease-
prevention grounds is clearly shocking (S. Baker).

One doesn't need to be an expert in surveillance to grasp that
if the technology is available it will be used, and one doesn't need
to be a futurologist to know what's coming down the line. The
merging of GPS and face-recognition technologies means that,
with the exception of hermits living in the remote wilderness,
everyone's exact location will be known to the state in real-time
(Mozur & Krolik). Some of the more dystopian consequences of

this are already a reality, as when jaywalkers in certain Chinese cities are seeing themselves, along with their name and identifying information, displayed on giant LED screens at busy intersections and automatically fined. The Chinese Government isn't accustomed to allowing public debate on the ethics of hi-tech surveillance (much less on the cutting-edge, province-wide laboratory of Xinjiang), or very forthcoming about the intrusive technologies it's implementing; it just implements them. One place with comparable developments to look to is South Korea, like China a homogeneous society with a largely conformist, obedient population but a more democratic press. To "reduce the strain on overworked tracing teams in a city with a population of more than 800,000 people, and help use the teams more efficiently and accurately," authorities in Bucheon are using "AI algorithms and facial recognition technology to analyze footage gathered by more than 10,820 security cameras and track an infected person's movements, anyone they had close contact with, and whether they were wearing a mask" ("South Korea"). If it's happening in South Korea, it's happening in China. China presently has one billion face-recognition surveillance cameras.

What's on many people's minds in China now is not the rapidly evolving omniscience of Covid-tracking. If anything, it will come as a relief when the technology reaches a level of accuracy and seamlessness that allows us to come and go without having to fiddle with our devices and QR codes every time we enter a shopping mall. The dystopian question, rather, is whether the Chinese authorities are planning on keeping all the Covid measures in place *post*-pandemic, in a perpetual state of vigilance, permanently on guard for the next pandemic. This won't necessarily require the constant scanning of health codes as we'll all be tracked in real-time anyway. Instead, the technologies will operate behind the scenes. As the population has now gotten used to the array of Covid measures, they can more easily acculturate to, internalize, and accept the next development: the knowledge that everyone is always already being watched. What happens when we get used to this state of affairs?

The Communists mastered social surveillance long before electronic technology. This surveillance has always been, at its core, not just the political surveillance one associates with totalitarian regimes, which actually involves only a handful of unruly agitators and dissidents, but sexual surveillance, which is designed for everyone. During the Cultural Revolution, many families were split apart and forced to stay in sex-segregated dormitories. In my close to three decades in China, I've been able to observe how hotels have served as morality enforcers and sexual gatekeepers of the state. In the 1990s, growing spending power allowed people greater mobility, and the private hotel industry developed along with domestic tourism. But only married couples were permitted to room together in hotels and had to prove their marital status upon checking in, a policy that remained in place until 2003. Curiously, the unmarried had long been allowed to sleep together in bathhouses, which had 24-hour private rooms (often with unlockable doors but police checks and busts were rare) and no registration requirement. This was freer even than in the U.S., where hotels require some identifying information such as your car's license plate. The bathhouse industry flourished in the 1990s and they were the go-to places for illicit, that is, extramarital sex until the authorities put an end to it around the time of the 2008 Beijing Olympics. All bathhouses thenceforth required identification upon entrance, though by that time unmarried couples could stay together in bathhouses and hotels as long as both registered with their national ID at the reception.

The 2003 milestone securing for the Chinese right to cohabit extramaritally in hotels has in the past few years begun to wobble—due to the little Big Brother in everyone's mobile phone. It's not just GPS that is to blame but GPS combined with the powerful WeChat (like Facebook, WhatsApp, Instagram, and every other app rolled into one), which along with the competing Alipay is used for buying things. China has been cashless since the mid-2010s. Cellphones are used for all monetary transactions, from buying a car to booking a hotel room to paying a prostitute or the migrant manning your favorite street-side snack stand; you need merely scan the seller's QR code. This convenience, however, comes at the expense of the state's knowledge of your every move. Compared to the somewhat scattershot identity indicators the U.S. Government has of its citizens (social security number, state driver's license, credit history, social media), the Chinese Government has a more centralized and orderly database, with the national ID number (passport in the case of foreign residents) being the sole indicator needed to call up every citizen's complete digital history and profile. People are cautious about being inflammatory on social media; WeChat users can have their account permanently shut down without warning for political commentary or rumormongering, though private sexting isn't interfered with.

In the decade of opportunity between 2003 and 2013 or so, before WeChat became so powerful and ubiquitous, exercising your sexual freedom at a hotel was still an anonymous act. The government could easily pay the hotel a visit and find you out if they had reason to, but trysts could be carried out in reasonable confidence no one would ever know. Nowadays, the phone calls or WeChat messages of your conversations arranging the tryst, GPS tracking of your respective locations to the hotel, the record of your WeChat or Alipay payment used to book the room, and your respective ID numbers presented at reception all align to document incontrovertibly your liaison with a member of the opposite sex. The police are too busy to be much interested in people's daily lives, including their sex lives. But although adultery is no longer a crime, it can easily be ferreted out and is of potential use to, say, HR departments, in a country where privacy protections are murkier and all medium to large-size companies, public and private, have a Communist Party office. The knowledge that the authorities have access to anything and everything is increasingly giving people pause before using a hotel to embark on an affair, at least those with reputations to lose.

Since the Covid pandemic, booking hotels has become a much more stressful affair for everyone, not just adulterers. Your booking is canceled if the city or city district your hotel is in goes into lockdown, which may involve just a single Covid case in the entire city; you are also canceled if the city you're coming from has an outbreak. Bribery has long been a last resort in China; no longer, as far as coronavirus authorizations are concerned. Once arrived, you aren't allowed past the hotel reception until you've electronically established your credentials with one or more health-tracking codes on your cellphone, filled out a police-mandated health form, and possibly required to present a negative antigen test within the past 48 hours. All these steps apply to any person accompanying you as well. They are interested not in adulterous affairs but in people infected with the virus. This means, however, that if someone in the same hotel is discovered to be Covid positive, or has been in contact with such a person, the hotel could go under lockdown without warning, and no one allowed out for days or weeks. The same applies if the district your hotel is in goes into lockdown. You and your partner will be questioned about your travel histories. While your adultery probably won't be of immediate concern, the questions will be awkward, and being cooped up with your secret partner for days could end up exposing you in one way or another. What if you're both from the same workplace?

If you feel it's no longer worth the hassle going through with a hotel tryst, you're not any safer from Big Brother's roving eye sneaking your lover into your apartment while your live-in is out. Facial recognition cameras at your complex's gate have you in their sights, and both your cellphones' GPS tracks you right into your home.

One business you might assume to be off-limits under Covid is massage, given the close physical contact involved. At the start of the pandemic, all massage shops were shut down, as were bars and other entertainment venues. Then a few months later they opened back up (and shut down again after each new outbreak).

The government has an obvious interest in keeping as much of the population employed as possible, and I doubt any country has more per-capita massage workers than China. Yet we are confronted with a paradox. In this most intrusive of surveillance states, the opportunities for intimate and sexual contact thrive even in the Covid era. Unless you're a well-placed Party member or belong to the business or entertainment elite, with a reputation on the line, nothing is bound to happen. There are far too many people having sex for the authorities to bother about. The Chinese Government today is quite lenient, surprisingly lenient, about people's sex lives. Like shopping, it's been legitimized as a social safety valve. Things could always backslide, of course, to the spouses-only hotel laws of pre-2003, but even the nanny state of that era was light-years away from the grim circumstances that obtained up through the 1980s when people could be executed or imprisoned for extramarital sex, and university students expelled for sex as late as the 1990s.

THE CASE OF THE USA

Unaccustomed to having their lives interfered with, Americans' insistence on freedom from Covid restrictions is having, by contrast, a very bad effect on their sex lives. The nasty conundrum forced on us by the Covid pandemic is that the only way to effectively combat it, even with vaccines and medicines, is surveillance. Only surveillance provides the knowledge of who is infected, where they are located, and who they have been in contact with. This knowledge diminishes the burden on the medical system, while its absence escalates the medical burden since testing and contact tracing are scattershot and impotent without it. There has been much controversy in books and the media, well before Covid, over electronic surveillance and the resulting erosion of freedoms in democratic states, but the hard truth is that surveillance is the only weapon at our disposal for fighting dis-

ease outbreaks. China is not the only country to employ sophisticated tracking of its citizens. In the wake of Covid, most countries are ratcheting up their surveillance capabilities. We are
also seeing hints of another dystopian sci-fi Rubicon we hope
won't be crossed, but a logical and perhaps inevitable outcome of
all of this, the implanting in people of microchips, as Prime Minister Benjamin Netanyahu suggested doing to Israeli children
(Sverdlov).

South Korea, held up as a model of national medical response,
is one example of overreach, when the state of the art collides
with traditional prejudices, namely against homosexuality. In a
coronavirus outbreak at a gay nightclub, hundreds who might
have been exposed were reluctant to get tested for fear the medical authorities would inform their workplace and they'd be fired.
In other words, further success in containing the virus hinges on
how willingly this putative democracy's leadership can let go of
its dearly held homophobia (Kim). Singapore had similar issues
with its discriminatory treatment of its million-plus migrant
workers from India and Bangladesh (Yeung & Yee). On the other
hand, sex-positive social attitudes can be turned to advantage,
and people whose job involves extensive networking marshaled
to assist the medical authorities, as sex workers in Zambia did,
but this takes a rare degree of institutional imagination ("Coronavirus: Zambia").

The American political system was no more structured to
handle the Covid pandemic than the 1918 Spanish Flu. Two
years into the pandemic, there has been no talk of reforming the
healthcare system such that it would bring it in line with the rest
of the civilized world. At the start of the pandemic, the U.S. Government couldn't even administer the paltry $1,200 stimulus
checks properly and fairly, sending them to people who didn't
qualify and denying them to those married to non-U.S. citizens;
not to mention feed the hungry (Fadulu). Though the nightmare
of the Trump Administration and its incompetence is over, its
confused gesturing was symptomatic of a more profound problem:

the inability of a cruel Victorian-style capitalist regime entrenched in a moribund imperialist ideology and run by cynical
and blindered plutocrats to deal with something beyond its comprehension—a pandemic.

The U.S. has bifurcated more starkly than ever into Republican "red" and Democratic "blue" as it adapts to the pandemic.
Conservative, religious, rural, and older, Covid Reds buy into
conspiracy theories such as that the virus is a hoax and vaccines
are poisonous, or simply chafe under any restrictions to their
freedom. In their refusal to get vaccinated, they have, predictably,
been losing their lives at a much higher rate than Covid Blues,
who belong to a more educated demographic. But if the latter
support public health measures and lockdowns, it's not just because they understand science; they can afford to lock themselves
down, having jobs that allow them to work from home rather
than in factories, warehouses, or the service industry. The sad
reality is that American society as a whole doesn't care much for
its most vulnerable, and this accounts for the highest Covid fatal-
ity rate in the world, over 800,000 deaths and counting: "Societies more known for valuing their elders, as is the case in many
East Asian countries such as Singapore, South Korea, China, and
Japan, have fared much better than the U.S. throughout the
pandemic, with fewer cases and deaths from COVID and some of
the highest COVID vaccination rates" (Gounder).

Meanwhile, the sight of young Americans blithely swarming
bars and beaches despite urgent warnings has caused much con-
sternation and outrage. Yet their nose-thumbing acts of freedom
nevertheless convey something of symbolic importance: it's a logical, appropriately sarcastic, middle-finger response by the hapless subjects of a failed state. Why try to protect themselves from
the virus when the Trump White House did everything in its
power to allow it to spread?[6] Why should they have to bear the

---

[6] Trump actively undermined efforts to control the outbreak for political
reasons (Weixel). The Biden White House reversed course but has been

burden of protecting the country when everyone is going to catch Covid anyway? These young people aren't the complete idiots they are made out to be. They recognize what's happening is a very bad flu season—well, ten times as bad—and despite their youth and health some of them will die. But their chances of surviving are pretty good, and many are asymptomatic. They are only carrying on as everyone will have to once the virus runs its course through the whole population, and they'll be the first to gain immunity.

If the sight of bars and restaurants packed with maskless patrons young and old strikes you as disturbing or pathetic, they'd likely respond, quite reasonably, that they are trying to preserve the only reality they have ever known as it collapses around them. This often means continuing to support businesses they've been patronizing their whole lives that are on the verge of folding, either from enforced shuttering or high turnover of overworked staff. Rallying around local business and stepping in to help the community, when avoiding crowds is called for, could even be regarded as a well-meaning if misguided expression of Americans' customary generosity, a generosity which, however, doesn't always extend to people who can't help themselves—the poor and elderly.

More pertinent to this discussion are the consequences to people's mental health of extended social isolation, in a country where psychological services are already inadequate and unaffordable ("Coronavirus pandemic"). Several phenomena converge on this problem: the atomized nuclear family, with friends and family separated geographically by long distances common in the U.S.; the alienating effects of communicating with people online; and the Covid pandemic, which has exacerbated all of these factors. "There is little awareness," writes Vinay Lal in *The Fury of COVID-19: The Politics, Histories, and Unrequited Love of the*

---

saddled with a patchwork national medical database, forcing it to rely on international data to track its own coronavirus outbreaks (Banco).

Coronavirus,

of how digital technologies, which claim to foster relationships and produce a highly interconnected world, produce
distancing....No one, in contrast, chooses to be lonely: it is
the fate of those who must live in a society torn apart by anomie, estrangement, and distancing—from one's self, community, and moral purpose. The gist of it is that, in the face
of COVID-19, we have been asked to "only disconnect"—and
this when isolation, self-absorption, narcissism, and social
distancing have all been the bane of our modern existence.

Bound up with loneliness but seldom discussed in conjunc-
tion with it is sexual loneliness. You won't find much in the way
of advice, except to avoid sex altogether. The conscientious would
stress that the act of lovemaking turns you into an efficient disease vector (if not quite as bad as choir singing; "Health authorities"). During AIDS this problem was solved with safe sex and
condoms, but there is no safe sex under Covid. No form of physical interaction is possible without aiding the enemy, one that
according to the medical consensus will be with us for good.
Covid is changing America and you are never going to be able to
party again, admonishes the superego. The only real way to contain the virus just happens to dovetail with—guess what?—good
old "family values": abstinence for teens and strict monogamy for
adults.

This new normal means adapting to virtual relationships.
That means dating is out, as it may introduce an asymptomatic
person, or a super-spreader, into your circle. If you cannot prove
you had a more legitimate reason for meeting this person, your
intent must have been sexual and therefore gratuitous and reckless, as a result of which either one of you may have singlehandedly just started a new local outbreak. Simply going out and infecting, or being infected by a person with the intent of sleeping
with them will make you guilty of abetting the pandemic. In

China, the state assumes the burden of worrying about who's infecting whom. It tells everyone to wear a face mask, and they obey; it tells everyone it's okay to remove their mask, and they remove them. If restaurants and hotels are allowed to reopen, people flock to them guilt-free. If the virus is still lingering and some end up getting infected, they'll shut the establishment down again. But no one is to blame and no one's conscience is bothered. In the U.S., on the other hand, individuals are duty-bound not to cause others harm, even from something as impossible to control as an airborne virus.

If you were to ask younger people what they feel about the new sexual normal, they might assert, again quite sensibly, that they aren't planning on curtailing their freedom one iota. To the contrary, the danger of catching the virus from sex might make it all the more exciting. The allure of sex is intensified by taboos against it, and defiance follows from an absence of moral exemplars. On the other hand, I can't imagine all the terrible family dramas Covid has spawned when teenagers going out of their minds rebel and flee their miserable bedrooms for secret trysts, only to get infected and infect their household in turn.

Covid has thus reframed the debate around sexual freedom in a fresh way. Even without Covid, there is no shortage of such concerns in twenty-first-century America. This is of vital interest to everyone, as the question of freedom from sexual repression becomes intertwined and inextricable from the question of freedom from fascism.

2

THE SEWAGE SYSTEM, OR WHAT IS FASCISM?

MANUFACTURE A MYTHOLOGY OF LIES

IN *THE RISE AND FALL OF THE THIRD REICH*, William Shirer depicts Hitler's chilling oratory and its effect on his followers:

> Now the 600 deputies, personal appointees all of Hitler, little men with big bodies and bulging necks and cropped hair and pouched bellies and brown uniforms and heavy boots leap to their feet like automatons, their right arms upstretched in the Nazi salute, and scream "Heils." Hitler raises his hand for silence. He says in a deep, resonant voice, "Men of the German Reichstag!"
>
> The silence is utter.
>
> "In this historic hour, when, in the Reich's western provinces, German troops are at this minute marching into their future peacetime garrisons, we all unite in two sacred vows."
>
> He can go no further. It is news to this "parliamentary" mob that German soldiers are already on the move into the

Rhineland. All the militarism in their German blood surges to their heads. They spring, yelling and crying, to their feet. Their hands are raised in slavish salute, their faces now contorted with hysteria, their mouths wide open, shouting, shouting, their eyes, burning with fanaticism, glued on the new god, the Messiah. The Messiah plays his role superbly. His head lowered, as if in all humbleness, he waits patiently for silence. Then his voice, still low, but choking with emotion, utters the two vows....

Donald Trump's oratory of pathos is of a less eloquent sort—shorter sentences, fractured grammar—but it casts the same spell and commands the same madness. In his rallies, his outbursts rotate among three targets, Mexican immigrants, Democrats, and the mainstream media. At a rally in Hershey, Pennsylvania,

Trump's bellows hands shift, horizontal to vertical; now he's chopping. "Brutalized," chop! "Murdered," chop! "Hacking," chop! "Ripping out, in two cases, their hearts." A man's voice somewhere ahead of me cries out "fuuuck!" More, like a liturgy, a horrible psalm of repetition, "illegal alien" and "rape" and "sexual assault of a child" and "alien," and "unlawful contact with a minor" and "rape" and "indecent exposure" and "sex crimes" and "animal"; "released by Philadelphia to wander free in your communities."

He gestures to the sectioned-off area where CNN and other news organizations are assembled, protected by a cage, and denounces them as "very bad people" and "scum" and "liars." "'Look at them!' he cries, pointing. His thousands turn to the cage to scream." As for the Democrats, one Trump fan conveys the prevailing mood to reporter Jeff Sharlet by bending over and "sniffing the wet blacktop like a hound," mimicking a supposed pedophile in the act of sniffing out children to molest. "Creepy Joe!"

cries another supporter. "Demons," he rejoins. A female fan expounds:

> "Not even human….It's too terrible to speak of." She turns away, to the happiness of a small circle of new friends she's made at the rally, a whole family decked out in Trump wear. But she keeps coming back. "The truth and the lies," she says. I don't know what she means. She turns away again, returns again, her eyes watery. "I'm going to say it," she decides. But she can't. She walks away. Her friends seem worried. She comes back, leans in. "*They eat the children.*" She shakes with tears. Her friends nod. (Sharlet)

In *The Fascism This Time*, Theo Horesh succinctly contrasts Trumpian-style demagoguery with its Nazi progenitor: "While early 20th-century fascism may have produced well-organized mobs of neatly dressed automatons marching in goose step to a vision of the future, early 21st-century fascism presents a slovenly crowd of obese retirees giggling over their own offensiveness. Yet, both inspire followers to be swept away by the crowd." Despite his buffoonery and his carnivalesque rallies, Trump and his supporters, Horesh notes (writing at the end of Trump's term in office), represent an ominous new national development. Examples indeed abound, from the expansion of Immigration and Customs Enforcement (ICE) concentration camps for the children of detained and deported immigrants (though 350,000 immigrants were already in ICE detention under Obama) to the January 6, 2021, attempted coup and attack on the Capitol building. Trump brought out the ugliness of the country's rightwing and supremacist sectors. But there is a tendency to place undue emphasis on the figurehead of Trump. I cannot but feel that his supporters are out of their league in the face of America's diverse majority and have only managed to expose themselves as a rather pathetic and incompetent bunch, despite the prospect of more violence to come, as his supporters and political cronies reattempt to wrest power by any means. Things are indeed liable to take a turn for the worse if Republicans reject the results of the 2024 presidential election, as Barbara F. Walter warns in *How Civil Wars Start*. And if they do succeed in regaining power, with or without a civil war, my thesis may turn out to have understated its case. This does not mean, on the other hand, that the country is not already on a fascist trajectory, one that began long before Trump. If this is not immediately evident, it's because it is all too familiar and close to home. It's called brainwashing, and brainwashing works precisely when it's not recognized as such.

A hallmark of fascism is the dumbing down of public discourse to a neat and tidy narrative of the nation's patriotic mission, typically calling for a return to a mythologized past imbued with pastoral signifiers. In the American case: rugged individualist cowboy types and devout Christian wives and children in their giant playground of a landscape devoid of Native Americans, Hispanics, and Blacks, though I'm sure there are white supremacists who are not averse to the restoration of slavery. While this nostalgia has historical roots, the gulf separating the fantasy of the past from the complex reality of the present requires much denial and distortion. The cognitive dissonance experienced amidst the chaos and change of contemporary society is too great to absorb and deal with. Half of the public rises to the challenge and the other half demands drastic action to halt the slide, to return to the past and preserve American life as they think they know it. The tension between these two publics has always existed in American society; Trumpian politics is just the latest twist. The immediate question is how much political power the mythologists currently possess and how much damage they are causing. Rejecting evolution in favor of creationism in the schools, subjecting the public to the daily display and brandishing of guns, charging mothers who miscarry with murder on the grounds of fetal neglect, and refusing face masks amidst a pandemic in the name of freedom, are a few of the recurrent mythologist causes fought over in the U.S. culture wars. They also serve to distract from a much more comprehensive, inclusive, protean deception long foisted on the public: the master lie of American exceptionalism.

American exceptionalism consists in and follows from the belief that the USA is the greatest country in the world. Conservatives and right-wingers take this notion for granted and uphold it fervently. Liberals and progressives tend to be more jaundiced and reject the balder forms of jingoism yet may still assume their homeland to be an example for the world to emulate. All countries have their points to be proud of. Few can approach America's rich legacy of popular music—blues and jazz, soul and country, rock and rap (though I'd add that a great musical tradition derives as much from social oppression and anguish as from the mixing of cultures, both found in abundance in the U.S.); technological innovation, which has given us computers, the internet, social media, electric cars and space travel; the counterculture, civil rights, feminist, gay rights, and ecology movements; or as vital and still vibrant a free press, from independent neighborhood bookstores to the online behemoth Amazon, which despite its reprehensible labor practices has succeeded in making millions of books available to people around the globe.

The dark side of all of this is an inherent, ingrained sense of American superiority—and a corresponding ignorance of the rest of the world. This is apparent at the top regardless of what administration is in the White House, from Trump's contemptuous dismissal of international agreements to Joe Biden's patriotic platitudes at a May 28, 2021, speech at Joint Base Langley Eustis in Hampton, Virginia: "America is unique. From all nations in the world, we're the only nation organized based on an idea....None of you get your rights from your government; you get your rights merely because you're a child of God. The government is there to protect those God-given rights." But exceptionalism is also apparent among ordinary folk of whatever political persuasion. It need not be affirmed because it's expressed implicitly. There are of course exceptions to this profound ethnocentrism (notably the well-traveled), this notoriously American apathy and indifference toward all things foreign. Yet whenever I go back home for a visit, I am struck by how little curiosity there is, how few people—otherwise openminded, well-educated people—bother to query me about the countries I have spent much of my life in. It's not just my own imagination but a phenomenon well known to American expats.

American exceptionalism also takes the form of a highly distorted understanding of how the U.S. is viewed abroad. Most Americans assume the world is envious of their country and everyone would live there if they could. This may be true in regions whose inhabitants are fleeing corrupt dictatorships, such as Central America or the Caribbean, and it may have been more commonly the case in impoverished countries in decades past. The uncomfortable truth, however, is that people not blessed with being born in the greatest country on earth are finding fewer reasons ever to visit it, let alone imagine living there. Friends and acquaintances I've known in my years abroad frequently express shock at the extent to which Americans are inured to the oppression they suffer under. In what other nation, for example, can you be arrested for dashing into a shop for five minutes to buy something while your kid waits in your car, or bounty hunters sue you in state court for providing a pregnant woman a lift to an abortion clinic? (K. Brooks; Keshner).

The notion that one's own country has nothing of interest to gain, nothing of value to learn from other countries and cultures is insidious because it makes it easier to overlook their humanity. It also makes people seem less human the more distant they are geographically. The fascist corollary is that it makes it easier to rationalize their elimination. An example of Americans' cavalier disregard for countries they don't like or understand is the casual use of the repugnant phrase "nuke 'em." This came close to actually happening under Trump (Foster).

Define the Enemy and Brutalize It

It is often said that fascist regimes require a charismatic leader with a knack for whipping up popular support and mobilizing nationalist aggression. But this is not always the case. A stolid, distant figure, Japan's Emperor Hirohito was never even heard on the radio until he announced his country's surrender in 1945. Yet the mere appeal of his name was enough to engineer the deaths of 15-20 million Chinese civilians. This genocide was carried out not just by means of the usual scorched-earth campaigns and attendant famine and disease, but a great deal of direct slaughter: shooting people in pits or roping together a dozen at a time and burning them alive with kerosene or gasoline. Something else was going on, which we shall attempt to examine below, to manufacture the kind of blind obedience that made Japanese farm boys and upright gentlemen with a taste for haiku and flower arrangement (which they were observed fiddling with in their barracks) alike gleefully rape pregnant women and disembowel them with their bayonets (Harmsen, *Nanjing*; Harmsen, *Shanghai*).

Japan's excuse at the time for the Nanjing atrocities of 1937, not to mention the much broader devastation of eastern China's cities and countryside, was that they "lost control of the army." But it's indisputable that much of the depravity was issued down from commands on high. Emperor Hirohito approved of chemical and biological warfare and signed off at least 375 times on toxic gas attacks in China (Gold). Hal Gold's *Japan's Infamous Unit 731: Firsthand Accounts of Japan's Wartime Human Experimentation Program* (which makes for as difficult reading as Vivien Spitz's *Doctors from Hell: The Horrific Account of Nazi Experiments on Humans*) recounts how for fourteen years beginning in 1932, a year after Japan's occupation of Manchuria, Chinese citizens were randomly seized and sent to secret medical experimentation centers (the flagship site near Harbin in Heilongjiang Province included crematoria), where they were dissected alive on the vivisection table, forced to have sex after being injected with syphilis, tied to stakes and blasted with various germs including the bubonic plague, and many other vile experiments. The expertise gained was used, among other bacteriological attacks, to drop a plague-outfitted ceramic bomb on Ningbo in October 1940; hundreds died but quick action by the city in isolating the affected zone prevented a wider outbreak.

The Germans matched, indeed exceeded the barbarism of the Japanese, being responsible for a comparable number of civilian deaths in Poland and the Soviet Union, some 20 million (a figure including most of the six million Jewish Holocaust victims). But the Nazis had an even more ambitious goal in the Hunger Plan, formulated in early 1941. By encircling vast territories and cutting off food supplies they would have deliberately starved to death an estimated 20-30 million Russians and Ukrainians (Stargardt). The plan was disrupted as the Wehrmacht got bogged down in Operation Barbarossa later that year and far fewer died than intended, though many millions of Poles, Slavs, and Jews were murdered by other means. Shooting people into pits was the dominant method in the early years of the war. As many as ten to twenty thousand could be shot at a single killing site per day, but that was found to be exhausting and traumatizing for the shooters. More effective means were experimented with, including dynamiting groups of people, also found to be inefficient (Mayer). One solution was to redirect carbon monoxide fumes into the vans ferrying victims to the killing sites and simply dump the lifeless bodies into the pits. More creatively still, in October 1941 in Konin, Poland, eight thousand Jews were thrown naked into pits filled with quicklime and melted alive; by the following morning all except the victims' heads had dissolved, their faces still frozen in their screams (Rhodes). Eventually, of course, the mass murder was sped up in the gas chambers and crematoria of the extermination camps, accounting for another three million victims.

An intractable question is how ordinary soldiers could be

compelled to participate in the indiscriminate, cold-blooded slaughter of civilians and defenseless troops alike. The Japanese army took few prisoners of war, and many of those it did were worked to death or succumbed to starvation and disease; for the most part, captured Chinese troops were killed outright. Germany made a pretense of keeping Soviet POWs alive, but several million of them starved to death in the concentration camps anyway. The comprehensive slaughter of the enemy was always warfare's operating principle. Julius Caesar had all of his captured troops put to the sword, matter-of-factly recounted in his *Gallic Wars*. Rape and pillage where civilians were seen as the victors' prize was likewise a timeworn practice, as were the scorched-earth campaigns of the Thirty Years Wars in Europe (1618-48) and the even more destructive Taiping Civil War in China (1850-64), the latter resulting in the deaths of tens of millions. The survival of civilians was long disregarded in the military calculus as being of any significance, morally or otherwise. Twentieth-century fascism operated as if it were still immersed in this past when war and slaughter were glorious for their own sake; it dispensed with such ethical encumbrances as the Geneva Conventions and relished in the spirit of total war. As Hitler oft retorted whenever any of his generals hesitated to pull out all the stops, "There is no room for sentimentality here."

Even in modern times, widespread civilian destruction is reserved as a last resort by all modern armies, to brutalize and break the enemy population psychologically and make them cave in, as in the Allied carpet bombing of Germany and the Americans' flattening of Tokyo, Hiroshima, and Nagasaki in WWII. The fascist state does the same proactively rather than reactively. Although the U.S. military, in its pointless and catastrophic war on Indochina, came to understand the importance of not alienating civilians in the South Vietnamese countryside to avoid pushing them into the hands of the Vietcong, it nonetheless gratuitously bombed North and South Vietnam, Cambodia, and Laos, resulting in one to two million civilian deaths—the largest

aerial bombardment in history (J. Gibson). Included in this devastation were hundreds of thousands of tons of napalm—gelled
gasoline—dropped on military and civilian targets alike, and the
four million Vietnamese exposed to the toxic herbicide Agent Orange, disabling or rendering gravely ill a quarter of them. To confuse the public, fascist states pay lip service in their propaganda
to acting only in the interests of defense and peace. Hitler always
claimed the Germans were only protecting themselves against
the worldwide Judeo-Bolshevik conspiracy and acted dismayed
when the Western powers declined to join him in his invasion of
the Soviet Union. The U.S. similarly banked on the bogeyman of
communist tyranny in its war of aggression against Indochina.

In order to turn an army into an effective fighting machine,
obedience is hammered into the troops down to the last man. For
those who might contemplate wavering, they have no choice: you
cooperate in killing because refusing to do so could result in your
own court-martialing or even execution for insubordination.
However, what needs highlighting is that not all soldiers are reluctant to kill. Many do so willingly, and this wrath is vented on
enemy civilians as enthusiastically as it is on enemy troops. To
explain this, we need to delve into a more stubborn kind of obedience, operating on a deep psychological level and instilled from
an early age, requiring a crushing and pressing of the immature
ego into the mold of group conformity. Once thus reshaped, individuals can be turned into sadists without their having much
conscious comprehension of this process.

Central to this indoctrination is dehumanization. Before an
enemy can be brutalized, it must be defined and identified, made
vivid, threatening, and larger than life, yet *less than human*. Dehumanization renders the enemy unique, separate, and therefore
expendable. It's easier to rationalize and compartmentalize murder and slaughter if one believes that what one is killing is not
really human. It also helps if the enemy is physically and recog-
nizably distinct, of a different race. This underscores the fact that
fascism is undergirded by racism. Thus, the yellow race of Viet-

namese "gooks" served as a convenient enemy for American ser-vicemen. For the German and Japanese fascists, race was a bit more problematic. Where the enemy was not racially distinct in a physical sense, it was simply declared to be so. The Japanese inculcated the absurd notion among its citizenry that they were racially superior to the Chinese. Subtle facial markers do distin-guish the Japanese from the Koreans and the Chinese, southern Chinese from northern Chinese, but East Asians as a whole are indistinguishable from one another. Russians and Poles are in no meaningful sense physically distinct from the Germans, yet by positing an imaginary "Aryan" race, the Germans convinced themselves they were superior to the brute-like Slavs on the one hand and the wily and cunning Jews on the other, both classed as *Untermenschen*—subhumans. It is telling that when a nation turns against its own people, the Other is often racialized and physical or hereditary distinctions created where none were be-fore. Being a mere descendent of a landlord branded one a land-lord in early Communist China. Landlords were also dehuman-ized by being depicted in the media as stunted, stoop-shouldered, and (like the Japanese and American enemies) mustached, all signifiers of wickedness. The peasantry was then unleashed on many innocent people, resulting in two to three million "land-lord" murders by Mao Zedong's own estimate.

If you still find it inexplicable that ordinary people can be brainwashed into believing in an enemy—a less-than-human and expendable enemy deserving of righteous death—consider your-self lucky that your indoctrination failed.

PRIORITIZE RAGE OVER RATIONALITY

In Philip K. Dick's alternate-history novel *The Man in the High Castle*, Germany and Japan defeat the Allies in WWII and divide up the United States between them. The intriguing premise re-sulted in one of the author's most popular works. Yet the book is burdened by a central limitation—its modest length. Whereas the majority of Dick's novels present tightly structured, self-contained worlds, here he was working on a canvas too large to be contained in its 200-plus pages. The multiple locations, characters, and backgrounds could be no more than sketched, and the resulting gaps begged to be filled in. Amazon Studios found the concept fecund enough to come to the rescue and flesh out Dick's broad brushstrokes into a magnificent four-season (40-episode) eponymously named TV series (2015-19). Creator Frank Spotnitz inserted new plot lines and devices drawn from Dick's own oeuvre (parallel realities, time slips) while staying true to the overarching narrative. No expense was spared in recreating a visually imposing Nazi and Japanese-occupied America as the triumphant fascists might have run it once the troublesome war was out of the way and the superfluous Jewish and African *Untermenschen* dispatched. There are indelible images: the smart black SS uniforms (in high-definition Blu-ray), the melting down of the Liberty Bell into a shiny copper swastika, the blowing up of the Statue of Liberty, Albert Speer's once-stalled plans for his Grand Dome (dwarfing in size the U.S. Capitol building) now rising awesomely over Berlin, the proud Reichsführer Himmler assuming the helm after Hitler's death in 1962 when the story is set (and the year the novel was published), and the like.

Dick's speculative novel provides much food for thought. I have a contrary thesis: a German or Japanese victory in WWII would have been impossible even under the best of circumstances, given the self-destructive and entropic nature of fascism. Fascism is predicated on and fueled by rage. Its very basis is unstable and unsustainable. Just as capitalism requires constant economic accumulation and expansion to avoid collapsing in on itself, so fascism requires constant expansion and growth, and it is this that drives its military ventures into the ground. There is no such thing as a calm, cool, collected fascism, capable of righting itself and achieving long-term stability. As huge and necessary as the combined Allied effort against the Nazi juggernaut was, it's arguable the Germans lost the war even before they began it, by building up armed forces designed for blitzkrieg rather than protracted war. Fresh off their conquest of France, so confident were the Germans of being able to subdue the Bolsheviks that they failed to make even minimal provisions for winter warfare in Operation Barbarossa, launched in June 1941 and expected to be wrapped up before the summer was over. As a result of this folly, by December, bogged down outside of Moscow, one million German troops would perish by either arms or, dressed in rags in subzero temperatures, exposure. The Japanese army likewise overextended itself in fighting on two fronts—China and the Pacific War. Yet before that, in 1937, some Japanese military advisers had warned their top brass not to proceed on to Nanjing after conquering Shanghai. As they predicted, the Jiangsu Province campaign, like the Nazi's Moscow campaign, turned into a costly diversion that eventually drained and stalemated their forces in eastern China, at the cost of millions of casualties on both sides (Harmsen, *ibid.*).

The dilemma of aggression versus realism was to reoccur in the European theater over the next several years as the Germans continued to lose ground against the Soviets and their shortages in manpower and materiel grew more acute. The horrific limbo of the Lodz ghetto illustrates this nexus of ambivalence. After the Nazi takeover of Poland in 1939, the remaining Jews of Lodz deemed healthy enough to work and hence spared immediate extermination were forced into the city's Jewish ghetto. By mid-1942, they had been reduced to 70,000, a third of their original population, manufacturing clothing on a starvation diet for the German army's upcoming second campaign on the Eastern front. Already the "pragmatist" faction among the Nazi leadership was warning that the Lodz Jews were dying of illness and malnutrition at a rate of several thousand per month, which was to rise to almost 5,000 by September, at the height of the battle of Stalingrad. Nevertheless, despite the Wehrmacht's desperate need for clothing and supplies, which were being provided at the time largely by the Jews in the Lodz and other Polish ghettos, the "exterminist" faction prevailed and finally swayed a vacillating Heinrich Himmler to order the remaining Polish Jews to be sent to death camps in June 1944, when the Soviet advance toward Germany narrowed the Nazis' priorities. Only 877 Jews were found alive in Lodz by the Red Army in January 1945 (Mayer). When we note that Himmler was wavering, this was not of course out of any moral concern over the killing of the Jews, but whether the meager food rations barely keeping them alive would be better apportioned to German troops then fighting under extreme conditions.

A more rationally minded military leadership might have fed their prisoners of war and put them to work in factories. That the Nazis never productively exploited more than a fraction of their millions of Polish, Soviet, and Jewish captives but murdered or starved them to death is one of fascism's key paradoxes. It thrives on violence but undermines itself in the process of expending its violence: a death-drive ideology.

If it seems presumptuous to style the United States as "fascist" in the same sense as German or Japanese fascism, the U.S., again, is no stranger to devastating, pointless, and failed military ventures, which moreover have a racist basis—the war on Indochina for one. But it's not necessary for a fascist state to engage only in outward aggression; it can just as effectively turn its aggression inward, as is the case in the U.S. This might not be immediately evident. On the contrary, many regard America as the world's beacon of democracy and the only counterweight to the forces of totalitarianism. Rather than address this mainstream propaganda head-on, my task here is to apply certain criteria I have observed in my study of fascism and see whether the American example fulfills them or not.

Returning to the question of irrationality's predominance over rationality, let's have a brief look at the extraordinary wastefulness of the U.S. economy, which is effecting a slow but steady nationwide degradation and deterioration. If the U.S. has survived as a representative democracy for two and a half centuries, it shouldn't be forgotten that its rise has always been tainted and its wealth stolen, formerly enabled by slavery and today by inequality and exploitation. Even without a war of aggression at present, U.S. military expenditure in 2020 was $778 billion, 39 percent of total military spending worldwide and far ahead of any other country, $392 billion spent on nuclear weapons alone (China comes in a distant second in military spending at $252 billion). The oft-stated rationale is that the U.S. needs to maintain overwhelming military dominance to protect not just its own interests but those of the entire "free" world. Even if nuclear weapons are never used, the knowledge of how many the U.S. has in store keeps hostile states in check through sheer intimidation. This symbolic power, by which America reminds the world of who's in charge, simply costs that much amount of money—it's expensive being the global cop. Or so we are led to believe. The *unacknowledged* rationale for this tremendous expenditure is the web of corporate relationships and profits in the military-industrial sector.

Reminding the world of who's in charge involves actual destruction as well. The U.S. drops an average of 46 bombs per day on other countries—a total of 337,000 bombs released between 2001-2021 (Benjamin).

Even more money is wasted on the business of incarceration. The U.S. imprisons more people than any other country—2.3 million in 2020 (followed by China with 1.7 million, but China's population is four times as large)—and keeps another 4.6 million on probation or parole (Oudekerk & Kaeble). While only $80 billion is spent annually on the operational costs of prisons and jails ("only" being relative, that is, to military spending), hundreds of billions of dollars are lost to the economy from the reduced or absent labor of the imprisoned, the paroled, and their families. The U.S. is unique among industrialized nations in sabotaging the reintegration into society of the incarcerated. Parolees have enormous difficulty finding employers willing to hire them, not to

mention for a decent wage, causing many to return to crime—
and back to prison—in order to survive and, in a vicious circle,
further impoverishing their families from lost wages. Compounding this vicious circle, the family's children, lacking positive role
models and burdened with psychological and developmental diffi-
culties, are also likely to enter a life of crime. Tallying up all of
these hidden debits, a Washington University study estimates
that for every dollar spent on incarcerating people, there are ten
dollars in social costs, adding up to one trillion dollars yearly—
more than the military budget (Ferner).

Maintaining the massive prison population is a huge financial burden. The costs are passed on not just to taxpayers, which
fall disproportionately on the poor, but directly onto the poor as
well—the families and neighborhoods that serve as the prime
source of incarceration recruitment. But it's not as if the industry
is actively looking for human fodder for the cynical sake of profit,
apart from the ten percent of America's prisons that are privately
operated and whose profiteering is very much in evidence (Bauer). On the contrary, prisons and jails are a big drain on state
budgets. They do provide employment (at low wages) for white
rural locals living in their vicinity, and private contractors profit
from the obscenely low wages paid to prisoners, an average of
eighty-six cents an hour; Alabama, Arkansas, Florida, Georgia,
and Texas engage in inmate slave labor for no pay at all (Brakke;
"Economics"). But these hardly offset the costs. Jackie Wang confronts this enigma in her incisive *Carceral Capitalism*:

> Although it's important to analyze the economic conditions
> that have been driving contemporary police practices, an
> analysis of prisons and police that solely focuses on the polit-
> ical economy of punishment would be incomplete. There are
> gratuitous forms of racialized state violence that are "irra-
> tional" from a market perspective. From an economic per-
> spective, the new sentencing regime that emerged alongside
> the War on Drugs—such as three strikes laws for drug pos-

session—make little economic sense: Why waste an exorbitant amount of public money on incarcerating nonviolent offenders, sometimes for life?

It's noteworthy that the prison industrial complex draws its
guards and prisoners from the same populations—uneducated
rural whites and disadvantaged urban Blacks—as the military-
industrial complex draws its recruits for the army. The underly-
ing motivation of this intertwined military-prison industrial
complex is, again, symbolic: to put people in their place. The rage
directed towards America's enemies abroad is simultaneously
directed toward America's *internal* enemies—minorities and the
impoverished. It's a political economy of irrationalism, for there
is no sensible explanation for the diversion of wealth and govern-
ance away from the nation's disintegrating infrastructure,
threadbare educational, medical, and social services, and paraly-
sis in the face of global warming. As David Graeber sums up the
function of irrational state power in his *Debt: The First 5,000
Years*,

> We are looking at the final effects of the militarization of
> American capitalism itself....the construction of a vast bu-
> reaucratic apparatus for the creation and maintenance of
> hopelessness, a giant machine designed, first and foremost,
> to destroy any sense of possible alternative futures....a vast
> apparatus of armies, prisons, police, various forms of private
> security firms and military intelligence apparatus, and
> propaganda engines of every conceivable variety, most of
> which do not attack alternatives directly so much as create a
> pervasive climate of fear, jingoistic conformity, and simple
> despair that renders any thought of changing the world
> seem an idle fantasy....Economically, the apparatus is large-
> ly just a drag on the system; all those guns, surveillance
> cameras, and propaganda engines are extraordinarily ex-
> pensive and don't really produce anything.

INCARCERATE THE ENEMY AT HOME

What's shocking about America's gulag archipelago of prisons is not just the sheer number of the incarcerated—over two million—but the general indifference toward them. As with Americans' lack of interest in other lands and cultures, there is a similar degree of ignorance about the nation's internal colony, distanced and dehumanized from its citizenry in its own way. Part of this has a racist basis. Blacks, Asians, and Native Americans make up 42 percent of the prison population; if Hispanics are counted separately from whites, the minority prison population rises to 72 percent, compared to the 38 percent of minorities in the country as a whole (U.S. Bureau of Prisons). The internal colony consists not just of the incarcerated but encompasses the transitional territory of the impoverished inner-city as well, which supplies much of this population and recycles it back into the prisons through recidivism and a counterproductive parole system. Wang describes the distancing process by which white America insulates itself from its domestically exiled legions and keeps them out of sight and out of mind:

> The urban landscape is organized according to a spatial politics of safety. Bodies that arouse feelings of fear, disgust, rage, guilt, or even discomfort must be made disposable and targeted for removal in order to secure a sense of safety for whites....The media construction of urban ghettos and prisons as "alternate universes" marks them as zones of unintelligibility, faraway places removed from the everyday white experience....What happens in these zones of abjection and vulnerability does not typically register in the white imaginary.

Conservatives claim that the skewing of the prison population towards minorities is unremarkable; they are the groups most prone to crime. What conservatives ignore is the historical context. The white majority has from the outset engaged in a centuries-long, unrelenting campaign of oppression against Blacks and other minorities. By the end of the Civil War, the U.S. had four million slaves. In the Reconstruction and the Jim Crow eras up through 1965, white vigilantes lynched some 3,500 Blacks, with almost no accountability. Slavery crept back in disguised forms. As Alec Karakatsanis reminds us, "for many decades, white elites in the South used the punishment system to transfer wealth, confiscate land, and preserve racial hierarchy through convict leasing—that is, criminalizing people so that their bodies could be forced to work for profit."

The mortality rate of convicts in South Carolina chain gangs in the 1870s was 45 percent. "We must not be held to too strict an accountability," intoned Alabama Inspector of Convicts W. D. Lee in 1890. "We have a large alien population, an inferior race. Just what we are to do with them as prisoners is a great question as yet unsettled. The Negro's moral sense is lower than that of the white man. We say that he has been degraded by three or four generations of slavery" (Bauer). In the Tulsa race massacre of 1921, 10,000 Blacks were left homeless and 300 were murdered when their neighborhood was destroyed by whites. Also, from the mid-nineteenth century through the third decade of the twentieth, thousands of Mexicans were murdered by white vigilantes in Texas, California, and New Mexico (C. Gibson). The treatment of Native Americans over the same period is well known, having been starved off their lands by the U.S. Army, who slaughtered virtually the entire national herd of 30 million buffalo, since "we were never able to control the savages until their supply of meat was cut off." Or as one army general put it, "kill every buffalo you can! Every buffalo dead is an Indian gone" (Phippen).

Then from the mid-1960s until the early 1970s, in response to decades of racial segregation and police harassment, American ghettos exploded in pent-up rage in some 2,000 uprisings. During a mass arrest in Cairo, Illinois in 1971 (which had been experiencing two straight years of conflicts between law enforcement and Blacks), after a white woman's purse had been stolen, the city police chief announced, "I want every nigger in Cairo rounded up, and if that means busting heads to bring them to jail, I want them brought in" (Hinton). During this same decade of violence, federal allocation of funds for police increased 2,900 percent to $300 million in 1970—not the most creative approach to repairing race relations. The urban uprisings were brought under control after a significant slice of the Black male population was transferred from ghettos to prisons by the expedient of vastly increasing the construction and capacity of prisons, whose population ballooned from 200,000 in 1970 to 2,300,000 by 2000. In recent decades, the mutual hostility has only become more entrenched with the targeting of Blacks by increasingly militarized police forces stocked with military-grade weapons, including mine-resistant tank-like vehicles and Black Hawk tactical transport helicopters, routinely gifted to police forces across the country by the army, while state and local governments now shell out about $250 billion annually on police, corrections, and the courts (Hinton; Whitehead). Over the past decade nationwide, police have shot to death 2,000 Blacks, many of whom were found to be innocent. Some of this lethality is due to police panic, elsewhere to execution-style killing. In December 2020 in Columbus, Ohio, a cop repeatedly shot Casey Goodman, a Black 23-year-old, in the back as he was entering his home, holding nothing in his hands but sandwiches (B. Brooks, "Ohio"). In April 2021 in North Carolina, police repeatedly shot a Black man, Andrew Brown Jr., in the head as he sat in his car in his driveway while they shouted, "Let me see your hands!"; body camera footage showed that Brown had his hands on the steering wheel the entire time (Szekely & Layne). A University of Washington study reported that the majority of police killings in the U.S. between 1980 and 2018 were misclassified or went completely unreported (Oladipo).

Hispanics, particularly "illegals," are also singled out for special treatment. Mexican immigrant Joel Arrona-Lara was pulled from his car by ICE agents in California while driving his pregnant wife who was in labor to the hospital, who had to drive herself the rest of the way ("ICE detains"). A Honduran woman's baby daughter was plucked from her breast—literally—by ICE agents while feeding her in a Texas immigration detention center (Madani). An innocent U.S. citizen, Laura Sandoval, was visiting an ailing relative in Ciudad Juarez, just south of the Texas border, and upon returning to El Paso apprehended by the Customs and Border Protection (CBP), which operates with impunity like a Gestapo. They took her to a nearby hospital where a male doctor subjected her to a vaginal and rectal examination for drugs, enforcing her bowel movement with a laxative. She was told that if she did not voluntarily indicate her consent on a form, they would charge her $5,488 for the hospital bill (Bosque).

The incarceration industry is not exclusively a racist enterprise. Whites who fall afoul of the law may be better positioned to avoid long prison terms or prison altogether if they are wealthy and well-connected, yet they experience the same fate once they disappear behind prison walls. A large, looming prison system, irrespective of who is imprisoned, is attractive to fascism. Fascism also relies on public support, without which it cannot acquire the power it does. Americans can be unforgiving toward those who cross the line into crime and are enthusiastic supporters of harsh prison sentences. When a government resorts to extreme forms of retribution out of all reasonable proportion to the crime and well beyond any civilized standards, we call this *symbolic power*. Symbolic power serves to show off the sovereign's or the state's power. It functions to instill fear in the populace, sending the message, "Watch out, you may be next." Its historical analog is the burning of witches at the stake and the public beheading of infidels and traitors, spectacles which magnify the agony of the condemned for the sake of general catharsis. Today it survives in the cruel mental and physical humiliation of the modern dungeon—U.S. prisons. The display of symbolic power is the prime activity of authoritarian regimes, as an intimidated population is easier to control and more amenable to fascism.

As we have seen, the U.S. leads the world by far in incarceration rates: 6,517,000 under some form of correctional control in 2019, or about three percent of the adult population. This breaks down into 631,000 in local jails (470,000 in indefinite pretrial detention), 1,291,000 in state prisons, 226,000 in federal prisons (450,000 incarcerated for nonviolent drug offenses in state and federal prisons), 879,000 on parole, and 3,490,000 on probation. An additional 400,000 are in indefinite immigration detention at the hands of ICE and CBP. Almost one million convicted sex offenders are on sex offender registries, many for life, while unknown thousands (states generally don't publish reliable data) more ex-sex offenders are incarcerated in "civil commitment" prisons after completing their sentences ("Crime rate"; Morris; Sawyer & Wagner).

Turning to minors: 44,000 are in juvenile detention, adult jails, and prisons. Children aged eleven to seventeen make up one-fourth of imprisoned sex offenders and one-tenth of those on sex offender registries (J. Levine; McKay). Over 400,000 children, many involuntarily, are in out-of-home foster care. Meanwhile, 70,000 migrant children are held in detention, many separated from their parents ("Detention"). Accounts of physical and sexual abuse of juvenile prisoners are rife. In one Texas detention facility, guards forced boys to have oral sex and got a girl inmate pregnant (Sandoval & Arango).

Much of the public—excepting of course the minority communities affected—is willfully ignorant about the reality of prison life. Several unique features of American incarceration stand out. We've mentioned the perverse practice of exploiting inmates' labor for absurdly low wages, putting extreme financial pressure on them and their families. There is also a shocking absence of hygienic, nutritional, and medical measures. Overall close to half of the prison population has a psychological disorder (the percentages vary between jails, state, and federal prisons); being ignored and left untreated in the hostile prison environment ensures their further mental deterioration. Lawmakers visiting Riker's Island jail in New York, with 6,000 inmates in indefinite pretrial detention, often for nonviolent offenses, "described seeing shower stalls being used as jail cells, fecal matter and urine lining the floors, and dead cockroaches next to spoiled food in the jail's hallways." Many inmates were characterized as suffering from mental illness (Francis). At Logan Correctional Center for women in Illinois, prisoners "are walking through raw sewage in their housing unit...living with maggots, mold in the sinks & showers, no bleach to clean...No cameras in their open living quarters with an all-male correctional officer staff" (Conway).

U.S. jails and prisons do not, as a rule, mete out dictatorship-style torture at the hands of officers (unless guard-administered beatings count), but they tacitly pass this responsibility onto the prisoners, who routinely engage in injurious or lethal attacks on fellow inmates using shivs (homemade knives), along with rape, while staff looks the other way. Other prisons can be absurdly draconian about sex, putting prisoners caught in a consensual embrace, handholding, or even gesturing fondly to each other, in solitary confinement (Bauer; Halperin). Up to 100,000 inmates are currently held in solitary confinement, though estimates can vary widely as prisons hide their data (Manson). The title of one recent news article captures what happens to some of them: "A prisoner was 'covered in filth and barking like a dog' after 600 days of solitary confinement in a Virginia jail" (Bhardwaj). Prisons and jails often refuse to comply with the federal government requirement to report the causes of prisoners' deaths, because to do so would implicate them in their medical neglect of the inmates as well as their enabling of prisoner-on-prisoner violence (Press).

It's a shibboleth that prisoners consist mostly of incorrigible types who need sequestering for society's safety and moreover deserve their lengthy prison sentences anyway. There are indeed many prisoners who fall into this category. But it doesn't follow that they should be treated atrociously while doing their time.

Purely as a matter of expediency, not to mention humanitarian-ism, reform is unquestionably superior to punishment, as attest-ed by innovative prison models such as Norway's ("Incarcera-tion"). Would you rather see angry convicts further hardened by lengthy incarceration released back into society with poor job prospects, or rehabilitated and employable parolees with newly acquired skills and trades? But equally important, many prison-ers are not in fact violent, indeed don't belong there in the first place. Slightly less than half of the prisoners in state prisons, 70 percent in local jails, and 94 percent in federal prisons are nonvi-olent offenders (Sawyer & Wagner). Many are there for drug crimes, some locked up for simple marijuana possession—at a time when the country is moving toward cannabis legalization. Thousands more each year wind up imprisoned for misdemeanor offenses which morph into jail time over failure to pay multiply-ing court fines that they lack the means to pay (Ockerman).

A single past criminal record, no matter how inconsequential, can doom a person to minimum-wage jobs, for the two-thirds who succeed in finding one; the remaining third remains unemployed. Seventy million Americans bear the invisible shackles of a crimi-nal record—a powerful means of social control provided to the state. A felony conviction disqualifies one from voting. Many ex-convicts are unaware of this, but instead of simply preventing them from voting, they are, astonishingly, sent back to prison for innocently attempting to vote (Lantry & Haslett; S. Levine). Of course, racist conservatives in states like Texas, Florida, and Georgia have an interest in disenfranchising Blacks by any and all means including imprisonment, as it favorably impacts Re-publican electoral outcomes.

MONETIZE PUNISHMENT

Let's start with the humble parking ticket and work our way up to more serious crimes. What interests me about this particular infraction is that everyone, the most conscientious car owners included, gets ticketed sooner or later, and there are many otherwise law-abiding citizens who, whether due to sheer carelessness or obsessional necessity of some sort, get ticketed quite often. There are those who accumulate so many parking tickets that they give up and stop paying them. Or let's take the speeding ticket. Sooner or later, everyone receives one of these too (or a moving violation for driving too slowly if you're a pot smoker).

While it would surely be interesting to see how drivers collectively conducted themselves in the absence of any rules of the road (forming posses converging on reckless drivers?), I doubt there is an anarchist or libertarian out there who doesn't support some basic traffic laws. Yet traffic penalties are imposed not for the common good but to generate cash for city budgets. In the U.S., some 25-50 million moving-violation tickets are issued each year, amounting to $3.75-7.5 billion in revenue, and an equal amount in profits for insurance companies, who gleefully hike the premium of their ticketed customers. As the National Motorists Association puts it, "No other class of 'crime' is as profitable for state and local governments as is that of traffic tickets" ("Traffic tickets"). Parking tickets generate a hefty cash flow as well. New York City alone earned $565 million in fines in 2015 (Mays). Delinquent driving is the perfect cash cow and the penalties are increasing year by year. They would skyrocket if it weren't for certain constraints, such as the law of the marketplace. When costs rise beyond a certain point, consumers stop cooperating. In the face of exorbitant fines, drivers tend to show up in traffic court, where they often succeed in having charges dropped, as courts feel a certain moral obligation to hold municipal avariciousness in check. Or drivers might simply start behaving themselves, causing an unacceptable plunge in public revenue.

More serious traffic offenses are monetized as well—speeding 25 mph over the limit, driving under the influence, leaving the scene of an accident, manslaughter while DUI—though the inci-

dence rate drops off significantly with misdemeanors and felo-
nies. The number of DUI arrests in the U.S. annually is around
1.5 million, a fraction of total traffic offenses. Still, the best of us
gets tripped up now and then. I have a friend who never had a
traffic violation in his life until he got pulled over after a couple
drinks and was booked for DUI. He was exactly at the 0.08%
blood alcohol limit (for Illinois) and not over. He fell below the
limit when he was again breathalyzed at the station a few hours
later while handcuffed to a chair, and with the help of a lawyer
managed to get the charges dropped. He still ended up with some
$5,000 in administrative and legal fees. He's lucky he wasn't
charged, which would have eaten up more in jail time or probation fees, not to mention a license suspension and a record.

In theory, at least, financial penalties for minor offenses are
a logical, fair, and transparent form of punishment. Like the
"sin" tax on cigarettes and liquor, they provide added revenue for
the government at no extra cost to the well-behaved citizen, placing the burden instead on those who take risks. A capitalist perspective takes things a step further and considers all possible
means of monetizing and profiting off unlawful behavior. You
could even describe risk as the ultimate product capitalism sells
to the public: "Today we live in a world in which risk is manufactured and made quantifiable by new technologies and new forms
of expert knowledge. Risk now inheres in everything we do, from
eating, investing, and driving a car to simply breathing. Risk is,
simply put, ideological" (Tomso).

The focus of interest here is not so much the petty or the professional criminal (theft, burglary, fraud). Less than five percent
of the population ever ventures into this territory, while less
than one percent commits assault and robbery, and far fewer still
rape or homicide ("Crime rate"). As we'll see, the American state
does indeed capitalize on all of these crimes, increasingly so. But
a more profitable enterprise would concentrate on the predictable
manifestations of human weakness, those which the general
population cannot help but fall prey to again and again: the irre-

pressible infraction or offense. Traffic violations are one; debt is another; illicit drug use and sexual misconduct are two more. These are the real cash cows.

In a more rational system of justice, no one would go to jail for any offense except violent acts. If punitive fines replaced jail time, the convicted could continue to work and be productive members of society. Fines would be graded according to the severity of the crime and wages garnished in proportion to one's ability to pay. That in itself would be enough of a punishment and a strong disincentive to repeat the offense, while repeat offenses would be punished more severely. Offenders would also be required to undergo some form of rehabilitation and community service. Violent criminals who must be sequestered for society's safety should be put to work in prison for reasonable wages to pay for the cost of imprisonment and to support their families.

For a monetary-based punitive system to make sense, people must have money to pay the fines imposed on them. The U.S. is unique in its grotesquely sadistic approach to punitive justice, in that it simultaneously incarcerates and fines the convicted, who thus lose the means to pay their fines once prison deprives them of employment. The U.S. as well, particularly since the 1980s when the prison population ballooned, locks up more and more people for a greater variety of offenses and keeps them locked up longer than anywhere else. There are, of course, nefarious regimes elsewhere in the world that are extremely brutal toward their citizens, but such tends to be reserved for political prisoners. U.S. domestic policing, by contrast, directs its brutality toward a much wider swath of the population.

A common refrain is that those in jail deserve to be there because they have a debt to pay to society. As for those who get off lightly with only a probation sentence, it can't be that bad, can it? Well, it is pretty bad, in fact. The system milks anyone who makes one false step—and their families—to the max. One Baltimore woman, a nurse's aide, incurred thousands of dollars in fines and repeated jail time for a single DUI offense that caused no accident or injuries (Dewan). An Alabama woman, a day-care center custodian, experienced similar financial hell from a single driving-on-at-expired-license conviction (Stillman, "Get out"). Both were poor and Black but gainfully employed until they lost their job due to jail time, which prevented them from paying their fines and pushed them deeper into the hole and back into jail—a vicious circle for people at the edges of respectable society.

Ever more inventive ways are devised to place an extreme punitive financial burden on the offender—known in the parlance as "offender-funded justice"—while depriving them of the means to pay. Underscoring their arbitrariness, the myriad administrative and correctional fees issued by courts, jails, probation agencies, electronic surveillance contractors, and so forth, vary among states and cities, some putting a greater burden on the taxpayer, others on the defendant. Typical rates that a misdemeanor offender will pay might include $2,000 to a bail bondsman, $1,500 to a lawyer, and $250 to the court. If the offender is able to avoid jail time and put on probation, there will be fees amounting to $80-$200 per month to the probation service, and another $300-$400 per month in rehabilitation courses, which can stretch from as little as twelve hours for first-timers to thirty months or more for repeat offenders. If electronic surveillance or house arrest is imposed, a GPS ankle-bracelet rental can run $300-$500 per month. Many sex offenders are saddled with electronic monitoring for life and struggle or fail to make these payments as they are routinely denied employment.

Another misperception is that we pay for prisoners, who hardly deserve the right to bask in the lazy comfort of a taxpayer-funded jail cell. The reality is that the taxes are eaten up by bloated prison bureaucracies and there is still a shortfall of funds. Since the 1980s, the jailed population has burgeoned beyond the capacity of existing budgets. Governments have thus turned to private companies and contractors who claim to operate prisons more cheaply, with resulting deterioration in conditions and kickbacks to powerful politicians (Korecki). Both private and state jails charge prisoners for everything from room and board and medical care to laundry and toilet paper. The average "pay-to-stay" rate is a hefty $68 per day or $25,000 per year. Some local jails in California charge prisoners as much as $100-$150 a day (Eisen). You might hope these high costs would guarantee a basic standard of care and protection for the incarcerated, expected of a developed country. But the quality of U.S. prisons is by all accounts dreadful, with threadbare medical and virtually no psychiatric care, along with beatings, arbitrary punishments, and 70,000 rapes annually (Gopnik).

The fees incurred by prisoners might be recouped through forced labor but for the outrageous crumbs for wages contemptuously tossed at them; Louisiana pays four cents an hour (Rabuy & Kopf). Working mothers or relatives often have to pay for an imprisoned family member's necessities (soap, toothpaste, phone calls, emails), at artificially inflated rates that can run up to $10,000 per year (Lewis & Lockwood). If the family can't support them, they go into debt while in prison, making it all the more difficult to get a financial foothold when they get out. Prisoners thus accumulate huge debts from years in jail. Collection agencies are hired to harass their families to pay up on their behalf, and they hound parolees upon their release, which in turn contributes to the high recidivism rate, as parolees have a hard enough time finding gainful employment and acceptance back into the community even without any indebtedness. Many prison debts simply go unpaid, for reasons that are not hard to understand: they have no bearing on reality.

JACK UP THE STATE OF FEAR

The most effective weapon for keeping a population docile is psychological terror: the ensemble of intersecting anxiety-inducing processes and effects dispersed throughout daily life. Because these forms of mass distress are normalized to appear as universal and inevitable, there is scant awareness of their collective function and little coordinated response or protest. We do not necessarily mean crude, Big Brother-style repression. Repression in its contemporary American incarnation is far more sophisticated and subtle. The best way to describe it is by breaking down the generalized, faceless terror into its components (*terror* here being distinct from *terrorism*, i.e., destructive acts carried out by self-identified terrorists).

Financial terror refers to the distress of being heavily burdened or rendered indigent by unmanageable or unanticipated financial pressures and hardships. Eighty percent of Americans are in debt to an average of $38,000, mainly auto loans and credit-card debt, while average mortgage debt per household adds another $190,000. The average student loan debt per undergraduate student is $49,000; 28 percent of those with student loans default. Master's degree graduates of Columbia University's film program have an average debt of $181,000, and some have debts up to $300,000 (Korn & Fuller). It's said that people have no one but themselves to blame for money problems since it's a personal choice. But this downplays the circumstances that force many to fall into debt in the first place, which may be to rescue themselves from economic constraints or crises or to help other family members. It also ignores the aggressive, predatory activities of financial organizations and educational institutions to induce people to go into debt. Capital One Financial Corporation, for example, earns $23 billion in interest each year with its bespoke targeting of the lower echelons of wage earners in order to "push people into debt who would have otherwise avoided it" and "profit off people's misery," as one former employee puts it (Botella).

It would be nice if society could acknowledge and take more responsibility for the ease with which it allows people to become indebted instead of smugly blaming them. Unfortunately for Americans, the tendency to hold the poor responsible for their own failures is long-entrenched and has religious roots going back to the Puritans, who "brought with them...a biblically prescribed view that God helps those who help themselves, that poverty is a kind of sin, the result of a willful failure to work and thrive" (Snedeker). But the problem runs deeper:

> The hold that debt has over our lives is not merely numerical. It functions as a disciplinary apparatus as we internalize the ideology that naturalizes indebtedness....We are, from an early age, socialized into a form of financial citizenship that compels us to accept indebtedness as inevitable and to constantly engage in self-disciplinary acts that authorize and extend the debt economy—whether it's pursuing a job as a corporate lawyer instead of a public defendant in order to pay off student loans or telling your peers they are irresponsible for not building their credit. (Wang)

Medical terror refers to the devastating impact of snowballing bills from sudden illness or accident. No one's physical well-being is exempt from peril but American medical terror is especially horrific, as it piles financial terror on top of a health emergency. It's hard to say which would be worse, a stage-four cancer diagnosis or the cost of that diagnosis: 42 percent of cancer patients lose their life savings after two years of treatment, averaging $92,000 per patient (Bandoim). Not surprisingly, catastrophic illness is the leading cause of bankruptcy in the U.S. (Graeber). Annual medical expenses for Americans come to $5,000, including those with insurance or patchwork assistance from Medicaid, Medicare, or the inadequate Affordable Care Act. That's the per capita *average*; it is much higher if we discount the many young, healthy people with no medical expenses. There is no shortage of news stories on the obscene cost of medical care—of hospitals price-gouging patients as much as ten times actual costs or springing inscrutable hidden fees (Sun; Kliff & Sanger-Katz). At first glance, it can seem as if such stories are concocted for entertainment value and hospitals are playing practical jokes on patients, as when one hospital charged a man $1 million for his coronavirus treatment (Kliff). The cost of a drive-thru Covid-19 test in Texas is $2,450; get the test done in an emergency room and it's $54,000 (Gleeson).

Meanwhile, Democrat politicians wring their hands and mouth protestations of outrage, Republicans sit back in sardonic silence, and the rest of the world shakes its head in incomprehension at the sad, sadistic U.S. medical system.

Compounding medical terror is pharmaceutical terror: the colluding of the drug companies, hospitals, and physicians in overprescribing medicines, especially to the elderly, for the sake of profit (Span). While 40,000 Americans sit in prison for cannabis offenses—a safe and natural plant medicine—drug companies contribute to the growing national annual overdose tally of 100,000 deaths and counting, from lethal opiates and opioids (Nir, "Inside"). Many of these deaths are due to illegal abuse, from such drugs as fentanyl whose safe dosage is very hard to control, but many users start out with legally acquired medication and graduate to illegal use only after their prescriptions run out and their only recourse to assuage chronic pain is the black market.

Social terror refers to the violence—and the fear of violence—which hangs over American communities like perpetual storm clouds. Commentators are fond of pointing out statistics showing that violent crime in the U.S. has actually decreased over the past couple of decades (due to a variety of factors it's not necessary to go into here), and therefore panic about crime is exaggerated and overblown. This misses the point that the violence is already way out of proportion to other developed countries and is comparable to places like Brazil, Colombia, South Africa, and the Philippines. Three hundred and sixteen people are shot every day in the U.S., one-third of them lethally; gun injuries rack up $1 billion in medical costs per year (Santana; Flowers). Private insurance typically pays for only a portion of victims' gun injuries, which average $96,000 per in-patient stay, that is, exclusive of emergency-room treatment; the remaining medical and rehabilitation fees are picked up by Medicaid (maybe) and the victims themselves (Fransdottir & Butts).

So great is the diarrheic flood of guns in the U.S. that Mexico is presently suing American gunmakers, who design their weapons to appeal to Mexican drug cartels, to stem the flow of guns into their country. A Colt special edition .38 pistol, for example, is engraved with an image of the Mexican revolutionary Emiliano Zapata (Agren). I was once robbed at gunpoint near the University of Chicago campus; it was an interesting experience but once was enough. It took place only three blocks away from where 24-year-old Dennis Shaoxiong Zheng was shot to death three decades later in a broad-daylight robbery, the third University of Chicago student to be randomly murdered in 2021 (Terry). If you've spent your entire life in this country without a gun incident you might think omnipresent gun terror isn't as bad as it is made out to be because you haven't experienced it. But the majority of the world's population live in much safer circumstances and go about freely without being shadowed by the specter of assault. In Canada, England, Germany, Japan, and China, countries where I have lived beside the U.S., a night on the town is a stress-free experience, for women as well, where they're much in evidence at late hours.

Whenever gun-control advocates get their news bite after the latest mass murder, they are quickly put in their place by soberer voices reminding us that meaningful gun control never stands a chance of legislative passage in this country, and they are probably right. What will likely change as guns continue to proliferate and fear of their use looms ever larger, is that everyone, in an attempt to turn this fear on its head, will have to arm themselves with open-carry weapons—exactly the gun lobby's goal. If this ensues, the only people who will want to immigrate to the land of the free anymore will be those fleeing impoverished countries even more violent than the U.S. International tourists may be frightened away, along with the $250 billion in annual revenue they bring in. Also financially ravaged will be universities, when the large cohort of international students vanishes, who supply another $45 billion in revenue. With a shrunken economy in an austere social landscape, we could witness the unprecedented phenomenon of a developed country reverting to a developing one: the future incarnation of the nineteenth-century American Wild West.

I am jolted back into the old malaise whenever I return to my hometown of Chicago, with the constant sound of police, fire-truck, and ambulance sirens at all hours of the night. You only begin to notice this if you've been out of the country for a while or live in a rural area. Foreign visitors are unnerved by this ominous, round-the-clock noise pollution. Sirens have a dual indexical function. First of all, they indicate—index—the presence of an emergency vehicle so that cars can get out of the way. But sirens also index a general state of emergency. Inured to it as a result of routine, lifelong exposure, we are unconscious of the phenomenon in its generalized aspect, and regard sirens as an inevitable feature of daily life. But there is in fact little need for sirens, except intermittently to clear traffic.[7] That these vehicles have nothing better to do than blast their siren down empty streets at night when people are sleeping bespeaks something else: state power's insistent affirmation of itself. You might be more conscious of this were you to imagine the standard sonic signature identifying emergency vehicles being replaced by air-raid sirens.

Another way to appreciate the face of state power is to be in a confrontation, however trivial, with the police. I was biking recently in Shanghai, China, when a police officer stopped me for violating a traffic regulation for cyclists. Gently placing his hand on my shoulder, he guided me over to the correct lane for crossing the intersection. This is America: one evening a few years

---

[7] I should qualify this: in the U.S. sirens clear people very effectively; Americans tend to pull over almost in a panic, whereas in China emergency vehicles are blocked by indifferent cars and pedestrians, a phenomenon that has fortunately improved in recent years.

back I was pulled over on a street in Chicago. Instead of calmly informing me that one of my taillights had stopped working, the cop resorted to yelling and cursing. I happen to be white. Being Black makes it much easier for police encounters to spiral out of control or erupt in instant gunfire. In an incident only days ago, Chicago police kicked in the door of a house in a Black neighborhood without announcing themselves or presenting a warrant. They pointed their guns at the parents lying prone on the floor and then at their two girls in the bedroom, four and nine years old, who wet their beds and have since displayed PTSD symptoms; it was the wrong house (Niemeyer). A young Black man describes another encounter with the Chicago police:

> Once my friend and I were walking down the street. We were at Wood Street and 45th and we had just come outside. Then the cops came. Deep. Three cop cars. Because my phone had a weed plant on the screen they wanted my PIN number to unlock my phone. But I said, "I'm not going to give you my PIN." So one of the white cops punched me in my stomach and put me inside the cop car. (Kaba)

Atlanta police were filmed kicking a handcuffed mentally ill woman in the face and down a hill, who had been brandishing a weapon (Marcus). Whether she was threatening people is irrelevant in regard to such police behavior *following* upon her being subdued. One hardly needs to be armed and dangerous. Bay Area police sicced an attack dog on an unarmed Uber driver, severely mauling his arm, when his rental car was listed as stolen after he had fallen behind on payments; video showed the attack to be entirely unprovoked (Anguiano & Bhuiyan). A Black woman in California stopped her car at the side of a road to change places with her father and was obedient when the police approached her. For no reason, they slammed her to the ground, knocking her unconscious (Weber). Police around the country have a knack for flinging people to the ground. A migrant woman was caught by a Border Patrol officer who "threw me to the ground in a very aggressive way. And he pulled me up three or four times, and kept slamming me on the ground," kicking her in the rib cage and lower pelvis (Sullivan). A white Louisiana cop was videoed lifting up a Black woman who had just been attacked by several boys and "slamming the 100-pound woman to the ground repeatedly. Witnesses say that at one point, the deputy slammed [her] head into the pavement so hard that several of her braids ripped straight from her scalp" (Germain). A deaf man pulled over in Colorado for running a stop sign tried to communicate with the police in sign language but was slammed to the ground, tasered, and jailed for four months, allegedly for resisting arrest (Burke). When a disabled Black man was ordered out of his car by Ohio police and protested, "I can't step outside the car, sir. I'm a paraplegic...I got help getting in," they were filmed dragging him out by his hair and throwing him to the ground as he screamed in pain (Zitser).

If I've been piling on more than a few examples of people being treated like rag dolls, when they aren't treated like terrorists, it's to point out that it happens far too regularly to be considered mere haphazard acts by rogue cops. Long entrenched in this country, gratuitous state violence is, again, a form of symbolic power. The police are enlisted and encultured into this ideology, without requiring their conscious understanding of it, to evoke and dramatize the state's power through countless intimidating displays and acts, whether it involves hurling people to the ground, punching them in the stomach or, as renowned Malian musician Ballaké Sissoko experienced after a recent American tour, U.S. customs officials destroying his priceless kora (Sawa).

As this behavior trickles down and becomes normalized, we see more people at the margins of society similarly act out on vulnerable people, as if mimicking it. Over the first two years of the Covid-19 pandemic, there were over 9,000 reported hate crimes against perceived Chinese in the U.S., many involving horrific, random attacks on elderly Asians—slammed on the head by bricks, shoved from behind, thrown out of their wheel-chairs. As if to explain away the problem, it's been noted that many of these assaults were committed by homeless and mental-ly people. But that only underscores the fact that it is sympto-matic of a violent society from the top-down ("More than 9,000").

THE SEWAGE SYSTEM

In business-as-usual America, government coffers are militariz-ing the police, expanding the jail population, providing employ-ment for the carceral complex, and solidifying corporate ties with private contractors in the electronic monitoring and surveillance industries. The state is happy to oblige in all of this, as it gives the bureaucracy and related sectors things to do and punitive profits to gain. With some eight million incarcerated, probated, and paroled under some kind of penal or protective jurisdiction, on top of the 70 million with a criminal record, we have what amounts to the physical or electronic shackling of almost a quar-ter of the American population. To be sure, some of the impris-oned are a threat to society. But most are not. Fascism sweeps up everyone. In the name of law and order, large numbers get put away in either human cages or digital cages, subject to criminal-record blacklisting, GPS tracking, and other forms of electronic carceral surveillance. As the technology develops and evolves, there is no telling how it may become employed against all of us in the future.

On the other hand—and this is also key to understanding fascism—the state cannot drag so many into its net without the approval and support of the population at large. With both per-ceived and real dangers all around them, the paranoid half of the American public is highly obsessed with law and order. Politi-cians exploit this to get elected and promise to follow through. The state again is happy to oblige and expedite this collective desire for ever more arrests for an increasing array of crimes.

And of course, the more crime there is, the more the public demands the sort of harsh state response that fascism trumpets. Oddly, nothing really changes, but what counts is the illusion of change, namely that the internal enemy is being packed off and society cleansed of its human waste, even when it's recycled back into society in the more toxic form of traumatized ex-convicts.

I use the metaphor of the "sewage system" to underscore that it's not merely a question of the object itself. Rather, sewage is the constituent product of a system, an economy, both politically and symbolically speaking. It's a political economy in that it is a real economy producing something, the criminalized and imprisoned, for consumption by its stakeholders—prison and police officials, contractors, prosecutors, and politicians—though at taxpayer expense and with collateral damage to the communities of the incarcerated. It's a symbolic economy as well in that it produces something illusory for public consumption—human waste—which furnishes the evidence of its own production, even if and precisely because real humans are involved.

But it's not enough to sweep things up once and for all to restore society to some primordial state of order. The public demands ongoing evidence, continual reassurance in the form of a constant flow of waste. The human sewage needs to be sent out of the way, but not to disappear. To provide the guilty with free room and board in which to do their time is unacceptable, and what happens to those dispatched to the carceral underworld needs to be made evident. They must be made to suffer throughout the duration of their sentences under the harshest possible conditions. In this sadistic theater, the line between those on stage and the audience is sharply drawn. If the question is what accounts for the enormous amount of human sewage the fascist state is compelled to produce, the answer is that there is something about this continuous outflow that is immensely satisfying. It serves them right, as the Nazis said of the Jews: they had it coming to them.

3

THE STATE OF RAGE:
THE AMERICAN SEXUAL DYSTOPIA

LET'S SAY YOU BELIEVE that the heterosexual monogamous family is the only proper place for a sexual relationship, and virginity for women and sexual abstinence for both sexes before marriage is expected and even essential. You believe adolescents have no sexual rights of their own and must be shielded from sexual knowledge and experience before they reach the age of consent (sixteen to eighteen years in the U.S., varying by state). You believe casual sex, serial lovers, simultaneous relationships, and the like are reckless and dangerous. You believe sex to be not very important in fact, a mental obsession and addiction, easily suppressed with a focus on the more meaningful aspects of life. But you also believe sex to be enormously important, inasmuch as sanctioned sex is holy and unsanctioned sex is immoral and destructive.

If you hold to any of the above, I'd wager you're a traditionalist and fairly conservative, if not necessarily religious. Communist regimes find all of the above most salutary, and fascist states like Nazi Germany instinctively controlled sexual behavior through such strictures. But they can be found in many countries, and as one looks back in history, sex laws were even harsher. In Elizabethan England, for example, adultery was punishable by death; in Medieval Europe, the Church dictated which days of the calendar the married were permitted conjugal relations.

Now ask yourself if any of the following happens to apply to you. You believe that there is no place for family nudity, and women must tone down their raw allure by shaving their body hair and wearing a bra, while it's okay for men to go about topless. You believe the public sight of a woman's breastfeeding nipple is obscene. You believe perceived improprieties of any sort should be referred to grievance committees instead of dealing directly with the offending person (we don't mean criminal assault or rape when we must resort to the police). You believe sex work is degrading and prostitutes and their patrons should be arrested. You believe the police should be informed if teenagers close in age are caught having sex, above all if one is above the age of consent and the other is not, and that it's acceptable for children of any age to be punished and even prosecuted if they engage in sexual harassment or assault. You reserve special loathing for pedophiles, who if they can't be locked up for life, should be exiled from society, regardless of the severity of their offense; you would troll the sex offender registries for newly listed offenders and their families to hunt down and attack. You believe all of this while regarding yourself as otherwise liberal and enlightened, in our day and age, toward gay and transgender rights, extramarital sex, and other practices that only a generation or two ago were deviant or unlawful.

No single country has a lock on these sentiments, but what's salient about the American response to sexual prohibition is its fanaticism, its eagerness to find fault where there is none and the ensuing rage where it is found. In the name of being progressive, Americans are particularly susceptible to sexual fascism. As Theo Horesh writes, "liberals are carrying out their own paradoxical crackdown on sexual freedom. The criminalization of relatively minor infractions of sexual norms; the severe crackdown on borderline cases of sexual harassment; the pathologization of late-adolescent expressions of sexuality." With its Puritan-inspired legacy of intolerance toward the sexually rebellious— Hester Prynne in Nathaniel Hawthorne's *The Scarlet Letter* is the iconic example albeit one that pales in comparison to the punitive response toward today's sexual deviants—a legacy backed by widespread popular support, it's easy for the American state to latch onto sex law as a ready means of expanding its regimes of surveillance over everyone.

Now let's consider a few examples of sex crimes and their punishment, pulled off the news almost at random, there being no shortage of stories. We'll begin with an egregious yet not unambiguous case and work our way through more problematic ones. Several years ago, a 46-year-old Indian American physician, Shafeeq Sheikh, was convicted of the sexual assault of a 27-year-old patient whose breasts he had fondled while she was medicated but conscious and receiving treatment for asthma in a Houston hospital. He later reentered her room and had unprotected sex with her. He claimed it was consensual; she claimed she tried to report the assault by summoning the nurse with the call button but was too weak to do so until the next day. Mitigating circumstances led the jury to downgrade the rape charge, which in Texas carries a prison sentence of two to twenty years, to a mere ten years' probation. That Sheikh wasn't given any time behind bars sparked media outrage at the miscarriage of justice. News reports did take care to mention that he lost his medical license and would have to register as a sex offender (G. Banks).

The mention is significant, for Sheikh might be better off in prison, where at least he would be in a stable environment, protected from the elements (if not from violent prisoners) and provided with daily food and bedding. If the public understood what his punishment actually entailed, it might be a bit more persuaded justice had been served. Sheikh's listing in the Texas Public Sex Offender Website shows his photo, risk level (low), duration he will be registered (life), date of birth, address, crime (sexual assault), sex and age of his victim, and the date of the offense. Note that although his probation ends after ten years, he will remain on the registry for life, and his address will be ever available to anyone with an internet connection (he'll have to register each new address if he moves). As the offense didn't involve children, he and his family may be spared attacks by vigilantes set on driving them out of the neighborhood, say by throwing rocks through their windows. Crimes on the registry are stated in broad terms, so that, for example, an eighteen-year-old caught having sex with his seventeen-year-old girlfriend in a state where the age of consent is eighteen might be listed as having taken "indecent liberties with a child." Some state registries don't list the victim's age, so anyone viewing such an offender's profile could reasonably assume he is a dangerous child predator, inciting the community to force him out, if he's allowed to live at home to begin with (*No Easy Answers*).

Because the registry's purpose is to alert the neighborhood to potential predators living in their midst, all listed offenders are subject to the same community restrictions, regardless of whether their crime involved children. In every state, sex offenders must keep a specified distance from places where children congregate, on pain of a felony conviction for violating the restrictions. In Texas, they may not reside or approach within 2,000 feet of any park, playground, school, day-care center, video arcade, youth center, recreational hiking or biking trails, or public swimming pool. These restrictions are often designed with the express purpose of zoning offenders out of their community or city altogether, including from their home; they may not be able to live at home in any case if they're forbidden contact with their own children.

The restrictions placed on Shafeeq Sheikh would have been decided by his probation board and the Houston police. If he is allowed to live at home with his family, he can consider himself very lucky. If not, he will find it difficult or impossible to rent an apartment, not only due to residency restrictions; landlords do background checks and routinely reject anyone on the registry. Whether he will be able to find employment to help support his family and pay for the array of monthly probation and administrative fees he'll be saddled with is also uncertain: employers likewise all the way down to fast-food restaurants refuse to hire anyone on the registry. The upshot is that as a consequence of allowing his hormones to get the better of him—as he may have rationalized it to himself—while doing his rounds one night at work, Sheikh may be reduced to living in a rural trailer park or under a highway overpass not covered by residency restrictions, supported for the rest of his life by the very family whom he had been supporting before his arrest. If his wife herself is unemployed, if their home has a mortgage, then she and their child may themselves fall into dire straits and rendered indigent. If Sheikh is denied housing altogether, he could always join a roving band of fellow sex-offender vagrants adorned with GPS ankle bracelets as they wander from community to community, or city to city, to find shelter, their movements tracked by the police (homeless shelters often turn away sex offenders). Milwaukee was one such dumping ground until it tightened up its residency restrictions in 2014, forcing some 200 registered offenders out of the city before they were allowed back in 2019 (Faraj; Hess).

Was Sheikh's crime so heinous as to deserve such punishment? Measured against the worst types of sexual assault, say violent rape causing serious injury or death, clearly not. He may truly have misread the situation and convinced or deluded himself that the sex was consensual—and the jury seems to have given him some of the benefit of the doubt. This does not of course excuse his act, but suggests that it wasn't premeditated; nor does he fit the typical profile of a dangerous predator with a prior pattern of behavior. It is therefore hard to see how such a draconian punishment, reminiscent of something out of medieval history or a Third World theocracy, fits the crime and what it accomplishes in terms of public safety. In any other country, the punishment for the same offense would more closely fit the crime; even if incarcerated, the offender would be allowed to reenter society and be provided with the necessary support for doing so upon his release.

Another example of the momentous consequences of a stupid but fateful decision sprung from sexual temptation is the case of Jace Hambrick. A 20-year-old gaming nerd from Vancouver, Washington, he responded to an ad posted by an attractive woman in the "Casual Encounters" section of Craigslist. Oddly, in their initial exchange, she told him she was thirteen. He apparently didn't believe her, assuming some kind of a tease, as it bore no relation to her photo, the sophistication of her sex talk, and her knowledge of gaming. She invited him to her house. She greeted him outside and lured him in. Upon entering, he was subdued by armed officers. She was indeed the woman in the photo, a 24-year-old undercover police officer. Despite not getting anywhere near her, he was sentenced to eighteen months to life in prison for the attempted rape of a child. It didn't help that his electronics turned up nothing incriminating such as an interest in children. Most of those convicted in such entrapment stings do a minimum of ten years in prison (after plea-bargaining), regardless of prior history. Hambrick was lucky, though, and released for good behavior after two years. The terms of his probation as a registered sex offender, however, are onerous and career-destroying. Although he may live at home, he is not allowed to visit shopping malls, movie theaters, sports venues, parks, or anywhere children congregate; at home, he is forbidden from drinking alcohol and must inform a prospective partner that he's a registered sex offender. During his decade on the registry, he will have to pay the state $28,800 in probation and counseling fees. He has not been able to find work, apart from occasional weekend gigs. After ten years he can apply to be removed from the registry, with no guarantee he'll be approved (Winerip).

The next example of judicial sadism is more ambiguous still, or rather unambiguous, at least from a humane perspective since the actual offense cannot by any rationale be considered a crime. Caught having consensual sex with two sixteen-year-old boys at a summer camp in Idaho, where the age of consent is sixteen, eighteen-year-old Randall Menges was sentenced to seven years in prison, not for underage sex but sodomy. Upon his release in 2000, he was placed on the Idaho sex offender registry. Years later he moved to Montana, requiring him to register as a sex offender in that state as well. During all these years, he has been denied employment and housing, has had to live in "homeless shelters and had to sleep on the streets." Finally in May 2021, almost three decades after his conviction, a Montana federal judge removed him from the registry on the grounds that "the harm Mr. Menges suffered under Montana's statute outweighed the public's interest in keeping his name on the registry." However, this was appealed by a state prosecutor, and Menges' legal situation remains in limbo (Cramer).

The state's rage is no better exemplified than in the recent case of a seven-year-old boy in upstate New York who was arrested on a rape charge. The child's identity is being protected and no details of the case, presumably innocent sex play with another child, were revealed. But even if it involved, say, his sticking something into the other's orifice, this cannot under any reasonable grounds be considered criminal behavior. A defense attorney, "citing cognitive science data showing that young children lack a true awareness of what they are doing and the consequences of their actions," made the obvious point that "'the science doesn't support prosecution of second graders'" (Nir, "A 7-year-old"). In *The Feminist and the Sex Offender: Confronting Sexual Harm, Ending State Violence*, Levine and Meiners lament this astonishing penchant of the American state for branding young children as sex offenders:

> Toddlers as young as two were being labeled as children who molest and treated for "inappropriate" behaviors like putting objects inside genitals, pulling down their pants in public, or

masturbating "compulsively." Some were being prosecuted as sex offenders. In fact, almost everything these children do—rub their bodies against other kids, expose themselves, insert things into orifices—can qualify as normative children's play. And even those children who do harm to others sexually almost always show signs of aggressiveness in other ways as well—hitting, abusing animals, setting fires. The problem is the aggression, the cruelty, or the inability to control their impulses—not the sex.

Luckily, this seven-year-old is too young to be placed on the registry in New York, whose threshold is thirteen, but Arizona, Arkansas, Colorado, Kansas, Minnesota, and Texas register children as young as eight, and Massachusetts as young as seven. One-tenth of the 900,000 people on the sex offender registry in the U.S. are children (McKay; Stillman, "The list"; *No Easy Answers*).

In the public imagination, at least to those even aware of its existence, the sex offender registry is a well-deserved repository or garbage dump rightly reserved for monsters beyond the pale of humanity. But it has become remarkably easy for almost any normal person in a stupid or thoughtless moment to get on the registry. Innocently patting a child on the buttocks; mooning or streaking during a drunken night out; urinating in public even after taking precautions to conceal oneself but caught on camera; accidentally stumbling into a woman's restroom or unlocked apparel changing room with someone in it; teenagers of the same age having consensual sex or sexting their nude pics to each other; prepubescent schoolchildren caught pulling down their pants; sleeping with a minor who falsely claimed with a fake ID she was eighteen; a massage therapist who grazes a customer's breast; an unknowing family member or parent of a sex worker accused of aiding and abetting sex trafficking by living in the same home: these are some of the offenses that can get one put on the registry. Not that these acts will necessarily get you on the registry, but it happens.

Sex crimes vary in gravity from benign to violent, and the law attempts to reflect this. The national sex offender registry implemented by the Adam Walsh Act in 2006 distinguishes between more serious Tier III (aggravated sexual assault, sexual abuse of a child under thirteen) and comparatively less serious Tier II and I offenses. Yet sentencing varies widely and can be arbitrary and capricious, and states may and often do exceed the federal requirement with yet stricter registry restrictions; states may not impose restrictions less strict than the national registry (Farley). Clearly, when sex offenses by grown teenagers or adults are truly abusive or violent, the state's expected role is to determine the proper treatment for the offender and, if necessary, sequester him from the community. On the other hand, when politicians enact laws expressive of the public desire for retribution and when the state backs the public's desire for revenge and becomes at one with the vengeful public, the state itself takes on a vengeful cast. We are then on precarious political ground. This is what is happening in the United States.

We look to artists and writers to put their fingers on the pulse of the times. The South African novelist J. M. Coetzee captured the ease with which sexual improprieties can turn tragic in his 1999 novel *Disgrace*, featuring a university professor who sleeps with a student under ambiguous circumstances, neither wholly consensual nor wholly coercive. He is fired, not for the offense itself but for his refusal to acknowledge it. The rest of the narrative follows his mental unraveling and descent into poverty and degradation. An American version of the sex offender protagonist is the Kid in Russel Banks' 2011 novel *Lost Memory of Skin*, portending the 2017 Jace Hambrick case discussed above: a nineteen-year-old man meets a teenage girl online for sex and neglects to find out her exact age. The story is set under the Julia Tuttle Causeway sex offender colony in Miami-Dade County in Florida (which actually existed until it was dismantled due to public pressure), the only place the Kid is permitted to live after his release from prison, along with his pet iguana and portable generator for keeping his ankle bracelet charged. High schools are prime territory for sex scandals, as in the 2007 film *Look* (dir. Adam Rifkin), with its clever conceit of depicting the entire action through the lens of security cameras. A callous high-school teenager just under the age of consent sets out to seduce her teacher just to see if she can pull it off. She succeeds and sends him to prison. The high-school sex scandal in Zoe Whittall's 2016 novel *The Best Kind of People* similarly portrays a respected high-school teacher who is jailed for propositioning one of his students, though here the focus is on the devastation to his ostracized family in the face of the community's rage.

These authors have not needed to resort to invention, as if concocting unique little Greek tragedies for our moral edification. Their task, as chroniclers of our time, is not hard, and their tales are all clearly based on real events, of which there is no shortage. What makes them so foreboding in the American context is the collective fury proceeding from the community rather than the government. The rage of the state is one defining feature of fascism; the state of rage is the other, when the state offloads its rage onto the public, delegating to it the task of retribution. The less the public understands this and experiences this rage as its own, the more efficacious a tool of the state public rage becomes.

Daily news stories of capricious rage over sexual accusations abound, some wholly manufactured, such as the high-school teacher in Maine who was falsely accused of sleeping with her seventeen-year-old student and not rehired after being fired, despite being exonerated of all charges. She now works as a restaurant server ("Teacher acquitted"). Schoolchildren in the UK have found a way to spread baseless rumors on Tiktok that their teachers are pedophiles, causing them to quit in fear for their safety; one teacher said a malicious Tiktok post about him had 12,000 views (Bryan; Rogers). Not that this couldn't happen in the U.S., it just may not have been reported. One story recently reported was the resignation of transgender professor Allyn

Walker of Old Dominion University in Virginia, due to threats against his life over the publication of *A Long, Dark Shadow: Minor-Attracted People and Their Pursuit of Dignity* (U of California Press, 2021), a sociological study of the "coping mechanisms and mental health strategies" used by people who feel inclined toward minors and don't act on it, intended "to help prevent others who feel the same attractions from abusing children." His use of the term "minor-attracted people" led to the malicious assumption, fanned by rightwing Fox News host Tucker Carlson, that Walker himself was a pedophile (McDade).

The latter affair is, or should be, alarming for authors, academics, anyone with a role in public commentary. We seem to be entering a new era of intolerance turned fanaticism, where the mere mention of the topic of pedophilia, however it is problematized, draws suspicion upon oneself. Perhaps I too need to reiterate for the record that in condemning the U.S. sexual persecution regime, I am not thereby condoning adult sexual interest or activity with those under the age of consent.

To many, the sexual abuse of minors is a special category of depravity, the worst of crimes committed by the lowest of the low, who by their actions void their place in society and deserve the heaviest possible punishment. But righteousness blinds us to the larger view and a more comprehensive understanding of real injustice. Since sex crime against children is framed in terms of absolutes, it's hard to get outside of the frame. My overriding interest here concerns the human rights violations of an aggressive state apparatus testing the waters of full-blown fascism. The place to look for these violations in a fascist state is the scapegoated. In the U.S., the historically scapegoated are Blacks, Hispanics, and other minorities, but the country is now being torn against itself over the racism issue. Public rage is shapeshifting and ever on the lookout for new, uncontroversial enemies to rally against. The sex offender fits the bill. By his unspeakable, alien acts, he gives license to both the public and the state to coordinate the unleashing of their rage upon him. Short of capital punishment, the state's power to enforce justice for sex offenses is always seen as not enough. The community must step in to finish the job. Convicted sex offenders are caught between these pincers. The worse the offense, the greater the carceral retribution; the lesser the offense, the greater the community retribution.

It's commonly assumed, among those not fully apprised of the facts, that pedophiles need removal from society because they are incorrigible and will re-offend again and again unless locked up for good. The opposite is the case: convicted sex offenders have among the lowest rates of sexual recidivism. According to one study, the overall recidivism rate after three years for child molesters was high (39.4 percent), but this included re-arrests for all types of offenses, such as violations of residency restrictions; if only sex offenses were counted, the recidivism rate dropped to 5.1 percent (Przybylski). While the medical consensus is that pedophilia is an inborn, neurological disorder, those with a predisposition are considered fully capable of choosing not to act on their desires (Dastagir). You need not fear the worst in any case. Those imprisoned for violent sex crimes against children (Tier 3 offenders in the national registry) tend to be put away for a very long time. Upon completion of their sentence, they are then disappeared for good, to live out the remainder of their life in a shadow network of "civil commitment" prisons that operate without public oversight or accountability, in reported conditions of "guard brutality, solitary confinement, overcrowding, rotten food, negligent medical care, broken toilets" (Levine & Meiners). Meanwhile, sex offenders who do time aren't spared the public wrath just because they're secure behind bars; they experience it the moment they encounter their fellow inmates, the public's surrogate. Any child sex conviction consigns them to the bottom of the hierarchy, where they are ostracized and targeted for the bulk of prisoner-upon-prisoner beatings and rape.

Bleak and harrowing as the prison experience is for sex offenders, they are not released on the understanding that they have "done their time." The United States has already one of the worst recidivism rates in the world. Spat out into an unreceptive social void, parolees struggle to find employers willing to hire them and consequently return to crime to get by—and back to prison. They are the ordinary criminals who have served their time. Sex offenders who have served their time, by contrast, are released not into a vacuum of anomie but a cauldron of hostility. The message confronting the lepers is stark and aggressive: you are not wanted back. Those who avoided prison altogether and are on probation have it just as bad, if not worse, as they are presumed to have gotten off scot-free. Now it's the community's turn to take over the reins of punishment, armed with a tool provided by the state and honed for this exact purpose. The sex offender registry is no mere list, a resource that neighbors can consult to guard themselves against pederast ex-felons coming after their kids. It's a mechanism of the sort normally provided to secret police for flushing undesirables out from hiding. Those on the registry who have been zoned out of their communities altogether have it better in one sense. Being homeless or nomadic and banding together, they are less subject to attacks by vigilantes.

The sex offender registry is not a rational solution to a social problem but a legalistic abomination whose practical effect is to demoralize ex-offenders to the point of giving up entirely. Left without means of subsistence, many return to crime in order to survive. Some may try to get back at society by going after children, exactly what their punishment is supposed to prevent. The police in fact have been among the most vocal critics of the registry, if for no other reason than it's a major drain on their time with all the paperwork required to keep tabs on those registered in their jurisdictions.

It may be instructive to look at how the rest of the world handles sex offenders. Many countries, including Australia, Indonesia, Russia, South Korea, and the United States, chemically castrate the most intractable—those who readily admit their predilection and even cooperate with the authorities in treating it (Cochrane). Only a handful of countries have a sex offender registry, and they are, interestingly, mostly English-speaking: Australia, Canada, New Zealand, Trinidad and Tobago, Jamaica, South Africa, the UK, and Israel. All of them share a key difference from the U.S. version, however. The information on the registry is not available to the public but only to the police, and where the community is informed, they may not hinder the right of ex-offenders to get on with their lives. Barbaric in its exceptionalism, the U.S. is the only country that banishes sex offenders from the community after serving their sentence, either by geographically zoning them out or allowing the community to drive them out, even assault them with virtual impunity (J. Levine; *No Easy Answers*).

When it comes to sex, the U.S. stands apart. As Roger Lancaster in *Sex Panic and the Punitive State* puts it, "Americans make sex a key criterion of their moral hierarchy with a zeal that is not equaled in any other industrialized democracy." No other criminal offense unleashes the collective rage as the sex offense. American culture's unique hostility toward the sex offender finds contemporary expression in perpetual national anxiety over the specter of the "imperiled child" (Lauren Berlant, cited in Lancaster). It's too early to assess the #MeToo movement's impact on sexual mores and codes of conduct. The outing and shaming of people in authority who have exploited those under them for sexual gain is laudable. But rewriting ever broader forms of sexual misbehavior into law only gives greater discretionary power to the courts and the police to expand the population of offenders beyond its already staggering scope. The public clamors for greater vigilance and ruthlessness against sexual offenses, politicians and judges are elected on platforms promising just that, and the prison-industrial complex, in turn, feeds on increased funding and sanction to apply their powers with greater indiscriminateness to the population at large. If the purpose of sex law is to make the consequences of violating it so terrible that no sane person would dare contemplate exercising sexual freedom in any form, the result is a society living in fear of itself.

I suspect that most people—educated, civilized people—could hardly care less about the fate of convicted sex offenders. After all, they only got what they deserved. They constitute a small enough slice of the population to be of little concern to the rest of us anyway. Their punishment, though harsh, sends a signal to the law-abiding majority to stay clear of this most volatile of society's hazard zones. If their example succeeds in keeping such offenses in check, then it is of practical consequence. In any case, our sympathies should lie with the victims of sexual abuse and assault, not the perpetrators.

I have a different angle on this. Persecution of hated groups is one of the defining features of fascism. Once underway, oppression's tendency is to deepen, multiply, and encroach on ever-larger segments of the population. It is a dynamic, reinforcing process, enlisting the cooperation of the masses. Even the most dictatorial and tyrannical of regimes seek some legitimacy in popular support to justify their policies. Fascist regimes tap into the social and economic discontent caused by these very regimes to focus and direct popular rage at scapegoated groups through crude nationalist or racist demagoguery. By doing so, they lift the bar of state power and enlarge the parameters of control over the entire population.

It doesn't just stop at one group, such as Hitler's persecution of the Jews; the Nazis also singled out Communists, gypsies, homosexuals, and the disabled. The more categories of the despised there are the better: they allow the dominant group to define itself against them and feel good about itself, which shores up more popular support for the state. The state in turn gives surrogate expression to the public's inchoate rage and renders this rage articulate and eloquent. As the public relies on the state to explain reality, people are dumbed down in the process and made more susceptible to brainwashing. They do the state's bidding in channeling back this articulated rage toward the hated groups. The result is that sexual persecution is becoming as American as apple pie.

4

AN AMERICAN TALISMAN[8]

A TALISMAN HAS APPEARED in 21st-century America, one with astonishing magical powers, a glass amulet utterly bewitching and miraculous, fitting in the palm like a mini crystal ball. To young kids submerged in the dreamy developmental phase of childhood, it is a veritable Wonderland of miniature toy stores and colorful games. With the touch of a finger, it can do all kinds of things, summoning and bringing people to life on its screen and commanding toys and snacks to be delivered to one's home. Then when they reach their early teens, kids begin adapting to the adult world of reality. The talisman soon becomes jaded and the magic fades. Still, it remains an impressive, multifaceted toy, capable of shooting videos and photos with incredible ease and realism, playing movies and music from an infinite list, and packing more information at the fingertips than the city library.

If someone from the future had attempted to describe this mysterious thing to me back when I was a teenager in the 1970s, I would have found it pure science fiction and more or less in-

---

[8] Reprinted from Isham Cook, *American Rococo: Essays on the Edge* (Magic Theater Books, 2017).

comprehensible, as we all would have. I refer of course to the smartphone, now the most mundane of objects. In the U.S., however, this talisman has a very peculiar status and function. For American teenagers and American teenagers alone, the smartphone retains its magical and untamable powers—of the black magic variety. It is a very scary, indeed terrifying object.

You're a fifteen-year-old female and thus below the legal age of consent, which is sixteen or eighteen depending on which state you live in. Annoying males at school have been sexting you revealing pics of their bodies. Because you have no interest in them, it's easy to tag them in the dung heap for potential reporting. But one day the very guy you've got a serious crush on sexts you his erect member. He invites you to reciprocate. This is a whole new ball game. What he did was outrageous and a major turn-off. At the same time, it makes you drunk with desire and afraid—of yourself. He promises never to show your pic to anyone, but you know he very well might. If anyone does get their hands on it, your boobs will be burned on the retinas of thousands of students and you'll walk into class tomorrow as the school slut. And on the retinas of teachers and parents and then your own parents as well. On the other hand, you have his pic too. Doesn't this mutually assured destruction guarantee he won't share your pic? Nah, still too risky.

Whew! Survived that one, the first of an ongoing barrage of sexting temptations. They just keep scrolling in. Only another three years to go before you reach eighteen.

It's a good thing you've hardened yourself early on to these attacks. Being the school slut will be the least of your problems, and I mean the least of your problems. For starters, don't forget to quickly delete all those nudie pics the guys are sending you. By possessing them even momentarily, indeed simply by receiving them at all, you are breaking the law. You are committing a felony: possession of child pornography. And certainly don't reciprocate with a nude selfie of your own, as that would make you a co-conspirator in the manufacture and distribution of child pornography. But wait, you say. It's only older guys and creeps who do child porn, right? How can someone underage violate kiddie porn laws? Doesn't being underage protect me?

Well, no. Not since the Adam Walsh Act was signed into law in 2006. It's understandable you might not know about this. Your parents probably don't know about it either, or they would warn you. Most people are too busy getting on with their lives to be pondering the latest changes to juvenile sex laws. While the law is supposedly there to protect you from adult pedophiles, it can be turned against you. Consider what the legal age means. It is the age at which the state considers you old enough to participate in adult activities. It's not just what others may do to you; it's what you may do to them. For instance, the primary purpose of the drinking age is not simply to prevent others from corrupting you with alcohol but to prevent you from corrupting others with alcohol. Similarly, the age of sexual consent is not just there to keep others' hands off you but your hands off them. You are not allowed to have sex with anyone in any form, physically or vicariously (webcams, porn) until you're eighteen. It's a total, blanket ban on sex because it's *you* who is the danger.

What about those so-called "Romeo" laws exempting teenage couples close in age? Such laws do exist, but only in twenty-one out of the fifty states. Do you know where your state stands on juvenile sex? You should. Because if you're in one of the unlucky states and goof up, welcome to the sex offenders club! It's quite a group. That's right, for being caught with your fifteen-year-old classmate's cock shot, or for having consensual sex with your boyfriend of the same age, your new circle of acquaintances will include everyone from prepubescent kids caught playing doctor, to streakers, public urinators, and baby rapists.

The law doesn't care how young you are or the circumstances of your offense (children as young as nine or ten can get on the sex offender registry in some states). It's enough that you violated it. Courtesy of the Adam Walsh Act, you will be classified into one of three categories, Tier 3 (violent sex offenders), Tier 2 (less severe but includes the manufacture and distribution of child pornography), and Tier 1 (a vague catchall category for remaining offenders). If you're lucky you'll only be a Tier 1 offender, which keeps you on the registry for only ten or fifteen years. Note that these categories apply nationally. No state may alter them to make them less severe, but states are at liberty to make them more severe, as severe as they like. In some states, a Tier 1 offense will put you on the registry for life, with no possibility of appeal. The registry is public and accessible to anyone with an internet connection. It lists everything about you, your mugshot, home address, phone number, email, and license plate. On the other hand—and this is crucial—the registry is vague about your actual offense. It defines you as a "sex offender" without necessarily detailing the specifics of your case or even what Tier you're in. Anyone keeping tabs on new offenders in the neighborhood and discovering you on the registry has no reason not to assume you are the worst of the worst and an extreme danger to the community. There are also vigilantes who make it their life purpose to hunt down sex offenders around the country. They will soon come to harass or attack you, and you will be hounded out of the neighborhood along with your family.

Even if your name is eventually expunged from the public record, you'll still be on it for life anyway, because private companies collect this information and sell it on the web. So while you may eventually be removed from the registry, you can't really be removed from it.

Take a moment to consider the consequences. Almost every state requires your school and employer to be notified of your sex offender status, regardless of when you were convicted and what for. Even if your school allows you to stay, everyone and their parents will know, and they will be very unhappy to have a sex offender on-premises. It won't help to move to a new school, as they will soon find out all about you as well. They will make it unbearable for you to remain in school.

When you are old enough to have a job, good luck trying to

find one. It's pretty difficult for a sex offender to find a job, any job, ever. That means it's going to be very hard for you to pay all the fees you've incurred as a result of your conviction. There may be initial court-ordered fines and administrative expenses running in the thousands of dollars. By law, you will be required to undergo a variety of regular tests, such as monthly polygraphs, administered by private probation companies. They are doing great business these days, as they can pretty much set their own fees, which can amount to hundreds of dollars a month. If you're a Tier 2 offender, you may be required to wear a GPS ankle bracelet for years or the rest of your life, and you'll be billed several hundred dollars a month for its operating and replacement costs (planned obsolescence is built into them too). You'll also need your own electricity supply to keep it charged around the clock; they are alerted as soon as your signal stops and this will promptly send you to jail. How ironic that the same GPS technology used to track sex offenders' whereabouts is also celebrated for its various applications in cellphones—enabling you to track your friends, for instance. This makes the smartphone a glorified ankle bracelet, so you're already used to the technology.

You take for granted a ready supply of electricity at home, but you may not be allowed to live at home. That's due to residency restrictions for sex offenders, which have gotten stricter over the years. They solve the problem of how to kick pedophiles out of the neighborhood by simple legal measures. Most states now prevent offenders from residing within 1,000 feet of schools, daycare centers, playgrounds, bus stops, parks, churches, swimming pools, and any other places where children congregate. As there are few places not covered by these zones, the restrictions can effectively lock you out of your entire town or city. If any legal residential pockets still remain, lawmakers simply extend the distance to 2,000 or 2,500 feet (half a mile) or add new venues to the list, such as stores and shopping malls. Or they create parklets or "pocket parks" to fill in all possible gaps.

Once exiled, where can you live? By the way, if later you

want to get married and have children, they will either have to live with you in your rural trailer or away from you, though in more lenient cases you may be allowed daytime visiting rights to your family's home.

If you remain unconvinced this could ever happen to you, it's understandable. As a teen, you are naturally rebellious and you should be, as it's a healthy sign of independence. You also tend to disregard dangers not immediately apparent, which require a certain maturity and foresight to anticipate. That's the lovely thing about childhood, being wrapped up in your innocent bubble and allowed to put off adult worries and responsibilities until later. When I was a teenager, for instance, it would never have occurred to us we couldn't experiment sexually with our peers.

Children become sexualized as part of their natural biological development. The idea itself is put into their heads earlier or later in various cultures. In North America, beauty industry values start burrowing their way into the consciousness of prepubescent girls quite early. The process is well underway by twelve or thirteen, sanctioned by peer pressure and parental approval—lip gloss, mascara, makeup. Years before boys take an interest in girls, the latter undergo extensive indoctrination and training to look attractive, and by senior high are expertly decked out and ready for the kill, already pros at the seduction game, when boys start turning their attention to them. Both boys and girls by this point have acquired quite a bit of lore about sex and gab about it with friends and classmates. Today you see fellow teenagers all around you having sex, girls boasting about their boyfriends, and everyone and his brother sexting each other their homemade porn.

A few advances in technology aside, things weren't all that much different in the past. I can't speak for earlier eras, such as the proverbial prudish 1950s, but I can attest that sexually open discourse has been a feature of Western society since at least the 1960s-70s when I was growing up. I suspect it always has been if not for the bias of the present. This bias holds that we are ever-

evolving toward a freer zeitgeist and leaving the repressive past
of our parents' generation behind. How misleading and untrue
this is. I recall one day in my last year of junior high while living
in Canada, aged fifteen. While waiting for the teacher to arrive
for chemistry class, we listened raptly as a classmate, Linda, related in graphic detail all the sexual positions she had tried with
her senior high boyfriend. Two years later in Germany, my senior
high classmates invited me to go skinny-dipping with them on a
Sunday picnic. Yep, both sexes. Also in Germany, where there
was no strict drinking age, a skimpily dressed thirteen-year-old
girl in a teen bar once came on to me. We danced a bit, and that
was all. I recall at the time finding it odd to be with someone so
young, as I preferred girls my age or a bit older. Yet it wasn't all
that surprising considering that German teens are sexualized at
an earlier age than most other cultures (the legal age of consent
in Germany is fourteen).

Draconian sex laws in the internet age are a relatively recent
phenomenon. That's another reason why you haven't heard about
them. They are unprecedented and exist almost entirely in the
United States. Some countries do have sex offender registries but
they are confidential and known only to local law enforcement.
No other country has residency restrictions and drives offenders
into exile, and no other country convicts juvenile sex offenders as
adults or bars them from gainful employment. If I have difficulty
wrapping my head around these new developments, I can understand you do too, in your youthful credulity and ignorance.

Let's agree that these criminal penalties bear no relationship
to any reasonable form of justice and are immoral and evil in
their very conception. It has something to do with the contemporary capitalist trend of extending profitable markets into childhood, all accelerated and enabled by computer technology and
internet commerce: first fast food, then the sexualization of children through teen mags, cosmetics, and fashionable teen wear,
and now the private incarceration industry, which is increasingly
accommodating juveniles. The result? A society that is itself per-

verted and schizophrenic, dangling sexual temptations to ever-younger people and then punishing them brutally.

Of course, the courts can't prosecute all teenagers. They don't have the resources to, not to mention the country can't afford to gut the future of its youth. There would be a widespread public backlash if too many teens were convicted of sex crimes. Yet the justice system only needs to pick out a few delinquents to make an example of. Your chances of being one of the examples are on the whole fairly low, but not by any means negligible, and the consequences are disastrous. Mom and dad won't be able to help you. They might inadvertently be responsible for getting you in trouble in the first place, if for instance, in order to ferret out all parties involved, they were to inform the school about the sexual content another student sent to your cellphone.

Kids, take my advice and ditch this toxic talisman that can turn your life upside down with one false step. Reject the smartphone. Get one of those ancient Nokia phones that had no camera or photo apps. Disable the camera on your laptop and iPad as well. And, most importantly, don't date or have sex. It's simply too dangerous these days in America. Do as Asian teenagers do and study your ass off to get into a good college. Before you know it, you'll be safely delivered to your eighteenth birthday and ensconced in a nice university where you can fuck your brains out to your heart's content (though vigilantly check the IDs of any fellow freshmen you've got the hots for who may still be seventeen!). I can tell you, computer technology is overrated. You don't need it. When I was growing up, we had our own form of social networking technology that worked just fine: an address book we pulled out of our back pocket.

5

TOILET TERROR

UTOPIAN CONSIDERATIONS

THE PERFORMING OF ABLUTIONARY activities openly in a shared social space had long been the norm before the individual's right to seclusion became something sacrosanct and inviolable. People used to bathe and go to the toilet, in other words, in front of each other freely and unselfconsciously. In our day and age, however, the right to bodily privacy is so ingrained and taken for granted that it's inconceivable why anyone would ever question it. Only in exceptional institutionalized settings—the army, the prison—is this right taken away. Yet it's only been a right in modern times, one that grew out of bourgeois "separate-spheres ideology" (Yuko) and Victorian preoccupations with the sanctity of the female sex over the last century and a half or so. It's also an out-moded right despite being clung to so tenaciously, as Mary Anne Case writes: "Separate public toilets are one of the last remnants of the segregated life of separate spheres for men and wom-en...now that the rules of etiquette no longer demand that the women leave the men to their brandy and cigars after dinner in polite company." Yet it remains very much alive today and is on display whenever the ladies get up on cue to go do their ritual restroom thing.

The bodily right to privacy developed, more precisely, in tandem with the late nineteenth-century technology of private plumbing, enabling at first the wealthy, and decades later most residences to be outfitted with their own bathroom, although as Alexander Kira reminds us in his classic book, *The Bathroom*, bathtubs designed for two could be found among the European gentry as far back as the seventeenth century.

I am sorry to have to turn all this on its head in what follows, but it's about time we disburden ourselves of the privacy fetish. This requires a drastic shift in cultural attitudes. As radical as it sounds, toilet liberation is wholly practical economically speaking and easily implemented, if not now then over a generation or two, as younger people enlightened and versed in ecological imperatives take over the reins of power.

There are already signs among scattered visionaries of a relaxing of the strictures and regimes. One household fashion trend, among those who can afford to tear down walls in their home or uproot their plumbing, is the "open-concept bathroom," a large bathtub or jacuzzi as the centerpiece of a spacious bathroom or even the living room, the bather or bathers visible to family or friends. More exclusive hotels offer something comparable though the rationale may be different; the point is not to lure exhibitionist guests but rather to enable you to watch TV while you bathe while keeping an eye on the fast company hoping to rifle through your pants (more commonly, open bathtubs in hotels sit in a standard bathroom behind a clear glass wall, with a shade or curtain to accommodate the shy). An attractive selling point in new homes, the beautiful bathroom meant for more than one never really went away, at least in Europe. One such exquisite specimen and its wine-drinking naked couple is featured in the Hungarian film *The Piano Player* (1999, dir. Schübel), set in Nazi-occupied Budapest.

A bolder proposal yet would eliminate private toilets and

bathrooms altogether and, in their place, encourage communal living arrangements with shared bathrooms. Anyone who has ever stayed in a no-frills dormitory or cheap hotel or hostel has experienced the shared hallway bathroom. While an annoyance if you're not used to it, it is quickly accommodated with revised expectations and a little mental agility. People with special bathing needs—the elderly, infirm, and disabled—would especially benefit in a communal household, as they have people watching over them.

A hotel in Changsha, China

The public restroom too is deserving of beauty, elegance, even grandness, but not as a mere cosmetic gesture. A garish example is an entire temple-like WC at the White Temple complex in Chiang Rai, Thailand. The hugely popular haunt got some bad publicity years ago over an ill-advised decision to open up a separate WC for Chinese tourists, some of whom had been observed trashing the "Golden Toilet" with their messy toilet habits; the decision was reversed, and the majority of the tourists remain Chinese ("Thai temple"). The Golden Toilet invites access with two entrances each for both sexes. The interior is rather prosaic, with nice décor touches but nothing in the way of creative use of space; the upper floor is for offices. Mere ornamentation slapped onto a conventional structure is indeed a waste of space. A true restroom design aesthetic would expand outward, organically, from the urinal. In other words, the standard urinal is itself an object of beauty, with its perfect fusion of form and function. Public restroom design should follow that.

The Golden Toilet at the White Temple complex, Chiang Rai, Thailand

While functionalism implies ease of access and use, it must also be informed by egalitarianism: something functions well because it's accessible to all. Existing public restrooms just about everywhere remains a strange agglomeration of culturally imposed sexism and puritanism. In one UK study, women spend 34 times longer queuing for the toilet than men ("The Peequal"). If, as a man, you've always wondered why this is the case, imagine how your access to the men's room would be impacted with the urinals removed. Even still, it's easier for you to urinate in a stall by simply unzipping and peeing all over the toilet seat, whereas women often have to fiddle with layers of clothing when they don't have to clean up after you if it happens to be a unisex toilet.

Men's urinals in the Golden Toilet

One solution is the female urinal. I can't think of a more eminent solution to an intractable problem that throws up more flak of resistance, one that merits some discussion. Germany has been at the forefront of these innovations, indeed has been experimenting with female urinals in public restrooms since the nineteenth century. The rationale is not only to give women equal access but to save water; women waste three times as much toilet water as men in the multiple flushing required to clean and make clean contact with toilet seats. To use a female urinal (or urinals adapted for both sexes), a woman must either face the wall or face forward, depending on the urinal's design. The urinals pictured in the gorgeous women's restroom below are evidently intended to be used facing forward. In either case, she must pull down her pants and pull aside her panties, legs astride in a semi-squatting stance, thus exposing her groin from the front or rear, though she might drape her nakedness with a dress. Or if facing the wall, the use of a handheld device such as the Pee Easy funnel would make it possible to keep her buttocks covered like men, but she would need to carry such a device around with her and be comfortable using it.

In Germany as well, some cities are converting gender-segregated to gender-neutral WCs, with the ultimate goal of replacing men's urinals altogether with gender-neutral urinals. What the etiquette would look like in a unisex restroom with women using the same urinals as men is anyone's guess. It's already delicate enough in men's rooms. There are unspoken rules. First, it's unacceptable to use a urinal next to another user if other urinals are available. Second, it's unacceptable to glance, however momentarily, at another man's penis. There is a third curious injunction, unconsciously observed: it's expected to acknowledge the presence of others with subtle signs, such as ad-

Female urinals, unknown location, Germany
(Prince Grobhelm – Own work, CC BY-SA 3.0,
https://commons.wikimedia.org/w/index.php?curid=3003594)

justing your posture when a newcomer arrives or a partial glance in their direction without eye contact. This is to mutually affirm the boundaries; not to do so might imply you're intending to subvert them with perverted designs. The presence of women in a unisex public WC would enormously complicate this etiquette, as female users would have to compromise themselves in front of the men milling about.

I suppose most women would regard unisex urinals as beyond the pale and refuse to use them, even when outfitted with emergency alarms and a divider separating male and female users (among other ameliorating measures). Even many men might be intimidated from entering such a restroom. Ruth Barcan speaks to the fear and resistance that would need to be overcome before coed public toilets could be socially accepted:

> For just as the spatial separation of men and women into different rooms aims...to reduce male violence against women, so the free circulation of sound is part of women's defenses against that same threat of violence. Knowing that your screams can be heard outside was the first thing matter-of-factly mentioned to me by a woman when I asked some of my friends whether they thought sound was an important factor in public toilet design.

The irony is that coed public toilets might be the best of all solutions since the presence of others would guard against aggressive males. Why then are public toilets segregated in the first place? This historically burdened question confronts us with the unfortunate fact that the segregation of the sexes reinforces and justifies its own consequences. As Gershenson (citing Richard A. Wasserstrom) puts it,

> Sex-segregated bathrooms...are just "one small part of that scheme of sex-role differentiation which uses the mystery of sexual anatomy, among other things, to maintain the prima-

cy of heterosexual sexual attraction central to that version of the patriarchal system of power relationships we have to-day." The same patriarchal system that envisions sex as a crucial binary category insists on the sexual segregation of bathrooms.

There hasn't been much news about these German restroom innovations since a flurry of articles appeared in the scandalized international press in 2017 (e.g., "Berlin's new toilets"). Were the proposals stopped dead in their tracks after massive public resistance? Or perhaps subsequent developments have slipped under the radar? Germany is a country known for its healthy tolerance and respect for public nudity, as shocked visitors discover when they stumble upon topless pool-side bathers in their hotel and full-blown nudist parks in city centers, such as the Englischer Garten in Munich. There may be adequate public support for unisex WCs with unisex urinals, but municipalities are likely constrained by their growing population of conservative communities, predominantly Muslim immigrants, not to mention the many tourists unacquainted with liberal German attitudes. Any viable changes would need to be two-pronged and incremental: outfitting women's WCs with female-adapted urinals, and merging or replacing segregated WCs with unisex WCs, all the while keeping enough gender-segregated WCs operating to provide people with a choice. The Germans have long freely gone naked among strangers in coed saunas, and over time, one assumes, male leering and harassment of female users would dwindle as coed toilet use became the norm. Then if enough women could be recruited, unisex WCs could all be outfitted with unisex urinals. This would also solve at one go the problem of safe toilets for trans people and would render moot the question of whether trans females should be allowed in women's restrooms.

Germany presents us with an instructive test case of the limits of the progressive imagination. The Germans may seem shocking by prudish American standards, but they are quite reasonable people who beckon toward what is possible. We might place Germany at one end of a continuum representing degrees of tolerance for bodily freedom, America in the middle, and hidebound societies that regard women as inherently dirty (e.g., the practice in Nepal and Ethiopia of forcing menstruating women into huts) or as unassailably pure and needing protection and isolation (which amounts to the same thing), at the other end. Far from being inconceivable or intolerable, unisex urinals and WCs do exist. They are being implemented or in the planning stages by municipal governments not only in Germany but elsewhere, though still largely confined to Europe. The reason for this growing shift toward sexual equality in public toilets, however slow and scattershot on a global scale is, again, the sheer logic of it. Above all, it's an environmentally and ecologically sound policy. Converting segregated WCs into unisex WCs saves money and space, and widespread adoption of the female urinal saves water—at a time when global water shortages are becoming acute. And, of course, unisex facilities provide women the same ease and speed of use as men.

Egalitarian public restroom design (as opposed to its successful implementation) has a long history and I can hardly claim to be proposing something original. While I've culled insights from the experts, such as Alexander Kira and Harvey Molotch, the following design for a "grand public restroom" is my own. The structure is imagined in the round, to spotlight its aesthetic and functional self-sufficiency, though I'd stress "functional" here in the more generous sense to distinguish it from the "American preoccupation with compulsive 'cleanliness,' devoid of any enjoyment, which results in our minimal 'functional' bathrooms." As Kira continues in a more positive vein, "one can find examples today of bathrooms that are treated as family rooms, private sitting rooms, libraries, offices, formal drawing rooms, art galleries, garden rooms, beauty parlors, gymnasiums, and so on."

Grand public restrooms would stand out in the urban horizon

with a telltale dome-shaped skylight or cupola, yet each would be architecturally unique. They would come in different sizes depending on population density or local demand, and there would be smaller versions with fewer amenities, scattered around the neighborhood, some consisting of no more than several toilet rooms accessed on the outside and unisex urinals on the inside, with attendants on hand 24 hours in the larger versions.

They would be free, open to all, well-maintained, clean, and safe. Ideally, they would be strictly unisex, but as I must ground this in our day and age, my illustration shows a transitional version

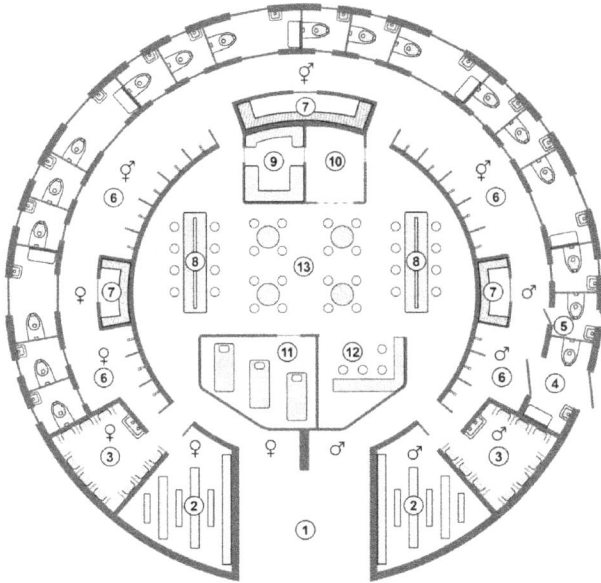

Bird's-eye view of a grand public restroom: 1) entrance, 2) changing rooms, 3) urinals, 4) large toilet rooms, 5) small toilet rooms, 6) showers, 7) saunas, 8) trough sinks, 9) lactation room, 10) attendants' office, 11) massage room, 12) espresso bar, 13) recreational tables. The symbols ♂/♀ indicate male/female segregated sections, coed when combined (concept and design by Isham Cook).

with both coed and sex-segregated sections. As in conventional public restrooms, the divided entrance requires women and men to enter separately. If one just needs to urinate, there are segregated urinal rooms adjacent to the main entrance on either side. If one needs to defecate, there are two options. First, private-use toilet rooms line the outside circumference of the structure, larger wheelchair-accessible rooms each with a baby-changing table, toilet, and sink, alternating with smaller rooms containing a toilet and sink. A sign on each door indicates whether the room is occupied or vacant (as in airplane cabin toilets), but with a big "O" or "V" so that the sign can be read from a distance. There is also an electronic display at the main entrance showing the occupancy of all the numbered toilets at a glance, enabling users to locate a vacant toilet. Attendants would be aware of which toilets are in operation and could notify those who are hogging toilets. Likewise, if the user has a medical issue or emergency the attendant can be alerted and spoken to via intercom.

Alternatively, the outer toilet rooms could be accessed within the building from the circular corridor lined with shower stalls and saunas. If a toilet is in use, its inner and outer doors are automatically locked and become unlocked when the toilet is vacant. But one cannot access the corridor from the outside via the toilet rooms; only users inside the building have access to the toilets from the inside. This enables the staff to monitor the visitors present and prevent men from entering the women's section and vice versa. The larger share of the shower area is coed, however. This is to give both sexes greater access to shower and sauna space and absorb spillover from the segregated sections. It's also to accustom people to coed use and lower resistance to the sight of the naked opposite sex.

Also offered are saunas, a massage room, and a segregated lactation room (though women could breastfeed openly as they wished), double-sided trough sinks with mirrors, recreational tables (with chess, checkers, Go sets), even an espresso bar. This is to encourage people not only to feel comfortable and at leisure but to hang out and socialize. Other grand public restrooms could offer different options and facilities. The largest might accommodate hot and cold pools for recreational bathing, as have long existed in Japan, Korea, and China. As in Germany and a few other European countries, many spa and hot-spring resorts are both coed and clothing-optional, so it's not such a stretch to imagine this degree of institutionalized freedom.

If the grand public restroom progressed to become fully coed, obviating the need for separate male and female sections, the interior could be streamlined with a single set of urinals, showers, and saunas for all genders/sexes to use freely, safely, and shame-free.[9] Granted, the more exotic brand of European spa aside, existing public restrooms remain a long way from the "utopian vision of men and women and people of all sorts sharing toilet space and shaping social life....As the sex ratio of users changes, one gender can spill over into the facilities ordinarily over-selected by the other, while, as the need arises, managing glance in an appropriate way" (Molotch). Indeed, there is growing awareness of the need for a new approach, and piecemeal improvements are already happening in many cities and countries. And there is always constant, bustling change, often for the better, occasionally for the worse. In what follows, I present examples of change in two countries, one exhibiting dramatic change for the better, the other dramatic change for the worse.

THE CHINESE EXPERIENCE

When I first arrived in China in the early 1990s, toilets were so squalid it was hard to imagine anything worse. A telling instance was a lunch stop in one mountain tourist town, Wutaishan, famous for its sprawling Buddhist temples. We chose the most

---

[9] By "all genders/sexes," I take my cue from Anne Fausto-Sterling's famous article, "The Five Sexes: Why male and female are not enough."

promising among a strip of shanty-like restaurants, all lacking a toilet. I was directed around back to the public WC, if you could call it that. It consisted of an open pit of raw sewage with a rickety wooden plank laid across to squat on while defecating. The pit was set back from the street but unsheltered and its occupants visible to passersby. Throughout my naked squatting ordeal, a male travel companion stood nearby and stared out of protective concern but also impatience. This had a most inhibiting effect. I gave up and resolved to hold in "the uneasy load," as Gulliver described it, denied use of a privy by his Lilliputian hosts. Nervously gathering up my belongings, I managed to drop my camera into the excremental sludge and fished it out with my fingers. Back at the restaurant, there was no sink or even soap. I had to make do with a pan of water to restore my hands and the camera as best I could. I'm not sure how they washed their dishes.

In the nation's capital of Beijing, public WCs of the era weren't all that much better: dark, dirty cinderblock cells with facing rows of squatting holes. Low dividers separated you a bit from adjacent users but not from those sitting opposite; some WCs lacked dividers altogether. This was after all a more social culture, where people felt less awkward about the communal witnessing of all aspects of daily life including the bodily functions, where the concept of individual privacy was less refined than in the West. I had no choice but to get used to being stared at by curious males whiling away the time with their cigarettes, newspapers, and chitchat, sometimes quite overtly about me, assuming I had arrived in the country that very day and couldn't speak the language (after decades here some still call out to me on the street, "Welcome to China!"). If you were out for the evening, you could always use the restaurant toilet, if again it had one, and you didn't mind soiling your shoes in the inevitable puddle of urine, spit, cigarette butts, and stray feces surrounding the squat receptacle. So extravagant were these examples of national performance art that they attracted comment. Like David

Sedaris on a trip to China in 2011 and Arthur Meursault in his wicked satire *Party Members*, I found these public potty displays, for want of a better word, funny.

Once the country opened up in earnest to foreign tourism and the Chinese themselves started traveling internationally, they became educated on the sanitary standards found outside the Middle Kingdom. They grew acutely conscious and embarrassed about their public WC problem, so much so that the Government trumpeted the country's urgent toilet development plans, citing such mottoes as "You can judge a nation's civilization by the quality of its public toilets." And they indeed worked hard on this. Over the past decade, there has been a sea change, though you can still find remnants of the past alongside progress. In order to maximize their limited space, tiny public WCs in Beijing's old lanes maintain adjacent squatting toilets without dividers (see below), but these are kept spotlessly clean throughout the day. Some WCs even provide toilet paper from a single dispenser in the entrance (locals are long accustomed to carrying their own tissue). Instead of aiming their waste into the obscure sewage holes of yore, users now position themselves on the polished metal platform and stamp the flusher with their heel. In case you haven't been following the latest health news, squatting toilets do a better job at evacuating the body's waste than sitting toilets. If knocking knees with your neighbor takes some getting used to, you can always grab onto his leg for support.

The national measures are being ramped up throughout the country. I was walking through a nondescript neighborhood in the third-tier city of Changchun not long ago and stopped in a public WC. In years past, it would have been a ghastly sight. But the toilet stalls now had locking doors and were spic-and-span. Chinese school lavatories too are kept cleaner than before, although their unshaded windows still give facing classrooms a clear sightline into the male urinal areas. In the newer shopping malls, the restrooms are ever larger, nicer, and gender-friendlier. In Beijing's China World Mall shopping plaza, for example, am-ple restrooms are at hand wherever you turn. One male restroom has eight toilet stalls (with a choice of squatting and sitting toilets) and ten urinals; the female restroom facing it has twelve toilet stalls, somewhat making up for the lack of female urinals.

One troublesome aspect of public toilet use in China is that, unlike the U.S., there is no law requiring food establishments to provide a restroom. Most restaurants do as a matter of course, and no bar would be foolish enough not to, but most cafés don't. The waitstaff will point you to the nearest WC in the mall or down

Men's public WC with squatting toilets in a Beijing lane, 2021

the street, or they arrange with a neighboring restaurant to let you use their restroom. But even in posh residential complexes like The Place in Beijing with its $3,000 per month rental apartments catering to foreigners, the commercial space at ground level wasn't designed to have restroom plumbing, and few of the many fine food and coffee establishments lining the concourse have their own restrooms. From certain locations, one has to walk the equivalent of a football field to get to the nearest public WC. On the other hand, restaurants, office buildings, and hotel lobbies never object to anyone slipping in to use the restroom, whether you're a patron or not; staff tends to be relaxed and not inclined to interfere. This stands in contrast to restaurants and businesses in American cities, which often display a sign in their window prohibiting restroom use for non-paying customers. Ironically, there is a greater need for non-patron use of restaurant restrooms in the U.S. since there are comparatively fewer public WCs. This brings us to our next country.

THE AMERICAN EXPERIENCE

As with many features of American life, amenities and facilities are distributed up the socio-economic ladder: you have to pay for the convenience. I don't mean the token fee as commonly charged in public WCs in Europe. You're expected to patronize an establishment before being granted use of the restroom, whatever cost it entails. Shopping malls provide restrooms for public use, but then it's assumed you're there to shop, and the unkempt may be approached by guards and escorted out. McDonald's and other fast-food chains present an interesting exception. They are often hangouts for the large homeless population in many cities, who are generally allowed to stay as long as they purchase a coffee; you can still get one for a dollar or so. Some shops may look the other way even if you don't buy anything. For all the criticism they receive for their unhealthful food and low pay, the fast-food chains perform a needed public service in functioning as daytime shelters for the poor.

The relative scarcity of clean, safe, accessible public toilets in the U.S., as compared to other countries, has long attracted frustrated commentary by visiting foreigners and domestic sociolo-

gists, if not by untraveled Americans who have no basis for comparison and don't know anything else. Everyone, though, is
acutely aware of the inconvenience of being stuck somewhere
with a bursting bladder or bowels and no idea where the nearest
toilet is. The assumption is that you have only yourself to blame
in not planning ahead and taking better precautions, in not leaving that bar, party, sports event or outdoor concert before giving
yourself enough time to fully clear your bladder, in not anticipat-
ing the long haul home or drive ahead. Or don't drink so much.
Or carry an empty plastic bottle in your car if you have to. Or
find some bushes or a dark corner in a park to relieve yourself in.

By this point, you may be assuming my title refers merely to
the nuisance of being caught in public with no WC in sight. I
don't mean to trivialize the word, but it does have metaphorical
scope to encompass the little things in life that bother or "terrorize" us, the many minor hassles we blow out of proportion in order to characterize a fleeting yet momentarily excruciating situation or event, which of course bears no relation to real terror—a
shooting, a bombing—or other life-threatening cataclysms. But
this is actually not what I am getting at by the "toilet terror" of
my title. What I lay out as follows refers rather to something, if
not quite life-threatening, far worse than our desperate search
for a toilet. By an order of magnitude worse. And it is unique to
the USA.

We can start by recognizing that there is an etiquette to public toilet use. This etiquette is not confined to the toilet itself—
this may be counterintuitive—but extends beyond the facility to
encompass all urban space, indeed the entire town, suburb or
city. You can get into trouble by using a toilet stall against the
rules, when for example being espied by security while dealing or
shooting drugs or having sex in one (that's what that half-inch
gap between the door and the hinge is for), or even inadvertently,
as when stumbling into a poorly marked entrance for the wrong
sex. You can also get into trouble for not using a public toilet.
Public urination constitutes the greatest violation because it's

interpreted as the most flagrant, ultimate rejection of something society, American society at least, upholds to the absolute strictest of standards. This becomes apparent when these standards are violated. In the U.S., as Kira notes, "privacy demands and sex segregation are strictly enforced by both legal and social sanctions and...casual public elimination can lead to swift arrest." As "technologies of division and separation," public toilets, adds Barcan, are a "form of segregation...at once immensely naturalized and immensely policed, the most taken-for-granted social categorization and the most fiercely regulated."

Most countries have penalties for public urination, typically fines equivalent to several hundred USD, though in some locations such as Singapore the fines can go up to several thousand dollars for blatant acts like public defecation. In Germany, on the other hand, there is no law against public urination. The law in most countries is rarely enforced unless the act is performed openly in broad daylight or otherwise deemed flagrant. In China, where I've lived for decades, I've never heard of anyone getting into trouble for public peeing, nor have been warned about it. In civilized Japan, salarymen can be seen urinating outside without discretion, but then they're dragooned into enforced after-hours drinking sessions with the boss; they're seen throwing up on the sidewalk and in the subway station as well. It is also grasped that incontinent people afflicted by age, diabetes or various colon conditions may have to let go in an inopportune spot before they make it home, and allowance (one hopes) is made for medical reasons. But as for young partiers who have no such excuse, is it really necessary to slap them with a $500 fine, on top of potentially much worse consequences, if they make at least minimal effort to relieve themselves out of sight, such as in an alley or behind a tree?

The land of the free has little tolerance for public urination. This has led to gross distortions of the law, to an extent poorly understood by the very public that's so ruthless in fingering offenders. Public urination signifies no mere rude display but is identified in the American psyche with depravity: obscenity and pedophilia. Whereas the law is wise enough to distinguish between public urination or disorderly conduct on the one hand, and public lewdness or indecent exposure on the other, not all people do. That includes the police, who are at complete liberty to interpret an act of public urination as lewd or obscene. The police are expected to uphold and enforce the law, but when it comes to sexual offenses real or imaginary, they have wide latitude to do whatever they please. They also have quotas to fulfill and an incentive to err on the side of severity. As everyone who reads the news knows, American law enforcement has a habit of overextending its reach, when for example they shoot innocent but suspicious-looking African Americans. But whereas the public is turning against racist police brutality, nabbing sex offenders has its unbridled support.

Sane, reasonable people, people with a solid grounding in reality, can grasp that while public urination occurs and can be a nuisance, the number of those who urinate with the deliberate intention of exposing themselves is certainly minuscule. Public paranoia, by contrast, is vast and volatile.

A sobering way to gauge the frequency with which public urinators are charged with lewdness is a Google search of "public urination laws by state," where a host of law firms crop up offering their services to bewildered defendants. These sites patiently and methodically explain what is happening and what you should and should not do to avoid worsening the quicksand you are in. For time is fast working against you, and an experienced attorney is needed to negotiate with the prosecutor and the police and prepare evidence before things proceed to sentencing. To avoid appearing soft on crime, U.S. states have almost unlimited scope to apply the harshest punishment for the most minor of sex crimes. In Michigan, for instance, the minimum sentence for public lewdness is one day in jail, the maximum life in prison ("Should I be worried"). In at least thirteen states, the distinction between urination and lewdness doesn't even apply: urination automatically results in an indecent exposure charge—and possible registration as a sex offender (*No Easy Answers*). Note that it's "at least" thirteen states. The caveat is that all states are at liberty to charge your simple act of urination as a sex crime at the discretion of the police. Being witnessed masturbating is an automatic sex crime, and a serious one. I assume you would never have any intention of doing that in public, but men usually jiggle their penis when squeezing out their last drops, and someone happening to catch this out of the corner of their eye could misconstrue it as masturbation. A citizen's claim to have seen you in any state of exposure, even if you were taking the utmost precautions to urinate where you thought you were unobserved, could likewise result in an indecent exposure charge, one that escalates into a sex crime conviction. A child's claim, if it bubbles up to the police, and it's all over for you.

A good lawyer and a sympathetic judge might help extricate you relatively unscathed from the quicksand, perhaps only several thousand dollars poorer from legal and court fees but saved from the sex offender registry. Once on the registry, your offense is unlikely to be listed as mere "public urination" but rather the sinister category of "public lewdness," and you'll be stuck on the registry for a minimum of ten years, possibly for life, with likely attendant loss of job and housing, and forbidden contact with children. As a *Men's Health* article puts it, "when you have to urinate so bad that holding it is no longer an option, you might want to consider just peeing in your pants. It may ruin the rest of your night, but the rest of your life will be spared" (Levitan & Bettmann/Corbis).

When the state multiples crime by creating new categories of crime; when it singles out groups for disproportionately punitive treatment and enlists a duped public to collaborate in the name of safety and security; when the state inventively deploys the latest technologies (comprehensive databases, GPS tracking, facial recognition) in the service of prosecuting crime; and when out of all of this emerges an atmosphere of fear designed to intimidate and terrorize the population including those supporting these measures, fear not only of the state but of one's neighbor, fear of the racial or sexual predator, down to the fear of being caught without a toilet in public: we have arrived at fascism in its contemporary guise.

6

AMERICAN MASSAGE

SEVERAL YEARS AGO, the largest massage chain in the U.S. got the biggest marketing boost of its fifteen-year career with a dour *BuzzFeed News* story, "More than 180 women have reported sexual assaults at Massage Envy" (K. Baker). The findings, from interviews and testimony of aggrieved customers, exposed appalling behavior indeed. Many had their breasts or genitals casually violated while being massaged, but there were more violent incidents, such as one masseur who held down a customer's mouth as he fingered her vagina and another who raped a customer with his fist and ejaculated on her face. The offenders in these two cases were convicted, but few of the other accused were, what with the difficulty of pressing charges amidst conflicting allegations over what took place in private rooms without witnesses. The masseurs named in the complaints were all terminated and blacklisted in the industry, and there may still be ongoing civil lawsuits. Massage Envy was expected to ride out the crisis, though the chain came under fire for having been slow to respond to the complaints until the scandal broke and not having in-house protocols in place to deal with them at the outset.

Now, I applaud the outing of harassment and assault wherever it has heretofore lurked. But I make it a matter of principle never to take media outbursts or social hysteria at face value, above all regarding sexual politics and practices. I have no vested interest in Massage Envy, but in defense of the chain, the occasional slip-up at the hands of a few bad apples was only to be expected, given the sheer scale of their nationwide operation. I don't believe they would knowingly have employed sexual predators. Rather, displaced responsibility combined with denial in the face of the truth ruled by default before it took a scandal to reveal the extent of the problem. I also suspect that many offenders, at least not the worst of them, were otherwise decent people whose only real failing was their inability to understand workplace compliance. Not wholly clear about their role or just badly trained, they gave in to human weakness while oiling the naked flesh of a hot body. They then may have repeated the behavior once they saw they could get away with it, or deluded themselves into thinking customers were invariably into it too.

Uncomfortable as it might seem to those unfamiliar with the massage business, it's a fact that many customers are drawn to massage due to the powerful urge to be erotically teased, manipulated, even violated. At the same time, of course, many more have no such fantasies and are deservingly outraged if it occurs.

I would ask not why these massage workers succumbed but how the chain has managed to pull off its overall success rate. With 25,000 therapists at 1,200 branches nationwide performing literally tens of millions of massages every year (with a typical load of five to six customers per day per therapist or up to 100 massages a day at each shop), there have *only* been 180 reported complaints. True, for every reported complaint there are likely many more unreported incidents—25 more on average according to Massage Envy's own guesstimate. There must be many false reports as well: customers who imagine they have been inappropriately touched when they have not. Standard guidelines (at least during my own massage-therapy training decades ago) allow stroking up to an inch away from the breasts, genitals, and pubic hair. Some customers may perceive the therapist's fingers as being more intrusive than they actually are, for instance, while being massaged along the sternum between the breasts, which is generally permitted. Further complicating matters is ever-present contradictory signaling and misplaced body language, leading to honest miscommunications and mistakes. Without videotaped evidence, the presumption of guilt in most cases will lie with the therapist. Meanwhile, therapists may be sexually harassed by customers as often as the other way around. For their own protection, a strict, indeed hyper-paranoid professionalism is the rule, and this out of greater concern for their job than any loyalty toward the company.

If you're a female customer looking to be manhandled less than professionally, you'll probably have to spend thousands of dollars on countless massages before encountering a single masseur willing to take that risk and fast-track himself to termination, not to mention the risk of being busted by an undercover cop posing as a customer. Or if, on the other hand, absolute safety is your concern, you can always ask to be massaged by a masseuse.[10]

*

I am not expecting any erotics for my own session at one of the many Massage Envy branches in my hometown of Chicago.[11] They are booked up when I walk in and I schedule a session a few days later. They have several 60-minute and 90-minute

---

[10] A note on the words "masseur" and "masseuse," which have historical connotations of the old prostitution massage den and are rejected by the industry: I find "male massage therapist" and "female massage therapist" unwieldy and employ all available terms.
[11] To preserve anonymity, I provide no names or addresses. Readers are at liberty to do their own research.

blocks open with different therapists. I get a first-timer discount from the regular $100 to a mellower $70 for a one-hour session. They kindly inform me, though, that the 60-minute massage is actually only 50 minutes since five minutes at the start and end are set aside for disrobing and getting dressed. If we adjust to a full 60 minutes of hands-on service plus the expected fifteen to twenty-percent tip, their regular rate amounts to more like $140 an hour—twice as much. Not cheap, particularly if you're used to massage in Thailand, which offers the same quality of service at ten to fifteen dollars per hour.

In the lobby, they hand me the intake form on a tablet computer for ticking off a list of my known ailments—to absolve the company of responsibility in the event of some kind of seizure or heart attack—and a map of the body for indicating the parts requiring the most attention, apart from the groin area which is of course blacked out. I join two white female clients in a waiting room. My masseuse, who is Black, arrives and leads me down the hotel-like hallway to a room. The typical American massage chamber is decked out in a pleasant, indeed dramatic fashion, with gentle lighting, hushed music (a vague mash of Middle and Far Eastern), fresh taut sheets folded open at an inviting angle, and U-shaped face pillow and cylindrical knee pillow at the ready, the massage table itself positioned diagonally to increase the room's sense of space, or to forestall any associations with the rectilinear operating table. I slip under the sheet face down naked. One nice thing about American massage, as in Thailand, is you are invited to disrobe completely—none of those loathsome disposable briefs compulsory in many Asian countries. Though as we shall see, the draping procedure in the U.S. is so strict and prudish that one might as well be wearing briefs. And there's the rub.

Massage must be recognized in all its singularity to be at once the most ordinary and the most bizarre of professions. Despite the polite massage industry's insistent claims to the contrary, the practice inexorably pushes into sexual territory. It's not like other forms of bodywork—physical therapy, hair-dressing, nail salons—which need not encroach on this territory. A fitness trainer may place his hands a bit lower on his trainee's hips than called for; a hairstylist may brush her boobs against her male customer. These are extraneous, gratuitous acts, not essential to the job. By contrast, the massage therapist cannot avoid approaching the erotic zones. The more thorough the massage, the more these zones loom up. As the therapist's sensuous hands glide inward over the belly, thighs, and buttocks, with each potentially disastrous stroke he or she must decide when to pull back. Some push the envelope and go right up to the allowable inch away because that's what most customers want, at the risk of the rare customer who doesn't—and an accusation of molestation. Others stay a safe three to four inches away to forestall the slightest possibility of a customer complaint. My masseuse is at the more conservative end of this spectrum: she stays a good six inches away from my body's hazard zones. While she is skillful on the sanctioned parts, I can't help feeling shortchanged, though not so far as to be upset, as I scarcely expect anything else from an American massage.

I'm curious about her job, eager to compare working conditions here with China where I've been living for the past two decades, and we chat a bit.

"Can I ask you how much you earn?"

"I definitely can't tell you that."

A very pretty receptionist with subtle Latin features dashes up to me when I'm dressed and back out in the lobby. "Well, how *was* it?"

This exemplifies a cultural difference between the U.S. and China, a country where service is less refined and you are seldom queried about your experience in massage shops, restaurants, or other establishments where customer service matters. It's nice to encounter these stock yet reassuring acts of kindness again. But the way she asks the question is odd and disarming. Rather than cheery and routine, there is concern in her eyes, as if something might have been amiss and she's inviting me to lodge a dreaded complaint. Perhaps this particular masseuse has problems I'm not aware of? Or all of them do?

"The massage was fine," I respond casually. She can see I wasn't blown away by my massage, but I don't wish to complain. A single customer complaint in China can get the masseuse fired. More than once has a masseuse I was looking forward to seeing again been dismissed after another customer had complained about her. If I'm really disappointed in the service, I just won't ask for the same person again. But after literally thousands of massages throughout East and Southeast Asia, I've become a bit jaded and impatient. While my Massage Envy masseuse was adept enough and I'm not about to endanger her job, hers was a generic, underwhelming, one-size-fits-all massage.

The pretty receptionist sits down with me in the lobby, and I chat about my being back home after living in China for so long. She's attentive and friendly, and I'm finding my interaction with her more worth my time and money than the massage. I'm tempted to ask her why she herself isn't a masseuse, but I leave it at that.

What I'm after is a friendly massage. I try a place that should be able to deliver, a massage shop for men in an upscale, gay neighborhood in north Uptown known as Andersonville. They are almost booked up. One therapist has an open slot an hour later and the same therapist again later in the evening. I worry he's the least popular of the lot but take a chance on him and reserve the first slot. They hold my credit card number and warn me they reserve the right to charge the full amount even if I cancel ahead of time. After a coffee at a sleek café across the street, I return to the shop and fill out the intake form in the lobby. The receptionist points out a waiting lounge down the hall, which has sofa chairs and a mini-fridge stocked with free beer. He shows me the locker room. There's an electronic code to open the locker, a sauna, and a shower. Once I'm cleaned up and wrapped in the provided robe, I head over to the lounge. My masseur, a gay white guy, is waiting for me, shakes my hand, and leads me to the room before I can have a beer.

What I receive is a replica of my Massage Envy treatment, except that it didn't quite manage that. On the one hand, the slow graceful stroking, the hallmark of the so-called Swedish or "deep tissue" technique (some venues now differentiate between the two, charging higher for the more intensive labor of the latter). On the other, the very particular draping, which has the sheet tucked taut under the inner thighs, and the prudishness. No matter it's a gay place. Twice he asks me if I want more work on certain parts of my body. "Yes," I twice reply, indicating my buttocks, thighs, and stomach. "No problem." Each time he proceeds to disregard them. With only a few minutes left he turns me over, works my chest a bit, and time's up. Does he ignore my requests because they're naughty code for the libidinous? Or because I don't have the torso of a twenty-year-old athlete? Even chatting seems an imposition; he doesn't invite conversation. I'm not the point; his job is. If massage is an architecture, his is earthquake-proof. By staying a good hand's length away from my body's danger zones, he makes himself inviolable against any accusation of impropriety. At the receiving end, the massage is expensive, perfunctory, and disappointing, so much so I wonder if I'm not the butt of a joke, as if to say, "You *knew* the massage would fall short of your expectations, yet you went ahead and blew $100 on it anyway. How lousy does our service need to be before customers like you get it?"

A puritanical society expresses its conflicts over the body in mocking ways, and massage is a good example. There is the seedy carnivalesque tradition, like the foreboding "Thai" massage parlor I once visited in San Francisco, which operated in a basement behind a steel door with a peephole, middle-aged Vietnamese masseuses, and rats in the rooms. And there is the virtuous answer to this—the polite, New Age massage. Many governments see the patent absurdity of massage for what it is— a sex business trying to pretend it's not—and ban it outright, or place heavy restrictions on it, such as permitting only fully clothed massage or only on the back and feet, medically approved procedures for muscle ailments, specially designed robes with flaps to access body parts (as I experienced in South Korea), and so forth. Where full-body oil massage is allowed, therapists in the U.S. are expected to internalize the strictures on pain of career disaster. The massages that result are paltry distortions of the ideal, a twisted practice shaped not around prescriptions but proscriptions.

In Chicago, massage was long outlawed through a combination of community intolerance and police intimidation. In the 1980s, dedicated training schools began to appear and licensed therapists sprung up in luxury hotels or did house calls. Street-front shops were few and far between, but the business thrived unseen, while a few Korean-run handjob parlors lurked in the dingy far West Side of the city. Only in the past decades has it taken off in a visible way. I refer not just to Massage Envy but its main competitor, the Chinese, who are branching out from their restaurant niche and rushing in to fill a vacuum, given their legacy in the massage arts. With each visit back to Chicago, I see more new massage shops sprouting in almost every neighborhood, though they remain vastly outnumbered by less ominous forms of bodywork—hair salons and nail "spas." Apart, again, from the Massage Envy chain, almost all massage establishments are now run by the Chinese.

I try out one of them in another upscale neighborhood in the Lakeview community. In her 40s and attractive, the Chinese proprietor speaks confident English and has a cultural grasp of the quirky needs of the American client. She's got the business formula down and the stream of mostly female customers suggests it's working: the New Age music and decor—the lobby coffee table has a toy Japanese rock garden with little rakes for drawing patterns in the sand—competitive pricing at $60 per hour, and experienced masseuses. At this shop, they hail from China, Vietnam, Mexico, and elsewhere. Mine is from Mongolia.

She performs a respectable treatment, edging a bit closer toward my erogenous zones than I received from the previous two venues though not quite enough to incite me to come back. Then again, all that matters from the business's point of view is that most of the customers come back.

Evanston is an upper-middle-class suburb at Chicago's northern edge. It's known for its antique street lamps, lovely churches, and wealthy Republican constituents. The town was long dry despite the presence of Northwestern University; until recently alcohol could only be found in restaurants. It's the last place you'd expect to find a massage shop. Or maybe not. Things appear to have loosened up. I now see that several have popped out of the woodwork since my last visit here, evidently to accommodate bored housewives migrating over from the hair and nail salons. The one I happen upon is Chinese-run and staffed. My masseuse is in her 40s and speaks no English. She becomes effusive when I use Mandarin. From Dalian, she's been in the country for a year and a half. She works every day from 10 am till 9 pm, similar hours to massage workers in China (who tend to start at noon and work till midnight), but with tips can pull in much more income in the U.S.

Despite their previous experience, America-bound Chinese massage workers have to be retrained in the polite massage routines and the slower, deliberate stroking favored by customers here. Her training seems not to have succeeded, for she pushes all the way down over my belly to my pubic hair and the base of my penis. She stops short of grabbing me outright. It's just affectionate teasing of the sort common in parlors in China and Thailand. She repeats the move. My cock jumps to life and pokes out from the edge of the laxly draped sheet. If this were taking place at Massage Envy and I was the sort to take offense, she might now be out of a job. Working in a Chinese-run establishment, she's a bit safer. In the unlikely event a male customer ever complained, they'd deny everything and quietly shunt her to another massage shop in the extensive Chinese network. And she'd likely have wondered whatever the hell went wrong; all she was doing was intuiting the kind of treatment her customer wanted and delivered it. Inadequately schooled in U.S. massage etiquette, she was simply doing the job she thought she was hired to do, or the boss expected her to do. By inciting male customers back with these little erotic gestures, she is from the shop's perspective the ideal masseuse. When things go wrong (and they do go wrong) it's more often a female customer who has been inappropriately handled by a careless masseur, compounded by a communication breakdown when he doesn't speak English.[12]

I get similar titillating treatment at a larger venue in Lincoln Park. From Changchun, this Chinese masseuse is in her 30s and attractive as well as technically skilled. Only the latter is important but a pretty face does sweeten things. She too lets her fingers slide under my penis while working my hips and continues to do so once I become erect, though again without caressing me. There is a subtle line that's not to be crossed: too deliberate and it's not only dangerous for them, but it's boring for the customer. It's the glancing moves while attending to the massage, the collateral stroking that electrifies things, the finely calibrated erotic massage that stops just short of sexual massage. I return to try another masseuse there who, in contrast, plays by the rules with a prim and proper treatment. Most of the customers I see coming and going at this shop are white males. Perhaps the place is acquiring a word-of-mouth reputation and there are finer masseuses I have yet to sample.

Back in Uptown, there's a parlor that offers a different sort of encounter. It's decked out like your typical New Age massage shop but I have to be buzzed in the front door. An attractive but

---

[12] A Google search of "massage" turns up a mixture of massage websites promoting their services and the latest among a constant stream of police busts of massage parlors around the country; most of those busted are Chinese.

stern-faced Chinese scrutinizes my credit card and driver's license—to ensure I'm not an undercover cop intending to entrap her into offering extra services and then bust her. The last time I was required to show my ID for a massage was in Singapore, where the police require parlors to record customers' identification to protect the masseuses from violence. Here it's to protect masseuses from the *police*. Satisfied, she lets me proceed. Once on the table and draped, I start speaking Mandarin. Now she whips off the towel and goes for my privates without formalities. I don't like this approach, as again I find handjobs unexciting and it will double the session's price on top of it. We chat as she listlessly kneads my flesh. She's from Shenyang and has been Stateside for four years. I suppose if she were more technically adept, she could garner more customers. On the other hand, there are surely enough handjob patrons to bring in decent business—unless she gets nabbed by the police. She is taking a risk: any parlor locking you out so they can look you over calls attention to itself.

There is no typical Chinese massage. If you can get anything at the hands of Chinese masseuses in the U.S., from an unadorned handjob to the fussiest no-nonsense therapy, it's because the same range of services exists in China. They too have big massage chains run top-down a la Massage Envy, such as Liangzi in Beijing and Yu Massage in Shanghai, which dispense a standardized product for customers who want that. Chinese massage in the U.S. is different in one respect: it can only supplant lingering stereotypes of the old Cantonese-run prostitution parlor by breaking into the polite massage industry. Yet even as it ventures out of the Chinatowns to set up shop throughout urban areas and adapts to the latest trends in the bodywork business, it eschews branding and keeps an intentionally low profile. Chinatown is still the main terminus of the immigrant pipeline, but they're spilling over into other communities. Whereas the masseuses at the Lincoln Park shop reside in Chicago's Chinatown seven miles away as they traditionally have and are bused in every day by company van, those I met at the other shops on the North Side and Evanston live near O'Hare airport. And they're coming from different regions back home, Liaoning, Jilin, and Heilongjiang Provinces in China's northeast rather than Guangdong and Fujian in the south as Chinese immigrants have traditionally hailed from.

America's relationship with its Chinatowns has long been fraught, when not hysterical—as in the riots and massacres in the 1880s stemming from the Chinese Exclusion Act. They continue to lurk at the edge of respectable society, not the abject poverty and destitution of the ghetto, but the grey area in between, a distant country ever trying to get a foothold in our own, never wholly welcome but one which serves up a cuisine we've developed a taste for. The Chinese know how to present you with only what you want to see, and if it happens to be Chinese food, then that's all you will see. They are discreet to a fault, if not inscrutable, and stay out of the way, apart from the blank-faced waitresses serving your food. The more intrepid and curious, however, can seek out evidence of darker goings-on not immediately evident to the eye—massage or sexual services perhaps—down side streets, unmarked passageways, labyrinthine basements, trapdoors, and smoky rooms. America sweeps its vice into Chinatown where it conveniently disappears, yet is accessible to those with patience and persistence.

The polite massage industry remains a challenge for the Chinese. For many American customers, there is something slightly sinister and scary about a Chinese massage shop, however comfortably decked out in New Age trappings. This partly accounts for the success of the Massage Envy chain, with its reassuring suburban-mall design motifs; and you don't see too many Chinese receptionists in their stores. In order to secure legitimacy, the polite massage business has struggled over the decades to divest itself of prior associations with licentious massage, and as we have seen, adopts sweeping zero-tolerance policies toward the latter. Yet loathe they would be to admit it, they need their uneasy Other, the Chinese. They aren't competitors so much as codependents, playing different roles in the industry's distribution of labor from which they both benefit. As the polite massage business grows and generates demand, more customers, in turn, expect a greater range of services than the conventional business can provide but which can be outsourced. To customers who only want a more affordable alternative to the big chains, the Chinese are happy to deliver. To customers of more exclusive tastes, there are adepts at the ready to offer up sought-after services on an invisible menu—at a shop coming soon to your neighborhood.

The March 16, 2021, mass shooting by a white gunman of eight massage workers and customers at several Atlanta spas threw a momentary spotlight on the Asian-dominated massage business. It also exemplifies how the bugbear of "trafficking" only opens up more crevices for law enforcement to insert its tentacles. The media attention did little to advance the public's understanding or sympathy for these immigrants from China and Korea—here we see racism at work—who struggle in a limbo of widespread suspicion and a hypocritical, schizophrenic fascination that at once pulls them in and pushes them away, while police conduct raids on their workplaces or more duplicitously, ferret out sexual activity through entrapment.

The renewed interest turned sour as major media outlets, blinkered by an operative vocabulary limited to the words "trafficking" and "prostitution," cast aspersion on the entire massage business and the many immigrants trying to make an honest living in the grey economy. In one irresponsible investigative piece, *USA Today* found purported fraud at certain cherry-picked massage businesses and implied by extrapolation that all massage businesses were fraudulent (Quintana). There is no denying sex work goes on in many massage parlors, consisting mostly of innocuous handjobs, and why not? What's wrong with erotic massage, which is legally tolerated in many countries? But the fact of the matter is that the vast majority of massage workers in the U.S. do not engage in sexual massage. There is much corrective journalistic work on the topic to confirm this (e.g., Lam; Macmillan & Bhattarai).

*

In the U.S., where massage is often regarded in pejoratively lascivious (if not criminal) terms, the very idea of going for a massage can be a frightful prospect. In China and other Asian countries, the practice is identified in most people's minds with the ancient art, even as it partakes of the sex industry; therapeutic and erotic massage may sit happily together in the same shop, while only the customers vary. But there is a third approach, one that views erotic massage as fully compatible with the traditional art, and the two shouldn't be sundered to begin with.

Americans are among the most innovative people on the planet, and I now turn to a more creative community, to be sought out in the noncommercial sphere, in clubs and people's homes. Although Tantric sexual yoga originated in India (and analogous Taoist sexual arts in China), Tantric *massage* supposedly developed in Germany in the 1970s. With all due respect to the Germans, this is as much to say that it developed in California, incubator of everything weirdly hip and cool, from Eastern spirituality to personal computers. Erotic massage in one form or another has been an American pastime for decades. The latest fad (I was always wondering when someone would come up with the idea) is "bondassage"—being shackled to the massage table. [13] A related and more established practice is internal massage, otherwise known as anal fisting. I received an introduction to this exotic art form at a private club holding regular gatherings in Chicago, attended by some 30 participants

---

[13] I proposed the idea, if not the term, in my *Massage and the Writer: Essays on Asian Massage* (Magic Theater Books, 2014).

performing it on each other. Americans may not have any particular claim to fisting, which has probably existed in secret societies for ages, but the U.S. does appear to have the most practitioners and experts, concentrated in the West Coast, New York, and Chicago.

I arrive a bit early and watch the guests trickle in through the kitchen backdoor. Not everyone is known to each other, and there's a safe for storing our valuables. I relax with a beer and watch a fisting video in the living room with a few other guests. Most are middle-aged or elderly white males, a few Blacks and Hispanics, and a couple guys in their 30s. It's an acquired taste. Though I suppose there's no reason why they couldn't participate, it's a gay event and there are no women. One dude I chat up turns out to be a "virgin." That's a relief. Not only am I a virgin, I am not even familiar with the lingo. He's looking for someone with smaller hands, but most of the guys are on the burly side, bears. I realize I need to find a set of small hands too. One of the regulars has smallish hands and agrees to initiate me.

We proceed down to the basement. The space would lend itself well enough to a BDSM dungeon. There are seven slings bolted to the ceiling with chains. A smaller "playroom" off to the side has a mattress on the floor and a fridge stocked with industrially appropriate beer—Bud and Miller Lite. Everyone is naked or in jockstraps or leather and is assigned their personal can of Crisco, which cannot be shared for sanitary reasons. People are quietly circling and negotiating their choice of partner, before the first fistee mounts a sling. I watch as his fister puts on latex gloves and smears vegetable shortening over his anus. He proceeds to work in two, four, then five fingers, before his whole fist disappears into the rectum and continues sliding in up to the elbow. I am told some take the arm in all the way up to the shoulder.

"Where does the arm go?" I ask in disbelief. "I mean, you're going to end up fisting the heart, aren't you?"

"Pretty much," says one.

Two septuagenarians are now going at it in a second sling.
The fister is slight and ordinary looking though with a kindly
mien; the fistee is fat and well past any semblance of male
attractiveness. Had this gathering a more competitive purpose,
he'd surely have hoped to latch onto a more agreeable physique.
But it's evident that is not the point. His only concern seems to
be that his partner extracts as much pleasure out of the
ceremony as he gets from delivering it. Flattened together as if in
prayer, he pushes his hands all the way in and out of the anus
one after the other, rhythmically rocking on his feet in unison
with the rocking of the sling. Trance-like he stares, like a priest
or shaman performing a devotion. Whatever the spiritual
purpose or lack thereof, he's having what can only be described
as a mental orgasm. It's awesome to watch. If your massage
therapist can take as much pleasure out of giving you a massage
as you get from receiving it, that's the one you want.

My fister is ready. I get on the sling naked. My ankles are
hooked up to the chains by cuffs, my legs spread wide. What I
need to do, he stresses, is breathe deeply. One finger slides in
with no more difficulty than the doctor's jellied finger during a
prostate checkup. Two fingers don't present a problem either.
Things start getting jammed when he beaks four fingers
together, thumb tucked in. Crisco is liberally applied, the spent
white gunk falling onto newspaper spread out on the floor, as he
wipes me off with paper towels torn from a roll on a post next to
the sling: something like the practiced, cyclical procedure at the
dentist's, involving pain as well, but with a more ecstatic
purpose. I have to stop, exhausted.

I later contemplate the aborted initiation. Though I'd
certainly be able to take in more on a second try, I'd make faster
progress in a private setting, as an apprentice to a master. I have
nothing against exhibitionism, on the contrary. But the thing
about theater is that your body—the rectal muscles to be
precise—experiences stage fright even if you consciously don't. I
felt a bit like what the virgin bride must feel in those proverbial

wedding ceremonies where the groom's friends are allowed to barge in and witness the consummation in the bed-chamber. In order for everything to go off without a hitch, she needs to be forced, and the sheets plentifully stained with her blood. My failure to be fisted was a failure to do my homework, to practice with someone somehow, on myself if necessary, with tools to break myself in to the point where I was ready, to experiment with the required aids and implements—prostate vibrator, dildo, poppers, whatever it took. Yet it was also a communication lapse on my part: I should have insisted from the start that he not stop. I should have better communicated to him my patience and the latitude to continue and the scope to push myself harder.

7

MASSAGE DIARY: LAOS, THAILAND, CAMBODIA, VIETNAM

A FEW HUNDRED KILOMETERS from the borders of Vietnam, Laos, and Burma lies Kunming in southwestern Yunnan Province, one of China's more attractive cities, and a convenient stepping-off point for a multi-country massage journey. There is a key difference between massage in China and massage in Southeast Asia, where massage shops proliferate wherever tourists are to be found, jostling for attention among all the bars, cafés, and restaurants with their catchy English-language signs and menus. China's massage industry, by contrast, geared as it is almost exclusively toward domestics, is indifferent to foreigners and tourists. In your typical Chinese city, massage shops are scattered uniformly throughout most neighborhoods, their shop signs are in Chinese, with the occasional "Massage" or "Spa" in English ("spa" being code either for the full panoply of massage services or a body-care salon for women; accompanying Chinese characters usually clarify which). There is no clear division between sexual and nonsexual massage services; you cannot tell from the outside of a shop much about what goes on inside. But it's not as if anything goes. In both policy and practice, most of China's massage venues are no-nonsense, nonsexual therapeutic services, functioning as a requisite neighborhood facility. As many women patronize them as men; the phenomenon of the Chinese female massage addict is not uncommon, attested to by those I see at the same shops I frequent as well as those who have confided the predilection to me.

At the lower echelon of the Chinese massage industry are the male and female rural blind. These "Blind Massage" shops are found in every city. The blind would not otherwise find employment and are grateful for the work, strictly therapeutic at that, though contrary to their alleged superior ability they are not always well trained or suitable for the job. I've never found a blind technician that can compete with the best seeing technicians ("technician" or *jishi* being the term many massage workers prefer to call themselves). he rural disabled tend to be poorly if at all educated and are dependent upon overseers in an austere organizational environment, with little opportunity or incentive to develop professionally.

Overt prostitution (sexual intercourse) is rare at massage venues; it gravitates rather to the KTV bars, "rest & relaxation" businessmen hotels, and house-call and escort services. Prostitution massage parlors can be found in the outskirts or seedier areas of certain cities, mostly in the country's south (Shenzhen, Dongguan), but they are not the norm. The fashionable falsehood pedaled by anti-prostitution activists that massage workers are routinely enslaved bears little relation to life on the ground. None of the hundreds of Chinese massage workers I've met over the years has ever told me they were either forced into the job or prevented from leaving it. Working conditions can indeed be draining, running ten to twelve hours a day, seven days a week, with one or two days off a month. To ensure adequate staff are on hand, some establishments don't let them leave the premises apart from their days off. Those no longer willing to put up with this are free to quit and quit they do, moving from massage in and out of other occupations—hairdressing, nursing, apparel, insurance sales—at will. It should also be noted that Chinese factory workers often labor under the same strictures: locked in company compounds 24/7. Many might prefer the comparatively relaxed routine of massage work (typically five or six customers per day) to the relentlessness of the assembly line.

"Sex work" is a clumsy term, too blunt to describe the ways massage is actually sexualized. There is a full gamut of possibilities along what can be termed the "chaste/erotic" continuum, from acupressure to "Euro-style" oil massage, erotic teasing, and finally the handjob. Different masseuses at the same venue may engage in all of these or not, or with some customers and not with others. Anything can and does happen inside doors, in the secret negotiations and personal vibes between massage worker and customer. It is this very drama and suspense that provides the Asian massage venue with its fascination. The astute masseuse knows that each customer has different needs and expectations. She likewise has her repertoire of techniques and her limits. It's a question of a good fit between technician and client. As long as she can satisfy enough customers with her skilled handiwork, she can do good business.

Within China, Shanghai has the best of everything, both in range and quality of services. At midrange shops a 60-minute oil massage runs around 300 yuan (USD $45); the more decked-out the decor, the higher the price. One chain, Yu Massage, specializes in a four-hands "Double Rejoicing" massage, performed by two masseuses who synchronize their stroking. The venue is popular with foreign couples. Yet single males might be massaged a bit more erotically, as I was when one masseuse reached between my legs and stroked my perineum—the *huiyin* acupressure point. Not that she was necessarily crossing the line of respectability. Such lines are notional constructs, more fluid and permeable in cultures outside the Western puritanical context. I say "might"; that was the only masseuse at this chain to caress me thus, which would otherwise wish to maintain its reputation for politeness among its largely Anglo-American clientele. The chain is located in the upscale French Concession area and was one of the first to cater to foreigners.

Elsewhere in China, the massage industry is at the mercy of the political weather and periodic police crackdowns and clean-up campaigns, with legitimate establishments unfairly caught up in sweeps and thrown out of business, only to pop back up under a new name or location. Kunming seemed to be having bad weather during my stay there in late 2016. Two days of scouring the city turned up nothing except a single shop specializing in muscle ailments. I would likely have found more shops had I been more at leisure, but I had urgent traveling to do.

LAOS: LUANG PRABANG AND VIENTIANE

With the exception of the U.S., no country seems to have a more fraught and conflicted attitude toward massage than Laos; or to be more precise, the government's conflicted attitude. Massage—along with guesthouses, restaurants, and ecotourism—is a cash cow in the expanding tourist industry and must be allowed to develop, yet at the same time rigidly controlled. Burma, which I visited in 2014, makes for a useful comparison here (see my *Massage and the Writer*). In that country, the massage arts had a long tradition until stamped out under the military regime. It was only then making a comeback, but there wasn't much. In Laos, by contrast, there's a thriving massage business in the country's prime tourist haunt of Luang Prabang, or I should say at least the trappings of one.

Luang Prabang is a lovely little city, with a mile of tourist guesthouses, restaurants, and massage shops spread out along the Mekong. On the main boulevard parallel to the river, a couple blocks up on Sakkaline Road, Buddhist temples with stacked roofs commingle with colonial-era homes built by the French. The French influence is still evident, as it is in Vietnam, in the high quality of the coffee and bread, while restaurants run by French proprietors offer a decent imported wine selection. A writer or romantic would find it an idyllic Asian haunt to hide away in, even without the prospect of a decent massage. I spent four days growing ever more flustered in my research.

I start off with a few shops on Khem Khong Road along the river. They all have open fronts. The masseuses sitting in the entrance at the first place I step into acknowledge me without evincing any hospitality. I am led upstairs to a shabby little room by a woman in her 20s with her hair dyed blond. She gives me an indifferent and wholly chaste massage with one hand while playing with her cellphone with the other; at one point she interrupts the massage to leave the room and take a call, returning a good five minutes later. At the next venue I take a chance on, the young lady massaging me is so inept that I am compelled to do something I rarely do, quit halfway through. I pay part of the fee and take off before any further dispute arises (in China when this happens, they'd demand I pay for the full hour, but I can handle them with my ability in the language).

At the far end of the town and around the bend where the Nam Khan River flows into the Mekong, the quality of the housing steps up, and the massage shops are larger and more upscale, some with a coveted TripAdvisor placard; many occupy the traditional A-frame teakwood housing you can also see in Thailand. I choose one. A variety of massage essences is offered, and the shower is elegant and immaculate, with fluffy towels. A competent and thoroughly unmemorable massage follows in the steep-raftered room by an attractive young lady wrapped in the Lao sarong, or *sinh*. I suppose if I didn't have such high standards and it was my first time, the experience would have been wholly satisfactory and stamped indelibly in my memory of the country. But when you've racked up untold massages in a variety of countries, you become picky. Hers is the old one-size-fits-all treatment, the same massage she gives to all of her customers. In the massage arts the usual notion of quality control—maintaining identical standards in a product line—does not and should not apply. She lacks, as all but the best masseuses do, the ability to read the customer and grasp what they want.

I try several more shops over the following days. The massages are all noted for their sameness, down to the way they always start working upward from the calves. There's no reason why one can't work upward from the calves, but it seems like they were all trained in the same state-run school.

I've long found that the older or less attractive a masseuse is the better, if only because she has likely come to terms with her profession and is able to relax into the job and focus on the customer. At another establishment in a lovely teak dwelling, a middle-aged masseuse produces something approaching a satisfying session. She gets her fingers into the ridges of my groin while refraining from any direct genital contact—delicious enough for me to request another half hour. With her nonexistent English, an amusing scene ensues. I try everything—pointing to the clock, writing down the times—but fail to convey my request. If an Asian masseuse knows any English at all, it's money-making words such as "another half-hour?" and "hour and half?" The Lao aren't yet savvy enough to anticipate the customer who simply wants to extend their massage. We have to interrupt the session while she goes off in search of her boss who is momentarily out, to get to the bottom of my strangely urgent query. She arrives back fifteen minutes later and conveys my message to the masseuse. By then the spell has been broken.

On the bus passing through one of innumerable mountain villages on the way to Vientiane, I am confronted by a shocking sight. A woman is standing in a tub by the roadside pouring water over her magnificent breasts, naked but for the *sinh* around her hips, casually glancing up at us as we speed by.[14] By "shock

---

[14] I'm not able to snap a picture in time. It can't be discounted, indeed seems quite likely, that she was something of an exhibitionist, given that

Mountain hamlet in Laos, like the one where I saw a woman bathing by the road

ing" I must underscore that I don't mean offended, only that it's the first time to witness the like. Laos is a traditional society and is hardly expected to be progressive and openminded. Yet in this one respect, they are freer than much of the rest of the world, above all Americans, so notoriously squeamish and so easily bruised, so quick to reject out of hand our natural freedom to be naked, so quick to demand freedom *from* the sight of the naked. According to this parochial mindset, unless young and of fine physique, the naked body is ugly by definition. There is no middle ground: the body is either highly sexualized and frightening or decrepit and offensive. The social force of these repressive attitudes is such that breastfeeding mothers are reluctant to expose their nipple in enlightened New York City, where public nudity is in fact per-

---

the bus would have appeared around the bend about the same time every day. Exhibitionism is discussed in Chapter 10.

fectly legal but only performance artists dare assert this right. To bare an American nipple for the baby's mouth thus amounts to a form of performance art and a radical act. There is no valid argument against public nudity. There is only the futile question as to why it's not universal.

Most of the passengers get off at the popular backpacker haunt of Vang Vieng, with its hiking, kayaking, and rumored opium dens. Your massage researcher is the only foreigner left on the bus for the remaining stretch. Hours later, we pull into the capital after dark. Somewhere near the city center in a tuktuk, I speed by a shop with the word "Massage" in English and another word before it, beginning with the letter "E," perhaps "Erotic"? No, it can't be. At that very moment, a shapely woman emerges out of the shop as if noticing me. In a sheer net dress, her breasts and panties are starkly illumined by the streetlight. It all happens so quickly I can't be sure I'm not hallucinating. If this quasi-communist state can't even turn up a single decent massage shop, I must be hallucinating. The tuktuk drops me off at a hotel with an inviting front restaurant, the Mixok Guesthouse. In the reception, I see a middle-aged white guy having dinner with an attractive Lao woman. That much is reassuring. Like China of the 1980s, the government here, I've heard, forbids women to consort with foreign men.

As with many authoritarian states, much of Vientiane's city center is swallowed up in broad boulevards, monuments, and billboards adorned with the country's leader. My guesthouse is located in the compact international nightlife area, a few criss-crossing streets several blocks in scope. There are plenty of massage shops around, but I don't partake, expecting more of the same. To be sure, I'd benefit from a few more days here to let the town soak in and things pop out of the woodwork, a few locals to meet and perhaps a woman to chat up and get friendly with. But I'm on a tight schedule and impatient to cross over to the other side of the Mekong where the action is.

THAILAND: NONG KHAI AND UDON THANI

A short bus ride downstream and across the bridge and I'm deposited at the Thai border in Nong Khai. I can't tell whether there are more Laos or Thais in the crowded customs outpost. In contrast to the stark border control upon entering Laos, with its stolid officers in their communist-era uniforms and high-peaked caps, the atmosphere on this side of the river is relaxed, the channeling of people efficient, and there are a lot more people to channel. A female customs officer with blunt bangs and seductive eyes directs the crowd into the right queues. It's my second visit to Thailand and my first to Isan, the country's least-developed region. What makes me curious about the northeast is almost all the masseuses on my previous stay in Bangkok told me they hailed from Isan. Their migration into the sex trade is not in dispute, but I envisioned swaths of arid farmland and the population living in huts and dressed in rags (pockets of rural poverty certainly exist, as attested in Aldous and Sereemongkonpol's account of Isan from 2008). I want to witness the place for myself. Laos has long been an insular culture and due to national inbreeding, the people often resemble one another. In fact, northeast Thais are ethnically Lao and you can see a resemblance in some. Isaners—and rural Asians generally—are stereotyped as dark-skinned and the well-bred as fair-skinned. But also evident is the same wide range of hues and facial features as in the rest of Thailand.

I have no idea where to stay in the small city. A tuktuk drops me off in the city center, several kilometers away from the border control. I step into a coffee shop to use their wifi, and my GPS map shows a concentration of guesthouses along one section of the river. The staff points me in the right direction, but I see nothing ahead but dusty streets. I go into a convenience store to ask for more help. An attractive customer at the checkout offers to drive me there. She's well-dressed and her car is new. I'm grateful for her kindness and would much like to get better acquainted, but I don't know how to break the ice when neither of us speaks a word of the other's language.

The foreigner enclave amounts to one narrow street stretching for a block, with a handful of guesthouses and open-air restaurants overlooking the Mekong. I can see that Nong Khai is going to be too small for me. Still, things get off to a brisk start, as I knew they would. The first guesthouse I step into displays a poster in the lobby advertising 400 Bhat/hr ($12) massage room calls. I get settled in my room and a masseuse is at my door a few minutes later. She's in her forties, hefty with huge hips, possibly pretty when she was younger but no longer, but that doesn't matter for, on top of having good technique, she soon drives things into erotic territory. A towel is draped across my midriff, and as she pulls my knees back to stretch my legs, she exposes my erect shaft. Now, a massage doesn't have to collapse halfway through. I prefer it's brought right up to the edge and held there in a state of arrested tension for sixty minutes. But this is Thailand, where massages have a way of devolving into sex—to mutual satisfaction. It's clear she enjoyed things and she doesn't ask for a tip. The house call is so unbelievably cheap I give her a generous one anyway.

I stride out of the foreigner enclave, my normal energy level now supercharged from the lightning encounter, to hunt down another massage. One shop, a bit off the expat strip, has a sign in English for "Oil Massage," but it looks more like a beauty salon. A sexy woman around 40 is attending to a female customer and points at the clock, indicating she'll be free at six. I backtrack down the street to a cozy little coffeehouse where I wait out the hour. When I return, she's ready, the shop to herself. She leads me to the massage tables in the unlit back end of the premises. At most venues in Thailand, you just strip and get on the table naked. If you're shy you keep your underwear on and a towel is usually provided to cover yourself with, but they're not in the least fazed if you take everything off. This is a barebones sort of shop and there's no towel, nor is she adept at massage, which is surprising since the place seems to cater to locals with therapeutic needs rather than foreigners, but she indeed gets right down to business and offers to fuck. She has a marvelous body and I offer to massage her instead.

An hour's bus ride south is Isan's largest city, Udon Thani. The U.S. military had a base there during the Vietnam War for staging operations in its secret bombing campaign in Laos. The main drag with all the pubs and go-go bars remains lively today, while the composition of the expat community has shifted to retired Brits. It's much larger than Nong Khai and the quality of the Western restaurants is impressive. During my two days in the city, I visit quite a few massage shops; there are scores of them. They run the usual gamut from no-nonsense chaste to the erotic. And as in China, what the shop looks like on the outside is no help; it all seems to come down to whether a masseuse takes a fancy to you. But already rather exhausted by massage at this point, I prefer to spend my time with the lovable middle-aged waitresses at the Smiling Frog pub, who look like they might have been sex workers during the war days, except they aren't quite old enough for that. They serve the best pizza margherita I've had since Otto Pizzeria's at the Venetian in Las Vegas.

Commercial massage is more relaxed and liberal in some countries than others, and Thailand is where the art of massage has been permitted to flourish more than anywhere else. All cities in this country have an endless supply of massage services, but Pattaya and Chiang Mai stand out. Pattaya is notorious as Thailand's swinging "sin city" (open-air bars, go-go bars, soapy massage), to be compared not with Bangkok but something raunchier, like Angeles in the Philippines. Chiang Mai, by contrast, is not known as a sex mecca. On the contrary, it tends to draw tourists who come to the country for all the other reasons, the "culture" and laid-back atmosphere, the golden conical pagodas and orange-robed Buddhists strolling the streets, the food. Yet the city crawls with massage. So much so that there almost seems something odd going on, as if every time you think that you have

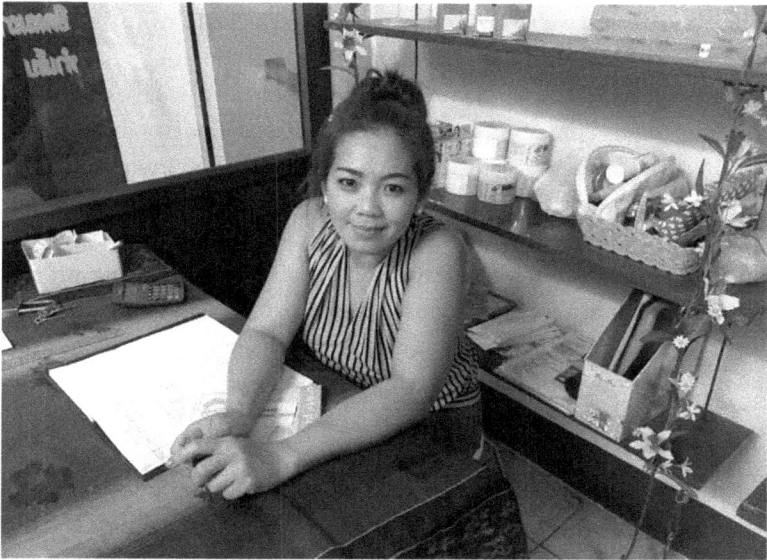

Massage lady, Udon Thani, Thailand

found a street free of any massage shops, yet another one peeks out with a good old "Hi there!"

To newbies, these shops can go from family-friendly to frightening in the space of a few meters. Most have open fronts, where you see couples and their children getting their feet massaged in reclinable chairs as you pass by. In the room behind or the floor above, floor mattresses are at the ready for Thai-style massage, performed by a masseuse who uses her body weight and her knees, elbows, and feet to elasticize you. You are clothed so there is no pressing need for privacy here either, but curtains partition each space to assuage the skittish Anglo customer anyway.

And then in private back rooms or cubicles, there is oil massage, performed on a dedicated massage table with a face rest. When the masseuse enters, she'll drape you with your towel, if you haven't done so. Once the massage begins the towel tends to come off unless you insist on keeping it on. In the presence of the

Thai masseuse, we're dealing with a special form of intimate social nudity. Male and female customers alike can expect a massage over the entire body, normally but not necessarily excluding
the genitals. Some masseuses keep things chaste; others are
happy to deliver more to those who want it. For men, this may
mean a laxer draping procedure, the inner thighs worked closer
to the groin, exposing your scrotum or letting your erection pop
out. From there on it's a dance of draping or sloughing off the
towel once and for all; the towel functions less as a veil than an
instrument of wordless dialogue, a gentle matador's cape. The
penis may be folded into the treatment and your semen squeezed
out—or not. She may ask for a tip beforehand or afterward or not
at all.

In the window of the massage shop next to my guesthouse in
Chiang Mai, a sign in English warns foreigners: "We only offer
proper massage here. Please do not ask for anything else." I am
led to a back room, and a masseuse begins to work my legs and
buttocks. Mysteriously, another masseuse soon shows up to take
over. An Asian version of Judy Garland around 40, Dang is fair-
complexioned with wide-set eyes, in a tight black shirt and blue
silk sarong. Guided by the supreme technique of mere thorough-
ness—if only all massage workers understood this!—she proceeds
to deliver one of the most explosive massages I've ever had. The
usual massage worker is given to fast stroking. I always have to
tell them to *slow down*. Dang is a master of slow massage. It
takes her only several hundred strokes to use up the hour. If that
sounds like a lot, the usual masseuse expends several thousand
strokes (and mangles her hands for good if she keeps it up day in
and day out). Dang dispenses with the towel early on, and I'm
naked when I turn over. She works my limbs to my solar plexus,
from the legs upward and the chest downward deeply, strongly,
and purposefully, as if plowing the soil, before terminating the
hour with a precise number of upward strokes along my shaft,
stopping just short of ejaculation. She's that rare poet of the
hands, building up erotic tension in layers and suspending it

there quaveringly without relief. It makes all my other massages in Chiang Mai pale in comparison.[15]

Females too should have this experience, though few women seem to go for commercial erotic massage, an unfortunate consequence of sexism. It is also a problem of the imagination—on the part of customers. Since so few women ever request such a massage, no masseuse (or masseur) dare venture there and risk causing a misunderstanding. I suggest that any female desirous of having a more deluxe-style treatment could start with a breast massage—few Thai masseuses have a problem with that and the practice is common in China as well—and if she intuits the vibes to be right, request more. A few masseuses may balk, others not.

Chiang Rai, up in the northwest corner of the country and a three-hour drive north of Chiang Mai, is a miniature version of the latter, with a smattering of famous temples, a handful of decent cafés and restaurants, and an expat-backpacker enclave a few streets in extent. It is also home to the extraordinary White Temple (mentioned in Chapter 5) built by the eccentric architect Chalermchai Kositpipat, who continues to add wild structures and futuristic ornaments to the temple complex. The temple and Kositpipat's gallery of paintings are worth a trip to Chiang Rai alone. As for the massage scene, it's an extension of Chiang Mai's, which is to say there's a lot, enough to keep one busy for days. Some strips closer to the main drag cater to single men or couples, those further back to men only. My guesthouse as well offers its own massage service. By this point, however, I am too massaged-out to sample any of them.

---

[15] Dang no longer worked at the shop when I returned to Chiang Mai in 2019. However, they called her up and she agreed to make a special trip, arriving soon on her moped and almost unrecognizable, now a Buddhist nun and completely shorn of her hair. She again delivered a massage as electrifying as her first.

Masseuses at a Bangkok massage shop celebrating their TripAdvisor promotion

CAMBODIA: SIEM REAP AND PHNOM PENH

I am due for a change of scenery and after a brief stay in Bangkok to see a friend, my Chinese girlfriend I grab a bus to Cambodia and my first visit to Angkor Wat, the world-famous, sprawling
ruined temple complex. The archeological encounter is thoroughly worthwhile but with volumes written about it, this is not the
space to add my own verbiage. The nearby city for accommoda-
tion, Siem Reap, I expected to be a dusty outpost in the impoverished and devastated country. It turns out to be one of the liveli-
est tourist cities I've encountered in Southeast Asia, a bustling,
disorienting congeries of chic restaurants, nightclubs, bars, cafés,
and massage parlors in every direction. I gather some expats like
the place enough to buy property and retire here.

The massage joints I sample are comparable to their Thai

counterparts in price and services offered but rather lackluster, with the exception of the room service at my upscale guesthouse. The central patio houses a pool surrounded by palm trees, crowded with tanned Western couples throughout the day and evening. The atmosphere is upscale, and I don't expect anything more than the primmest of massages. When my masseuse arrives at my door in a white uniform, I mistake her for my housekeeper. She has no problem massaging me fully naked and bringing me off and discreetly departs without asking for a tip. I make sure she gets one down at the reception.

The capital is grander and more populous, with an established expat crowd and lively nightlife scene along the Mekong riverfront. Phnom Penh has an old-world atmosphere, with bars on the gritty 136 Street named Pussy Cat, Olala, and Dirty Old Sailor (I am not making these up). There's a "Spa Bar" with liquor and massage on the menu, a novel combination, but the timing is off. I remain massaged-out from Thailand and not much in the mood. As well, I am still intoxicated by Dang's powerful massage back in Chiang Mai and enveloped in its lingering, perpetual glow; I want to keep the memory alive and avoid dissipating it in disappointing massages. Finally, I try out one shop next to my hotel with thin New Agey trappings but the massage is fussy. I'll have to do the whole trip again one day in reverse, beginning with Vietnam and Cambodia, starting out massage deprived.

The Tuol Sleng Genocide Museum makes a strong impression on me. The museum occupies the same high-school grounds used as an execution site by the Khmer Rouge. The horrible photos reveal the connection between state terror and sex.[16] Torture regimes the world over operate with remarkable consistency, stripping their prisoners naked and stringing them up in chains or

---

[16] See for instance *Nunca Mas*, a comprehensive report of torture, including sexual torture, under the Argentine military dictatorship. The ironic parallels between torture and massage are explored in my *Massage and the Writer*.

136 Street in Phnom Penh, Cambodia

binding them to tables, or iron bed frames as in this prison, male and female victims alike reduced to bloodied blobs of flesh at the hands of their male torturers. When terror is applied to individuals, it becomes perversely intimate. It's the sadomasochistic relationship with the playacting removed. It's sex at its most humorless. If rape is sex enraged, torture is the tragic corollary of massage. That's why massage is so frightening for many neophytes: to mount a table naked and surrender your genitals to potential attack.

VIETNAM: SAIGON

My first stop in Saigon is the War Remnants Museum, and more horrendous photos of mutilated bodies, this time at the hands of the U.S. military. It's still hard for me to fathom the massive disparity in deaths between the two countries from the war: two to three million Vietnamese, more than half of whom were civilians, versus a mere 60,000 U.S. personnel: 50 Vietnamese for every American. Most Americans aren't even aware of these statistics, let alone the profound moral aspects of the problem, the ease with which we can march into distant countries with our big military toys to teach the racial Other a lesson, blithely oblivious of the consequences and the scale of the slaughter and destruction.

This is my first trip back to Vietnam in ten years. I was previously in Hanoi, a crumbling but charming city, with a fledgling massage scene at the time. I heard Saigon was a crowded, chaotic urban mess, but I find it to be nicely laid out and pedestrian-friendly, at least by Asian standards. The nightlife street associated with U.S. troops back in the war, Đồng Khởi, is now lined with five-star hotels and exclusive boutiques. On that street, I sample an "Oriental" massage parlor next to an artisan coffeehouse. While awaiting my masseuse in the lobby, a male and female pair of police officers walk in and go over the store's account books at a table nearby. They speak to the proprietor quietly and pay me no attention. As expected, the massage is chaste, more expensive than Thailand but cheaper than China for the equivalent service.

I try out three other places over the next two days. Bùi Viện Street is now the main nightlife drag, packed with Parisian-style people-watching restaurants, fire eaters, and in the labyrinth of inner lanes, massage shops. In one such shop, oddly only a dry rub-down is on the menu—until the masseuse pulls out a bottle of baby oil in the last few minutes and offers more for an extra fee. I turn down happy endings if the massage itself is wanting, preferring to gamble my money on another masseuse. A shop on a street near my hotel turns out to be the best. A jeans-clad woman with shapely hips by the name of Thao leads me up a narrow staircase to a room with a molded massage table. She delivers a satisfying oil massage, to the tune of a Rachmaninoff concerto on her boom box. She speaks only a smattering of English but seems into me and the massage is good and I allow her to release me, at double the session's price. Even that isn't enough, apparently. Her boss, an older woman with youthful bangs, confronts her outside the door and they have a testy little spat, trying to keep things to a whisper; I am nonetheless spared further fees. We exchange contact information. I still get emails from Thao asking me when I'll be back in Saigon.

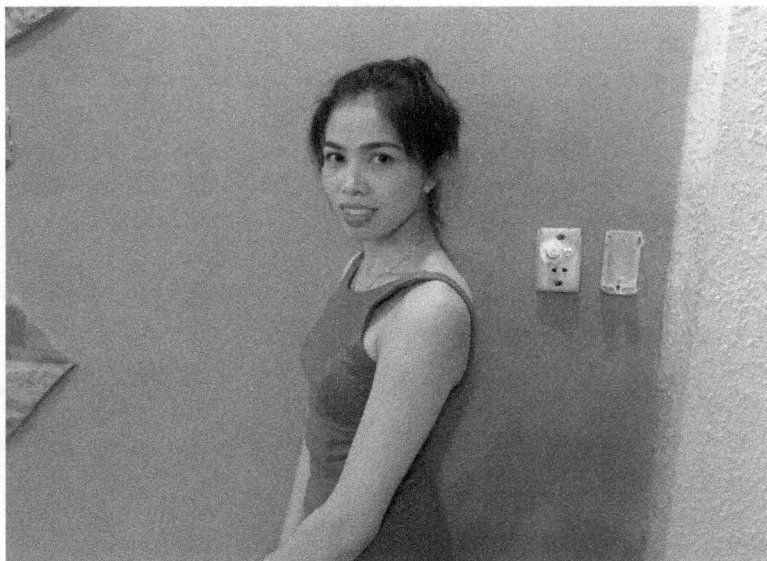

Massage lady, Saigon, Vietnam

I need a city large enough that it can never be exhausted. Between Bangkok and Saigon, I would choose Saigon to retire in. The Thai are renowned for their friendliness and hospitality, and their massage industry is vastly more developed, but a wall stands between. While they are very good at making tourists feel at home, all signs of the West disappear outside the foreigner enclaves. I also understand from those with experience in the country that Thailand is riven by class prejudices, and the well-bred are less enthusiastic about mixing with foreigners. My experience in Vietnam is also limited, but the place just feels familiar and more like home. This is presumably due to the formerly extensive contact with the West, going back generations (the French were here long before the Americans). Whatever the case, walking on the street, the locals look you in the eye more spontaneously than in other Asian countries.

On my last day in Saigon near the Bến Thành Market, I pass by a hot woman in her 30s in a tasteful silk dress. "Massage?" she says with a winning smile. That never happens in Thailand except when passing by a massage shop. It rarely happens in China, and they never say it with a smile but more of a taunt. It also happened in Hanoi on my previous trip, a young woman who rode up to me on her motorcycle, offering "Massage? Marijuana?" Unfortunately, I have a plane to catch and not enough time, or I'd immediately go with her.

8

THE BREASTS OF BALI:
AN UPDATE

And our women would have to cover their breasts as if they were whores.
Vicki Baum, *Love and Death in Bali*

IF YOU WONDER WHAT years of living in Bali—as opposed to Elizabeth Gilbert's four months of *Eat, Pray, Love* fame—might do for
the soul, long-time expat Diana Darling has bequeathed to us the
delightful novel, *The Painted Alphabet*, a lush reimagining of the
Dukuh Siladri folktale, from which I highlight the following quo-
tation. Sent packing by her parents to be brought up by the witch
Dayu Datu, the naughty eight-year-old Ni Klinyar is provided
with an assemblage of gifts to bear to her new guardian:

> Four sacks of raw rice, a black rooster, three batik sarongs,
> two thousand Chinese coins, several loops of cotton string
> (black, red, and plain white), a young yellow coconut and
> various other implements of Balinese ritual, plus several
> more unusual items—a size 32AA brassiere, a bottle of nail
> polish remover, and a Japanese-Indonesian dictionary.

Abandoned souvenir painting shop, Ubud, Bali, 2019

We have here in this odd collection of incommensurables an example of the Borges-style list—referring to the master Argentine writer's penchant for leavening his tales with bits of surrealism. Lest you assume this kind of invention is confined to the world of fiction, we find another such list of curiosities in Colin McPhee's memoir of his Bali stay in the early 1930s, *A House in Bali*. An earthquake has released evil spirits and his ill-protected house evidently becomes haunted. He seeks out a priest for advice. There is nothing intentionally playful about the list of sacrificial offerings the priest demands with a straight face McPhee must assemble if the purification is to be successful:

> For this you will slaughter one young bull, one goose, one goat, one dog with a three-colored hide, one duck with similar markings, one young male pig, one chicken with feathers growing the wrong way, five hens of five different colors, and

twenty-five ducks. You will also need six hundred duck eggs, six hundred bananas, and five thousand Chinese cash. The offerings prepared in advance will include two roast pigs, ten roast chickens, ten roast ducks, five baskets of rice, flowers and cakes, and five skeins of thread in the five colors.

Bali's age-old Hinduism, which is itself imbued with an even older indigenous animism, has given rise to one of the most mystically inclined of societies. The religious routine is thickly laid on everywhere: your dance-like moves to avoid stepping on the palm-leaf tray offerings scattered on every sidewalk, the ubiquitous split stone gates of street-front gardens signifying the parting of the material world, the shops that close for weeks as the owner attends a relative's cremation ceremony, the houses that can't be bought or built and the shops that can't open without an elaborate ceremony to appease the local spirits.

Yet when I consider the strange superstitions of my own homeland and how much of the population is stuck in a magical apprehension of the world, including a disturbing number of people I've met, I don't find Bali so alien. I refer to those who believe the earth was created 6,000 years ago and is flat, the dinosaurs were wiped out not by an asteroid but lack of space on Noah's Ark, a zygote is a person, nuclear war is desirable as it will hasten the Rapture, the first female Presidential candidate to win the popular vote ran a pedophile ring out of a pizza restaurant, and the sight of a woman breastfeeding her child in public is offensive. I always experience renewed shock by the last item in this American basket of bizarrables. With every fresh news report of a hapless nursing mother being harassed in public or even arrested, I seem to be encountering it for the first time, so astonishing and inexplicable is this taboo. We can lay the blame at the feet of one outraged Calvinist pastor from Boston named Hiram Bingham who in 1819, with the backing of the American Board of Commissioners for Foreign Missions, charged off to Hawai'i—presumably to see for himself—and almost singlehandedly succeeded in forcing the native women to don Mother Hubbards, upon reports they went topless. If there's one thing to be said about Bingham that resonates with males today, he was obsessed with the female breasts.

Two decades later, a young American sailor on a whaling ship sailed some 2,500 miles to the south into a tropical paradise, the island of Nuku Heva in the Marquesas, whose inhabitants were the ancestors of the Hawai'ians. Before dropping anchor, the sailors found themselves surrounded by scores of swimming beauties, the sashes wrapped around their hips the only nod to modesty as they climbed aboard. They then lay supine on the deck awaiting intercourse with the stunned crew, and we don't mean spoken intercourse. The sailor wrote up his experiences on the island after jumping ship and turned it into a book, *Typee: A Peep at Polynesian Life* (1846), which became a bestseller in the U.S. and the UK. The author, Herman Melville, knew of the events in Hawai'i and was thus able to appreciate his pristine setting before French missionaries in the succeeding decades would proceed to corrupt these islanders as well and achieve the prime objective of Christian missionaries the world over—the veiling and consequent sexualization of the breasts—along with other grand civilizing influences:

> Let the once smiling and populous Hawaii islands, with their now diseased, starving, and dying natives, answer the question. The missionaries may seek to disguise the matter as they will, but the facts are incontrovertible; and the de-voutest Christian who visits that group with an unbiased mind, must go away mournfully asking—"Are these, alas! the fruits of twenty-five years of enlightening?"

By the time the great Paul Gauguin set foot in the Marquesas, six decades after Melville, on the sister island of Hiva Oa, the female natives had long buttoned up, as they had throughout Polynesia, including Tahiti, where the artist had just spent the

Hindu-inspired art (early 18th c.), Klungkung Palace, Semarapura, Bali

greater part of a decade. This may come as a surprise given the plethora of olive-skinned nudes in his paintings. He had to coax them out of their clothes. He managed this by inviting schoolgirls in their teens and older, anyone he could manage, to his house to view his art. Strategically tacked on a wall of his studio were pornographic postcards he had acquired in Europe. Whenever one of his lovely visitors gazed curiously at the photos, for they had never seen the like, she would feel his hand creeping onto her buttocks as he propositioned her to pose for him. Most couldn't surmount their disgust at the oozing syphilitic sores on his legs, barely hidden by the Polynesian wrap around his hips, his sole article of clothing.

Gauguin has been reduced in our present politically enlightened era to a caricature more repulsive than pathetic (see for instance Ian Littlewood's *Sultry Climates*), not wholly without justification, as the prospect of fresh women in the backwater of

Ancient erotic sculpture, Monkey Forest, Ubud, Bali

the Marquesas who didn't know he was diseased was the very reason he made the move from Tahiti, where, as lore has it, he had been notorious among the locals.

You might suppose I'm being ironic in referring to Gauguin as "great," but not wholly. In defense of the man, an examination of the facts reveals a more nuanced situation. To begin with, syphilis was widespread everywhere, having coursed around the world like wildfire since its first appearance in Europe three centuries earlier. By the close of the Elizabethan era in England alone, most sexually active adults and many congenitally infected children were afflicted. Gauguin would not have been the only Polynesian resident to have the disease. On the contrary, Europeans stood as good a chance of *being* infected by native islanders, who first received the bacterium from Spanish explorers, as infecting them. Its general virulence had somewhat abated by the nineteenth century, but your beloved Ludwig van Beethoven,

Franz Schubert, Charles Baudelaire, Abraham Lincoln, Henri de Toulouse-Lautrec, Leo Tolstoy, Friedrich Nietzsche, Oscar Wilde, and many others were known or suspected to have been ravaged by it. There was, of course, no cure until the discovery of antibiotics. Being a syphilitic carrier was not necessarily regarded as a question of sexual morality or of morality at all, but as an unfortunate and pretty much inexorable bodily scourge. In the scheme of things, being spared the pox only increased your chances of succumbing to tuberculosis, typhoid, cholera, diphtheria or smallpox (the latter alone killed 300 million people in the twentieth century). And Gauguin's motives in moving to the Marquesas weren't all licentious. Those islands still maintained a Maori tradition of facial tattooing that had fascinated him for years. Meanwhile, it was his souring relations with the Catholic bishop, the gendarmes, and other enemies in Tahiti due to his political rabble-rousing, more than the receding prospect of fresh bodies, which gave him the excuse he needed to make the leap to the new island (Sweetman).

The story also goes that once the Marquesan women dried up, Gauguin made a last desperate appeal to any female passersby by mounting above the entrance of his dwelling a wooden sign carved with the words, "Maison du Jouir" ("House of Pleasure"), *jouir* being a double entendre for orgasm. The man was indisputably a lecher, as male artists often are. But what might seem nothing other than a pathetic personal ad writ large can be reevaluated as well. The placard was in fact an elaborate frieze of three-dimensional figures; its accompanying text would have been legible only to those who had approached the house and were literate in French. There was also a beautiful vertical pair of carvings along the sides of the entrance reading "Be mysterious" and "Be happy being in love," and two more laterally placed along the entrance floor. All five panels were rescued upon Gauguin's death in 1903 and are now displayed at the Musée d'Orsay in Paris.

Three years later in 1906, a major retrospective of several

hundred of Gauguin's works was exhibited at the Salon d'Automne, with a younger generation of painters present, including Pablo Picasso, Henri Matisse, Raoul Dufy, and André Derain. It was one of the founding events of Modernism. All were blown away by the riot of unencountered colors, the free play of forms, the pursuit of non-Western artistic media, the frank sexuality, and the striking idea of abiding in a culture on the opposite side of the planet for artistic inspiration. Gauguin's and several Cezanne retrospectives around the same time were the two decisive influences on the world's most famous modern painting, Picasso's *Les Demoiselles d'Avignon* of 1907.

So began the cult of Western expat artists venturing to distant Oriental utopias for inspiration. Matisse had to see for himself where Gauguin's colors came from and visited Tahiti in 1930, though he stayed for only two months. Next was Swiss artist Theo Meier who arrived in 1932. He stayed longer but was disabused by the reality of the place, far more priggish than Gauguin's paintings had led him to believe. Two years later Meier set sail for another location known for its naked maidens. He had heard rumors of an expat painter, the German Walter Spies, who had been on the Indonesian island of Bali since 1927 and was assembling an enviable cast of friends in his own "studio of the tropics" (Gauguin's phrase) in the town of Ubud, already an established artists' enclave on the island.

In the Western imaginary, all tropical paradises are essentially the same place, though Bali is as far from Tahiti to its east as it is from Istanbul, Turkey, to its west. Bali, however, delivered: the native women really did go about topless, and not only when breastfeeding or bathing in the river but in all their daily activities, the only exceptions being upper-class women who bore their status in their apparel, ceremonial dress worn at court, and dancers and theatrical performers, though toplessness in the royal context was once the norm throughout South and Southeast Asia: "Neither men nor women in the first millennium [C.E.] routinely covered the upper part of the body; this remained the case in non-Muslim parts of rural Southeast Asia (Thailand, Laos, Bali, etc.) into modern times, as in parts of South Asia itself. Court versions of women's clothing were often sexually revealing, as a vast body of evidence from Indian sculpture and literature makes clear" (Samuel).

Picture of traditional Bali scene hanging in my guesthouse in Ubud

Claude Lévi-Strauss's quip in *Tristes Tropiques* that "the tropics are not so much exotic as out of date" applies to Bali: it was the last of the island paradises to cover up. It's significant it was no longer the missionaries but a homegrown leader whose sexual propriety was shaped by Western puritanical morality, despite or rather because of his leftist ideology, when the dour nationalist Bagus Sutèja's first decree upon becoming governor of the island in 1958 was to banish the breasts (in Thailand it was the Hitler-admiring dictator Plaek Pibulsonggram who had put a stop to that country's toplessness in 1939). It didn't happen right away; there was much resistance evidently, as female natives struggled to understand the reason for having to confine their chests. During my stay in Ubud, my hired driver, in his 40s and too young to know anything firsthand, seemed to think women had all covered up by the 1970s when I asked him. It was probably a bit earlier, before the tourism boom. In any case, it's ironic that this transpired in the freewheeling '60s, when back in the 1930s Bali's tourist industry actively promoted its bare-breasted women (Vickers).

I should add that Western society had long had a relaxed attitude toward the breasts until the Victorian era. Throughout Europe in the sixteenth through eighteenth centuries (before that the historical record is more obscure), women were free to display their nipples in public, though there was an etiquette to it. Unmarried women were given more leeway. The "virgin" Queen Elizabeth was hence free to expose her breasts around Court and is known to have done so. Lower-class women who could not afford the "extreme décolletage" variety of bodice untied their chemise to let their breasts peek out. Numerous European paintings of tavern scenes reveal hands wandering on improperly secured bosoms. Upper-class women sitting for portraits could display one nipple to signal they were betrothed, both nipples if they were a mistress. With the historical evidence in mind, being upset at the contemporary "nip slip" on live American TV is a function of petty Victorian morality, prosecuted more eagerly in the U.S. than it ever was in England. And if this does apply to you, you can always visit more museums. But alas in our era, what the missionaries dreamed of but could not achieve is fast coming to pass through technology: the rapid dwindling of toplessness and nudity at nudist beaches the world over due to the ubiquitous presence of cellphone and face-recognition CCTV cameras. It could be that in the future the only place you'll be able to find women going about topless will be those scattered jungles and hill tribes where covering up has never quite penetra

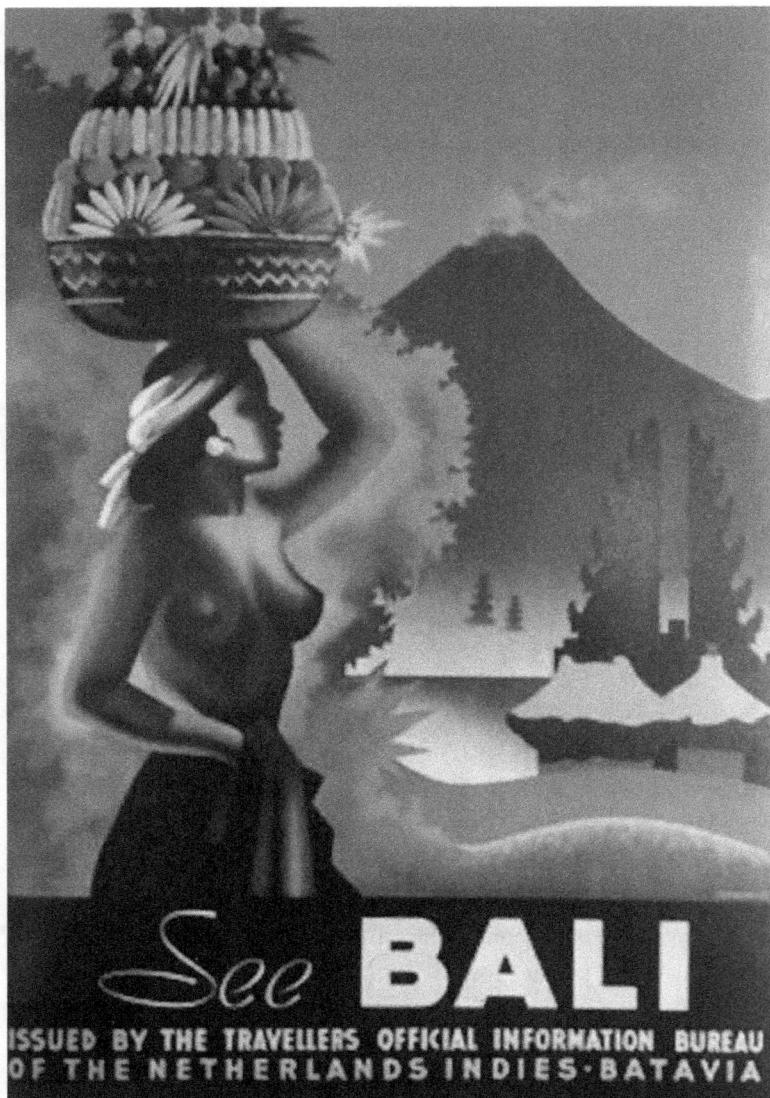

1930s travel poster by the Netherlands' Travelers Official Information Bureau,
printed in Adrian Vickers, *Bali: A Paradise Created*. Vickers' publisher used this
poster for the book's cover but covered up the woman's breasts.

ted, Laos for example.

In 1937 Walter Spies, the German painter, moved to the re-mote countryside of Iseh, near Bali's Mount Agung volcano, to escape his hectic socializing and concentrate on his painting. When Spies later moved back to Ubud, he let the aforementioned Theo Meier take over the idyllic house in Iseh. Over the next two decades, Meier netted scores of local female lovers, nude models, and several wives. He subsequently moved to Thailand to explore the female landscape there until his death in 1982. His paintings are now worth hundreds of thousands of dollars. This curious lineage of artists inheriting each other's houses continued when American expat Daniel Reid took over Meier's house in Chiang Mai in 1990. Reid was a classic hippie out of 1960s Berkeley who subsisted on LSD, opium, and whatever else he could get his hands on while vagabonding around the Middle East and India. This was followed by years in Taiwan where he claims to have slept with over 2,000 women, and then Thailand, by which time he had acquired expertise in Chinese medicine and sexual Tao-ism, popularized in *The Tao of Health, Sex, and Longevity*, and recounted in his memoir, *Shots from the Hip* (Reid had moved to a different house in Chiang Mai when I visited him in 2019, where he ran an internal-cleansing massage therapy business with his Taiwanese wife Snow).

As for Walter Spies, he had little predilection for female nudes; he preferred naturalistic settings for his art and teenage boys for his bedmates. Inspired by the jungle scenes of Henri Rousseau, his paintings were so gorgeous they influenced native Bali artists and now fetch over a million dollars at auction. He came to a tragic end when he was unceremoniously deported from Bali in 1938 for pederasty and was killed a day out of port when his ship was bombed by the Japanese. Spies' 1930s circle also included the anthropologists Margaret Mead and Gregory Bateson, the novelist Vicki Baum, and the Canadian composer Colin McPhee and his wife Jane Belo, one of Mead's proteges. McPhee's *A House in Bali*, cited at the outset of this essay, is a charming but enigmatic memoir of his Bali years. There is a great deal of scene painting and memorable detail on the local culture, but almost nothing about women or their breasts; nor does his wife merit a single mention in the book, though she was with him every day. McPhee regularly employs "I" rather than "we"; the reader unaware he was married would assume the occasional "we" refers to his servants. That McPhee was, in fact, gay partly accounts for this, though it seems he was a bit of a closeted one, or at least he chose to be more circumspect than Spies; there are references to the mundane activity of bathing in a nearby creek with one of his male servants and that's it. The nar-

Colin McPhee's private cook, Rantun, as photographed in *A House in Bali*

rative takes on greater clarity when one realizes McPhee's real passion was not people but the strange, dense murmur of the Balinese orchestra known as the gamelan. He traveled all over the countryside investigating every gamelan ensemble he could find (all villages possessed one), lavishing particular attention on the finer musicians and composers, in order to extract their music out of them, transcribe it, and work the exotic sounds into his own compositions. This music was his true love object, which he pursued with the relentlessness of an obsessive lover, and he sought to convey its effect on the reader in flights of erotically leavened prose:

> There was something dark and secret about their ancient craft, for they had to do with metal, cold mysterious product of the underworld, charged with magic power. For centuries they manufactured from the same substance the instruments of both music and death, the resonant gongs, the spears and thin-edged krises. In their craft the elements of life and death were strangely united. For a gong when struck can (or once could) dispel the demons, bring rain, wind; or give, when bathed in, health and strength. And music, which is the most ecstatic voice of life, rang from the bronze keys even as they were hammered out in the forges, over fires that had burned from time immemorial.

Vicki Baum, an Austrian author of a bestselling novel about Berlin, *Grand Hotel*, turned her 1935 Ubud sojourn into the historical novel *Love and Death in Bali*, recounting the 1906 Puputan massacre. Here the breasts are treated not with any special attention, except where their prominence merits mention: "The habit of carrying loads on their heads gave them an erect carriage and a rhythmic step, and their breasts and shoulders were at once soft and muscular." Elsewhere, the breasts serve to reveal the character of those reacting to them, such as the villager Pak's feelings about his wife, "how ugly [she] was with her untidy hair and hanging breasts." The breasts are never sexualized, and appropriately so, as the bare female figure was considered the most prosaic of sights, capable of being eroticized only through expensive clothes and adornment. But at the same time, Baum's novel is largely devoid of love and passion, despite its title; there is no obsession of any sort, let alone sexual, anything on the scale of McPhee's gamelan. Her scene painting and dialogue is workmanlike and often flat. The book's main redeeming feature is the fascination of its dramatic irony, as the protagonists, several Balinese families, comprehend all too slowly how the chain of events that began with a few fishermen grabbing some flotsam from a wrecked Chinese trading ship results in a Dutch naval invasion of the island and the slaughter of a thousand of their countrymen.

The Japanese occupation of Bali put an end to the first tourist wave (Theo Meier lingered on until 1955), and it wasn't until the 1970s, after decades of poverty, the devastating 1963 eruption of Mount Agung, and a protracted and vicious anti-Communist purge, that the island started to come to life again. Bali today has become popular with Western female tourists and expats, including some long-established ones such as the aforementioned Diana Darling, and an intriguing Canadian woman, Cat Wheeler, who has been living in Ubud off and on since the 1980s. I suppose what attracts foreign women to Bali more than other tropical paradises is its freedom from the Muslim restrictiveness of the rest of Indonesia, the absence of a garish Thailand-style sex industry, and a reputation for being a peaceful place where harassment of women is relatively scarce. Wheeler has written an eccentric yet not unenjoyable book, *Bali Daze: Freefall Off the Tourist Trail.* As expected, the book is free of a single reference to Bali's old reputation for its topless natives. She does have this to say, however:

In warm climates and cultures that are deeply social, the public water supply has been a traditional meeting place.

The pragmatic Balinese take this a step further by taking off their clothes and jumping in….Yet Balinese women consider the bikini top and tiny pair of shorts that some western women wear around Ubud unacceptably immodest.

Wheeler does not seem all that much interested in people, much less things like love and relationships. Her descriptions of her life center around her garden. The unflinching focus on her fish, birds, and insects, and her dogs, begins to feel claustrophobic in a sweltering hothouse way and reminds me of McPhee's pre-

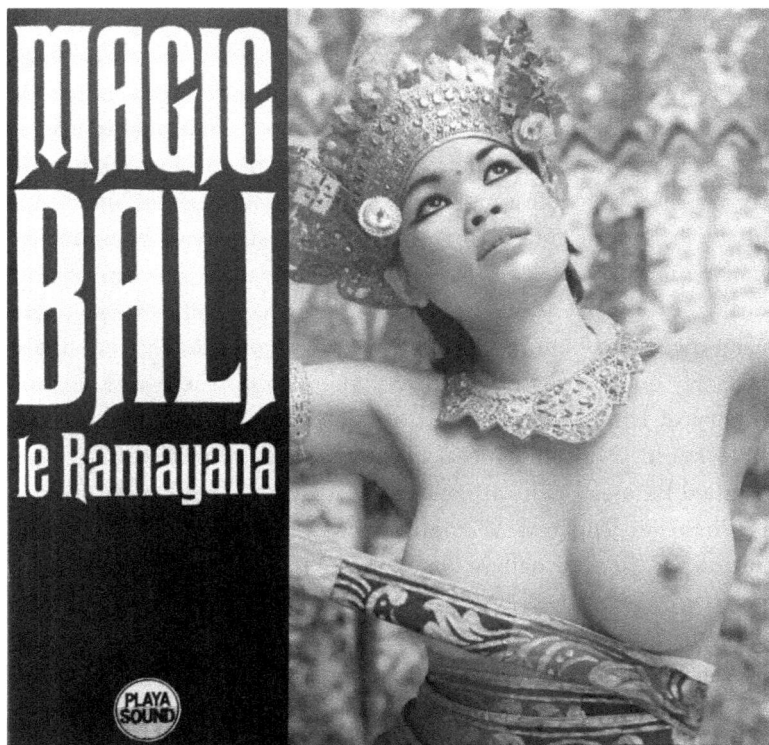

International release of Balinese gamelan music CD. You won't see traditional Balinese dancers going topless, but you can't fault the marketing savvy of this cover.

occupations with gamelan music. Readers noticed this absence of the human dimension, as Wheeler acknowledged in her follow-up book, *Retired, Rewired: Living Without Adult Supervision in Bali*: "If I wrote about the expats in Ubud, I'd have to leave town." Yet like McPhee, she does succeed in sexing-up her material in subtle ways, as if every Western writer on Bali cannot help but eroticize the island somehow, as when she writes of "copulating frogs" and the sex life of cucumbers. I have nothing against nature writing—will one day get around to Edward O. Wilson's *Naturalist* and Annie Dillard's *Pilgrim at Tinker Creek*, which have been sitting on my bookshelf for ages—but I was hoping to be more enlightened about the Balinese today.

I gave one more book a shot, Elizabeth Gilbert's bestselling *Eat, Pray, Love: One Woman's Search for Everything Across Italy, India and Indonesia*, the last third of which recounts her 2004 stay in Bali. A memoir about her career and relationship crises, the three countries are never more than an exotic backdrop to her internal psychodrama. The elderly Balinese healer she hangs out with, Ketut, indulges the attractive American woman and mouths for her spiritual benefit such platitudes as, "Smile with face, smile with mind, and good energy will come to you and clean away dirty energy." The book teeters on the edge of banality. Early on in her stay, Gilbert runs through the usual capsule history of the place. There is a sole reference to Bali's age-old toplessness: "Margaret Mead...despite all the naked breasts, wisely called Balinese civilization on what it truly was, a society as prim as Victorian England: 'Not an ounce of free libido in the whole culture.'" Gilbert's source for this Mead quote is Adrian Vickers' *Bali: A Paradise Created* (cited above). What Mead actually said was even more snobbish: "'Not an ounce of free intelligence or free libido in the whole culture.'" This was after all a rather insular group of Western intellectuals who had few close interactions with locals, apart from Spies who spoke the language. For all of Mead's groundbreaking work on indigenous sexuality in Samoa, it's an honest comment which merely reflects her status

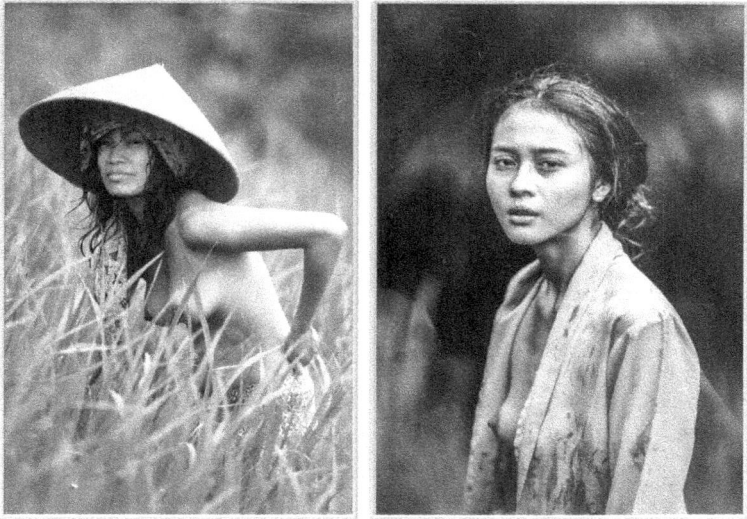

Idealized contemporary Balinese nudes photographed by J. P. Navicet
(Navicet Arts Gallery, Ubud, Bali)

as an outsider.

But there is one interesting development that threatens to thrust the narrative in a different direction, one protruding thread the extraction of which would cause the whole thing to unravel. Gilbert befriends another healer named Wayan, who runs a "Traditional Balinese Healing Center," where she seeks help for a bruised leg from a bicycle accident. The healer is an attractive and spunky female in her thirties with a pronounced sexual sense of humor. As her business barely brings in enough to pay the rent, Gilbert takes pity on the woman and launches a campaign among her friends back home to fund enough money so Wayan can buy a small house for herself and her daughter. She manages to raise $18,000, but the story takes an unexpected turn when Wayan inexplicably delays the purchase, using various excuses—this month or that plot of land wasn't spiritually propitious—only to ask for another $22,000. Gilbert suspects she's being scammed, but her newly acquired Brazilian boyfriend and Bali expat Felipe reassures her this is the normal way the Balinese negotiate. Wayan does finally acquire the house and it turns out well in the end.

The movie adaptation of *Eat, Pray, Love* elides these complications in the interest of conciseness. The movie also makes Wayan look much older, to erase her sexuality, employing an actress who looks to be in her 60s, and there is of course no reference to the true nature of Wayan's job, as described in the book:

> Then, to our lurid fascination, she described the different massages she does for men's impotent bananas, how she grips around the base of the thing and kind of shakes it around for about an hour to encourage the blood to flow, while incanting special prayers....But that's not all Wayan can do. Also, she told us, she is sometimes called upon to be a teacher of sex for a couple who are either struggling with impotence or frigidity, or who are having trouble making a baby. She has to draw magic pictures on their bedsheets and explain to them which sexual positions are appropriate for which time of the month....Sometimes Wayan has to actually be there in the room with the copulating couple, explaining just how hard and fast this must be done....But then Wayan confides something extremely interesting. She said that if a couple is not having any luck conceiving a child, she will examine both the man and the woman to determine who is, as they say, to blame.

If he's to blame, she spares him a loss of face by announcing it's his *wife* who has the problem and needs to be treated by her alone. In these sex therapy sessions, Wayan invites young males around the neighborhood to come and satisfy and even impregnate the wife, unbeknownst to the husband yet reassuring him of his virility when she gets pregnant. I guess I have to give Gilbert her due for not excising this content, content which contradicts everything the book stands for, as this side of Wayan's personality threatens to undo the integrity of the narrative, even as it renders her character more three-dimensional. Gilbert had to choose between maintaining a genteel façade of New Age propriety for her female audience or doing the opposite, scandalizing it by presenting a Balinese woman who is considerably more compelling and sexual than Gilbert herself. A more incisive female author (no male author could get away with it these days) would have exploited this extraordinary window into the sexual practices of one Balinese woman and devoted the entire book to Wayan, or even joined her life as participant-observer, business partner, co-conspirator or lover. So much for the Victorian primness of Balinese women.

I am cognizant of how "progressive" scholarship has trickled down into common discourse in the form of a more "political" or "woke" awareness, a heightened alertness to exploitation in all its forms. In our current, seemingly enlightened era, it is taken for granted that to entertain any sort of promiscuous motive while sojourning in the Third World is anathema and disqualifies the traveler from educated society. In the postcolonial conception of things, we have at long last overcome and outgrown a millennium-long regime of Western imperialism, beginning with the Crusades, directed against dark-skinned peoples who because they were physically "Other," alien and savage, were deserving of conquest. Conquest and control in turn feminized and sexualized these cultures as "virgin territory" and set the preconditions for the first wave of global sex tourism in the nineteenth century, pioneered by Sir Richard Burton, Pierre Loti, Paul Gauguin, and other English and French notables who ranged over distant locales on a whim and set up shop wherever they pleased. Thus were England and France able to "do with the territories what they would have wished to do with its women," and treat "the Orient as if it were the harem of the West" (Schick). Or as Littlewood puts it, "tourism can be used to buy the sexual privileges of a former age."

Benignly erotic souvenir paintings in an Ubud shop, marketed to Western tourists of prim sensibilities

Irvin Schick's study is informative and can be recommended for his illuminating research into the colonialist mindset and its inseparable female Other over the centuries. But while for the most part objective and analytical, the author can't refrain from a moralistic condemnation of the contemporary traveler, as when he writes, "Southeast Asian countries, especially Thailand and the Philippines, have become the new 'sex capitals' to which Europeans and Americans flock....to purchase partners with whom to indulge in pedophilia and other illicit practices." A reductive portrayal indeed. Pedophiles have been known to seek out minors in the Third World in the belief they can get away with it, but they constitute a minute fraction of the general population of tourists from developed countries. American child predators who are not intellectually challenged have good reason to refrain from even considering the idea. The United States has the most punitive child sex laws in the world, and any American caught engaging in such activities abroad is subject to U.S. law. Law enforcement in most of these tourist destinations happily cooperates with their American counterparts. International pedophiles are tracked by Interpol and the FBI and when caught are splashed all over the national media before their imprisonment and subsequent deportation back home, where more imprisonment awaits them in the grim U.S. penal system.

The adult sex business is undeniably vast and Southeast Asia is a hot destination for it. But it's not so easy to ascertain who participates and who doesn't. There is much overt prostitution in the well-known haunts of Thailand and the Philippines. But what about your average "massage therapy" establishment which serves clientele of both sexes? The female customer emerges from her treatment satisfied, while the male customer who is treated by the same masseuse an hour later gets a bit of erotic teasing or even a happy ending. This is the vast grey area of the global sex industry today, that is if "sex" is the right word since there is no clear definition of what constitutes sexual activity in many instances.

Bali is not presently known as a destination offering much in the way of red-light entertainment, yet its massage scene, as expected, falls in this grey area as well. I try out a number of massage shops in Ubud, Canggu, and Kuta on my visit.[17] Most are humdrum and disappointing, in terms of so many of the masseuses' lack of training and skill. With one exception: a shop in an upscale bungalow-style hotel off a busy street in Ubud, which I take my wife to. She chooses a spa treatment involving milk and lavender baths followed by a massage by the proprietor, an enticing woman in her late thirties, who would have been perfectly cast as Wayan in the *Eat, Pray, Love* movie.

For my own "four-hands" massage, the owner assigns me two

---

[17] This was in mid-2019. The Bali tourism industry has of course since been decimated by the coronavirus pandemic. We hope of course it can fully recover.

masseuses who arrive a few minutes later by moped. I am already face down on the table when they arrive. I try to guess what they look like from the feel of their hands on my body. The one working my upper torso is noticeably lacking in technique and an immediate letdown, but the one working my legs is skillful and far more thorough. Her strong fingers slip under my underpants (naked massage here being proscribed) and dig down to the erogenous zones around my ass and inner thighs. When I turn over, I am able to size them up. The inept masseuse is in her 30s, dressed in a blue silk kebaya and is very pretty, but I dismiss her. The expert masseuse is around 50, wearing eyeglasses, slacks and a T-shirt, fat and ordinary looking. I have trouble conveying to her that I want her for another half hour, with her lack of English. The boss interrupts my wife's massage and comes to the rescue to translate with her own limited English. Upon resuming, she proceeds to work her hands further down the lower belly and pubic region before lifting my erect member out of my underwear and applying similar techniques to it. There are only a few minutes left and perhaps uneasy at my wife's presence on the other side of the partition, she refrains from releasing me.

With female toplessness long banned in Bali, I might be asked at this point, why does the topic even matter? But it *does* matter, in the copious iconography of the female breasts all around me, the framed photos of topless rural women placed in guesthouses and restaurants to conjure up an atmosphere, the plethora of nude paintings in the many souvenir shops and galleries, the lore and mystique of this past on display in bookshops, the voluptuous Hindu naked goddess sculptures scattered along the streets, and in the intimate interactions with locals. It's everywhere, as if the traces of a repressed past have multiplied in myriad new guises.

9

A Modest Proposal Regarding Sex Work: Why All Sex Should Be Paid For[18]

MAIZIDIAN, THE OLD "wheat sellers" street in Beijing. This neighborhood near the embassy district hosts the largest concentration of massage parlors within the city, of both the chaste and erotic varieties (many more such establishments can be found in the suburbs). The main locale of German businesses, it's known to foreigners as Germantown; the Japanese are also active in the area. One of the more popular restaurants in Maizidian is Baoyuan Dumplings. It fills up fast during the lunch hour, though you can reserve one of their private dining rooms, as personnel often do from the American Embassy a short taxi ride away. The dumplings are succulent but their unique attraction is your choice of orange, green or purple wrappings—the dough in-

---

[18] Reprinted from Isham Cook, *Massage and the Writer: Essays on Asian Massage* (Magic Theater Books, 2014).

fused respectively with the juice of carrots, spinach or red cab-
bage. Like the colorful food, the waitresses change into a different folksy costume each day. Their cheerfulness and low turnover
bespeak good management. The owner plays cards with friends
at a table out front on the sidewalk when the weather is warm.
Since I order the same thing every time and the waitresses know
me, I need merely sit down at my favorite table and am soon
served.

One day a woman with high cheekbones and sexy almond
eyes fixes her gaze on mine as I step into the restaurant. Despite
her cheeks' youthful bloom, the shadows around her eyes suggest
her early 30s. She is much too aware of her attractiveness to be a
migrant, yet her unlikely rustic quilted cotton jacket and match-
ing pants coincidentally resemble the outfits the waitresses are
wearing. She is eating alone and finishing up her meal. A minute
later I casually glance over at her. She's packing up an order of
dumplings to go and meets my eye again. Not the type to affect
prudishness and plainly at ease in dealing with men. She gets up
to leave. As she passes by my table, she slips me a note with her
cellphone number and the English name Melody and says with a
smile, "Call me." I have a good look at her on her way out—
tallish with a narrow waist and full hips.

Rare is the woman handing out her number to a strange man.
Perhaps I've lucked out on my ultimate catch, a female with a
radical artistic consciousness who takes each day as an erotic
challenge (the closest I ever came was an affair with a professional Chinese acrobat I met on a bus, a porn connoisseur who
could eat herself out and in performance rotate her body from
supine to prone and back again while balancing lighted candela-
bra on her head, hands, and feet; I told her she really needed to
perform in the nude). More likely, she is a prostitute. But prostitutes don't have a habit of frequenting good restaurants. The
lower tier are served cheap boxed lunches or stir-fried cooked in
their dorm-style premises—breakfast actually, as they are just
getting up from late-night work. The more independent freelanc-

ers, by contrast, are too persnickety to waste money on something like fancy food: they expect to be treated to that by their clients.

I text her. She responds right away and can meet in the evening. She is not from the neighborhood and prefers to rendezvous at 10 pm in the lobby of the classy Marco Polo hotel in a northern part of the city some distance away.

"Can we make it any earlier?"

"No. I have to visit someone in the hospital and won't be free until then."

"What are you doing in Maizidian, then?"

"Delivering lunch for a friend in the hospital."

"The same hospital? Why come all the way down to Maizidian?"

No response.

"What are we going to do at the Marco Polo? It's pretty expensive."

"I live near the hotel."

After a late dinner, I ride up to the Marco Polo on my bike and wait in the hotel lobby. I'm worried her face in brighter lighting won't live up to my initial impression, and in fact am already regretting the long excursion when Melody walks in. Now brashly dressed in a low-cut black top, black tights, and an unbuttoned yellow sweater showing off her hourglass figure and big breasts, she's stunning. Far more attractive than on the first encounter and unmistakably beautiful. We move to the lounge, where I order Campari and sodas.

Her Chinese name is so common as to render it anonymous; not even Jane Smith or Susan Jones conveys its prosaicness, but in deference to privacy I'll stick to Melody. She is 29 and a graduate of the Ocean University in Qingdao with a degree in marine biology. She married a fellow student and went off with him to Germany while he worked on his doctorate. They fought a lot and got divorced. Upon returning to China, she found a gig as a music teacher in a primary school in Beijing.

She shifts closer to me. We caress each other. She gets to the point. Her father just had a stroke and the medical bills are sky-rocketing way beyond what she and her parents can afford; it's with them she's spending every evening in the hospital. She knows I want sex. She wants money—2,000 yuan to be exact. No way, that's too much. The most I ever spent on a prostitute was 500 ($75), which is what you used to be able to bargain things down to at the Pig & Thistle in the Lido Hotel or Maggie's in Jianguomen, with its midnight hoard of Mongolian hookers descending on expat males.

I tend to find sex with prostitutes boring and a waste of time and money, due to the lack of any genuine friendliness in the transaction. I must have a very good reason to bother, exceptional beauty for instance. The other reason I now feel myself teetering on the edge and willing to pay four times more than I have ever shelled out before is there's something uncanny about her. I can't read her; nothing about her makes sense. As a writer I thrive on such ambiguity, the raw puckered fold of mystery to wiggle my finger into and work into a story, perhaps an unpleasant one but one nonetheless worth writing about. She lowers the price to 1,500. If I agree, she promises to give me a freebie or two after that.

We walk over to her place. She has me wait outside for five minutes before going in separately, to keep her guests out of sight and "maintain a good relationship with the guard." The complex is in a decent-enough neighborhood and her apartment is what might be termed luxurious by average standards. The entrance opens onto a dining room. The centerpiece of the spacious living room is a king-size bed rather than the usual sofa and chairs—many Chinese like to turn their biggest room into a master bedroom. There's also a bedroom proper with another king-size bed, and a second smaller bedroom for her seven-year-old daughter, as I discover when I open up the room by accident (she told me she was childless).

The flat looks like a tornado hit it. Clutter and dust and unaccountable debris are everywhere: wooden planks from detached furniture frames, piles of long rolls of some paper product that might be inventory in some kind of business. I am relieved at least that it isn't rented by a madam or pimp and shared by rotating girls. She owns the place, she says, and I have no reason not to believe her, yet I can't figure out her circumstances. If she's still paying a mortgage she might indeed be in financial straits, but such a large apartment can only mean she's better off than most. For all I know, she gives men the same spiel about her father's stroke every time in order to keep the money she's invested in the stock market rolling in.

She emerges after showering with her robe hanging open, lies back on the bed, and spreads her legs wide to show off a freshly shaved vulva. "Chinese guys don't like it shaved but I know you foreign guys do. Here, eat me out."

"Oh, no! I need bush. I need unshaved. Why didn't you ask me first?"

I hastily put on a condom while I am still hard. She straddles me, which happens to be my favorite position, but she insists on keeping my hands on her breasts when I want to grab her ass and makes me maul them in a furious circular motion, apparently the only way she can get off. She yells loudly, and I yell at her to slow down. The mechanical contortions deflate my erection in seconds.

Apologizing for the fiasco, she invites me to spend the night, while warning me I have to leave early in the morning before she gets her daughter up at seven, not wanting us to get officially acquainted.

Her alarm goes off at 6 am and she gets up. I doze for another thirty minutes. After washing up, I find her fallen back asleep in the other bedroom. She jumps up and runs to her daughter's room to wake her up. I slip out the door into a cold November morning pouring rain and have to ride the hour and a half back home because while my folding bike can fit into the trunk of a taxi, finding a taxi in Beijing during rush hour in the rain is like winning the lottery.

I contact Melody a few days later to see if she's amenable to honoring her promise and stopping over at my place for a freebie. She agrees. But an hour before she's due to arrive she calls me. "It's too far to go to your place. Come over here instead. You can stay the night again."

Now we are at a crucial juncture, a battle of wits. It's not that she can't manage to make it over to my place. The problem is my proposing something, and that won't do. She feels it to be her prerogative to propose and my duty to accept. For if she can get me to agree to go back over to her place in spite of my reluctance, it means she can get me to do anything, including forking over more money on our next encounter and every encounter thereafter, despite the original terms of our so-called arrangement.

"No."

"Oh, yeah, come and fuck me! I know you want it. Oh, yeah, ooh, ooh, ooh, fuck me! Ooh yeah, ooh! ooh! ooh!"

I hang up on her.

As quick as a wink and we're enemies (a view I will later revise). But why should I be perturbed about it, when her actions merely confirm the eternal law of the prostitute, which I knew all along? A law that in its purity and logic can be described as a thing of elegance: the more unsatisfying the experience for me, the more satisfying for her (another view I'll later revise).

The ease with which instant sex can be summoned at the snap of a finger and a little money likens prostitution to a magic act. But the real magic is for the prostitute: the ease with which instant *money* can be summoned at the snap of a finger. The caressing of sensuous banknotes in exchange for a few minutes of fucking is more erotic than fucking. You've now succeeded in getting the world's two most tangible pleasures—sex and money—to realize each other. Once you habituate to this formula, there is no turning back. Once sex and money bind in this powerful chemical reaction, once sex is monetized and money eroticized, they can never be sundered. Money doesn't debase sex; it improves it, transfigures it. The sex-for-pay equation liberates precisely through its power to corrupt. You are compensated by a new form of pleasure that's more exquisite than sex itself. Once corrupted, you enter the exhilarating landscape of transactional sex, the heady sphere where it's men, not women, who are seduced and conquered.

The catch is that the sexual transaction obliterates all generosity. There are never any freebies. This is the central problem that I wish to investigate and work up a solution for.

Anti-prostitution feminists have fastened on this same problem but approach it differently, and I must first address this discrepancy to clarify my own stance on the issue. As they argue, the prostitute's loss of sexual innocence, her inability to enjoy sex without the expectation of payment or to enter into loving relationships, constitutes a grave violation of her human rights, even when she violates them of her own volition. They claim there is no legitimate form of sex work even under ideal circumstances— where the sex worker controls the conditions in which she enters into sex work—due to the psychological consequences of working in a profession whose nature is to grind away the very capacity for intimacy.

In addressing this argument, let's start with the tricky notion of intimacy, the deep, loving relationship. Most would agree that intimate love is precious, but must it be regarded as obligatory? If intimacy is a human right, so is the right *not* to be intimate. Intimacy is far from universal. There are many people who are not particularly fixated on love and relationships, or on the need to start a family, and would regard the pressure to do so as an imposition, indeed a violation of their individual autonomy. The same goes for sex. Everyone knows people who are utterly uninterested in their own sex life and are just fine being celibate, single, "asexual." They may have different preoccupations or obsessions—their work, adventure, sports, spirituality, creativity, health or even sanity and just getting through the day. For

countless others as well, money is more important than love or
sex. What's wrong with that? How is the sex worker's avarice, or
business acumen, any different from the entrepreneur's?

Nor does it follow that the absence of intimacy entails the
loss of the capacity to enjoy sex. On the contrary, some of the
most orgasmic women I have ever slept with have been prostitutes. A truth too few people realize is that sex can't be fully experienced and enjoyed *except* as hot sex, cleanly cloven from love.
There is something contradictory between liberated sexuality
and intimacy. When you cultivate sexual technique and enjoyment for its own sake, you arrive at the insight that the point is
not to please the other but to use the other to please yourself—
which, paradoxically, is the best way of pleasing the other.

The act of prostitution actually engenders a unique intimacy
of its own. When two strangers take their clothes off in front of
each other without any of the usual preliminaries of dating, acquaintance, talk or seduction, a special intimacy is revealed in its
barest essentials, stripped down and purer than any other type.
It's an edifying intimacy, one that teaches you how to deconstruct
yourself gracefully in front of the other. This is what you can
practice and work on when paying someone for sex or being paid
to have sex. In the process of humbling yourselves as equals, of
giving up a little of the natural shame shoring up your sense of
self and sharing it in mutual humility, you form a bond.

Why are sex workers so despised by the public and elicit so
much contempt? It surely can't be because they earn money, like
the rest of us. It can't be because they have sex. And it can't be
because they happen to combine these two activities in the most
logical way, which many of us already do in more subtle or indi-
rect ways ("payback" for a man's dating expenses; the wealthy
man who effectively buys his wife of choice). It has something to
do with the violation of intimacy, but it's more basic still than
intimacy. What I suggest really underlies social contempt for the
prostitute is her flagrant violation of privacy: not so much her
ability to relinquish her personal privacy at a moment's notice as

the rejection of the very idea of privacy, the whole tradition and ideology of privacy which has had such a grip on the bourgeoisie over the past couple of centuries. That the prostitute, and her client as well, are able to do this with ease flies in the face of virtually everything conventional society holds dear.

For a distinct minority, myself included, privacy doesn't have that aura of the sacrosanct about it. Indeed, the notion of "privacy" is itself unsettling, this at once so human and yet strange and artificial thing that is imposed on us, the violation of which, beginning with one's own privacy, becomes attractive and fascinating. What more effective way of outraging privacy, or rather liberating it, than turning it into an object of exchange?

Underpinning bourgeois sexuality and forming its fault line is the contradiction between two opposing ethical frameworks: that which regards sex, on the one hand, as a sacred commodity in short supply and that which regards it, on the other, as abundant and freely available. Conventional morality is obviously aligned with the former. People cannot handle this contradiction between everything they were brought up to believe and the contrary that keeps getting flung in their face. How can sex be so scarce and unattainable for some while so readily accessible for others? The tension between these two incommensurables creates a psychosocial schizophrenic split, an intolerable ambivalence. Hence the universal urge to resolve the split, to equalize and level the playing field, namely by eradicating not only prostitution but free sexual expression altogether, which of course never has and never will be achieved, unless through extreme draconian measures reminiscent of seventeenth-century Salem or the anti-prostitution campaigns in China in the 1950-70s. Such campaigns can be effective, but the price to be paid for total sexual repression is an intimidated and cowed population in whom fear of sex is so deeply automated that they lose the ability to engage in even conjugal lovemaking without shame.

Short of this goal, anti-prostitution feminists resort to casting aspersion on the entire sex industry, reducing it by association to the worst manifestations of sex work—the exploitation and violence of pimps, or the appalling practice, evidently common in some countries with extreme poverty (India, Bangladesh), of enslaving women in the sex trade from childhood—and lumping together in an implicational chain all those who aid the industry in any capacity, from child sex traffickers and pedophile tourists to the lonely guy who consumes porn or goes for a handjob, as fellow conspirators and "traffickers."

I categorically condemn the enslavement or coercion of sex workers whether by threats, violence or any other means. I also condemn the yoking together of incompatible phenomena that this fallacious argument is based on. The horror stories are a separate issue and should not be identified with sex work in general. Anti-prostitution activists refuse to acknowledge or understand that the vast majority of prostitutes are content in the sex trade, and if they don't exactly love their work (how many among the rest of us are lucky enough to?), they like the money.

This is apparent if you talk to the average prostitute, or to the men who sleep with them. If anything, their customers are a richer source of information about prostitutes than prostitutes themselves, since their variety of encounters gives them a wider-ranging perspective than any individual sex worker can provide (for the same reason, prostitutes are a better source of information about clients than the clients themselves).

Those who espouse an intolerant position on sex work predictably scorn to talk to either group—and betray thereby their general apathy toward the very issue they claim to be concerned about. They are suspicious of the men involved since as self-interested actors, men supposedly cannot be trusted to provide objective accounts or are pegged as perpetrators of violence by their very patronizing of prostitutes. They are suspicious of sex workers as well, assuming them to be victims of deluded thinking and false consciousness, even as they sympathize patronizingly with the worst-off victims.

Sex workers for their part are little inclined to open up to activists or researchers who appear to be hostile towards them. Nor will it do to approach them with a microphone, pay for their time and interview them disinterestedly in the manner of sociologists or ethnographers, with their sanctimoniously clear conscience. The only real way to get into the lives of sex workers, obviously, is to try it out and become one. But with all the legal and ethical barriers in place, female academics and journalists are locked out of this option too. Thus, a veritable wall exists between the world of sex work and the rest of society, with the patrons being the only mediators.

Men who write about their experiences with sex workers are invariably treated with derision. A recent example involving Chinese prostitutes is the critical hysteria that greeted Tom Carter's account of a brothel visit in his *Unsavory Elements: Stories of Foreigners on the Loose in China*. The author and some friends were driven to a so-called "teen street" in a shabby neighborhood on the outskirts of Beijing, where the taxi driver boasted there were no girls over the age of twenty. Though the women they hired seemed adult-enough from the account, the ambiguity about their age invited accusations of sex with underage girls, who moreover, it was assumed, were likely employed against their will—given the tenacious misconception in the West that all Asian prostitutes are enslaved. It didn't help that the author adopted a slapstick style of narration that worked quite well on its own but only seemed to trivialize what some readers took to be a serious offense.

When Carter's taxi driver boasted of teenage girls, he was probably exaggerating. In the usual career trajectory, rural girls leave home after graduating from junior or senior middle school to find work in factories, restaurants or shops in the cities. Some subsequently get interested in sex work through the persuasion of friends or peers and all the gossip about the money that can be made. If many are still virgins by the time they enter the business, it's not so much a result of the high value placed on virginity as the constraints of living in sex-segregated work dormitories (and high-school dorms before that) and the lack of leisure even for dating, due to the grinding schedules of factory and service jobs—typically twelve-hour workdays with one or two days off a month. When these girls finally do start their sex lives, as prostitutes or otherwise, they are already well into their twenties. In my own acquaintance with hundreds of Chinese sex workers, I recall only a single teenager among them, an enterprising girl from Anhui Province who had started up her own massage business at the age of eighteen when I met her.

China is not immune to human trafficking and its own varieties of slavery, though these primarily involve the underground "wife" trade (adult women kidnapped and married off to single rural males), the theft and sale of babies to childless couples, and the confinement of the mentally retarded in brick-kiln factories. These are horrendous problems, but they are distinct from the sex business. While inevitably there are pockets of degradation and abuse in the world of Chinese prostitution, the norm is a fluid migration to and from sex work by free agents acting of their own accord, moving from one job to another, returning to the factory when they're tired of the work and back into it when exhausted again on the assembly line. They move in and out of a thriving industry of spas, bathhouses, KTV salons, massage parlors, nightclubs, and hotels in every neighborhood of every city on a scale that few Westerners can comprehend.[19] The misplaced insistence among certain Western feminists that the millions of Chinese women who seek to better their material conditions through sex work should give it all up and go back to their lowly jobs or the farm, all for the sake of ethical considerations, smacks of the snidest variety of cross-cultural contempt, an insidious brand of "We know you better than you know yourselves" racism.

---

[19] E.g., the February 2014 clampdown on the sex industry in Dongguan in Guangdong Province cost the city estimated losses of US $8 billion (more than half the sex trade revenue for the entire USA) and up to one million sex workers temporarily out of work. Curiously, only 300 establishments were closed and a mere 67 arrested.

Many Chinese prostitutes I have met not only enjoy the work, they seem quite happy and at peace with themselves, and this shows in their typically cheerful manner. They may even be more psychologically sound than "normal" women. Not one has ever caused me any trouble. Some have gotten annoyed or angry due to a misunderstanding, but it was always a momentary issue we then resolved. They don't carry grudges. None has ever called me out of the blue to complain about something or harassed or stalked me. They show interest in me to the same extent I show interest in them. On the other hand, I have had more than my share of depressing, drawn-out, and frightening involvements with so-called normal women.

The pressure to be "normal" imposes enormous unconscious stress on a woman. The "normal" or "good" woman is above all she who is sexually irreproachable. Those who succeed in living up to this onerous standard and internalizing its strictures— monogamy, sexual fidelity, the sacrificing of self for family—are easily thrown into shock when things don't go their way. Males, for whom normality is defined in financial rather than sexual terms, tend to act out psychological stress (e.g., over career frustration or failure) with destructive aggression, domestic violence, or criminal activity, whereas females tend to blame themselves and self-destruct. The contradiction, the almost psychotic tension, between naive expectations and the crushing reality that follows when such expectations don't accord with reality makes many women desperately confused or frantic and pushes some over the edge.

Sex workers free themselves from this bind in one fell swoop. What is the most unforgivable thing a woman can do? What single act thrusts her more decisively into the worst of all categories, worse even than adultery? Engaging in prostitution. Becoming a whore. Yet this simple act of crossing over the red line into whoredom, or rather freedom, of receiving one's first payment for sex, has the power to effect something amazing on her psyche, puncturing and exploding the big bloated burden of guilt: guilt over letting society down morally, guilt over letting herself down sexually. It all washes away like so much placenta and a new self is born. Her new status won't absolve her in other people's eyes, but it re-rights her own internal balance. The rest of society can take it or leave it: she has emancipated herself. Freed of the burden of being "normal" and "proper," she can now relax into psychological health as if for the first time.

Invariably some prostitutes are influenced by all the relentless negativity, meanness, and humiliation (not to mention what jail time does to you) and reflect these attitudes back in mocking form or take a perverse satisfaction in their male conquests. We all too easily adopt the same cynical attitude, myself included, as when I earlier described sex with prostitutes as "boring and a waste of time and money" due to "the lack of any genuine friendliness in the transaction."

A more philosophical consideration of these issues over the course of writing about it has led me to reconsider my experience with Melody more sympathetically. After all, she invited me to see her again. It would have remained wholly on her terms, but who's not to say we might have taken to each other once we agreed on the financial arrangement? And then there have been the unaccountably friendly encounters appearing out of the blue, like the prostitute I once met in Taiyuan, Shanxi Province...

When we arrive in the city, we have no idea where to go, so the taxi driver takes us to a brothel street in the outskirts. On the way, he recommends stopping off at a pharmacy for some "sex medicine." My friend Jianwei goes in with him and returns with a box of erythromycin, a generic and largely useless antibiotic cheaply available over the counter. Jesus. Their medical naivete.

The strip was hastily erected on what had been recent farmland. The candy-colored prefab structures seem so flimsy that leaning against one of them, I fear, might send the entire street collapsing like Queen Carlotta's pasteboard castle in John Waters' movie *Desperate Living*. We check out the brothels one by one. It is still too early in the day, the madams outnumber the girls, and those who do appear aren't very attractive. One of the larger venues has a second floor, and drawn into its open mouth we go up inside, emerging into a dark karaoke room lined with black vinyl sofas. The house pimp apologizes that only one room for services is available at the moment but another will be free shortly. I tell him I want a voluptuous woman. He brings in a slim one for Jianwei, always readily available, as lower-echelon sex workers tend to be short and skinny. She leads him through a trapdoor in the wall into a crawl space large enough for an army cot—the hideaway designed with the hopeful intention of being overlooked during a police bust.

The pimp manages to produce a woman to my liking, surnamed Wang. While we sit on the sofa waiting for a free room, she unbuttons her shirt for me and massive breasts spill out.

Our room is scarcely larger than the trapdoor hideaway. Where a bed should be there is a dresser with toiletries on top and a wooden table, half the length of a bed, draped with a blanket. Wang doesn't want to strip but to just drop our pants without taking them off in case we need to pull them back on in the event of a bust. I lay down with my lower legs dangling off the table while she squats over me. Her nervousness is contagious and we fumble about for a few moments before I lose my erection. For the fiasco, she refuses to accept the fifty yuan she originally asked for. The price is so low I make her take 100 yuan anyway.

Back in the karaoke room, the sneaky pimp has doubled our house fee to 200, claiming we overstayed our session when in fact he purposely held up our room.

"Get out now, quickly," Wang says, shoving us down the stairs as she argues with the pimp and follows us out onto the street to hail a taxi. The pimp runs after us shouting. Wang jumps in the taxi with us.

"So you don't work there?" we ask her.

"No. I freelance. And it doesn't look like I'll be going back."

We treat her to dinner. She got into prostitution to pay back debts incurred by her family's failed nightclub, she says. I like her and we hold hands under the table and exchange addresses. I invite her to spend the night at our hotel but she has previous plans and leaves after the meal.

Months later, a letter from Wang arrives. I suspected she was illiterate when she got the waitress to write down her address for me at the restaurant. The generic style of the letter confirms this, a form love letter she must have paid someone to write with a few requisite personal details:

> Respected Mr. Isham:
> How are you? I'm writing to wish you good health and 10,000 other lucky things.
> I don't have a high education, let alone any knowledge of a foreign language like English. I have to express my feelings in my limited and simple Chinese.
> When everyone is celebrating the new millennium during this Spring season with the blooming flowers, it was such a pleasure to meet you in Taiyuan. This was the greatest joy of my life. Because China is now under reform and opening, the word *xiaojie* always brings dirty looks.[20] Out of so many *xiaojie's*, you chose me. Maybe this is what in Chi-

---

[20] If Wang did indeed have someone write the letter for her, she didn't seem to have any qualms about admitting her occupation as a *xiaojie*; her embarrassment was thus for my sake. Literally "young lady" or "miss," *xiaojie* is a euphemism for prostitute, and in the 1990s the term of address for female restaurant servers as well. As the association became politically incorrect in restaurants, *xiaojie* was replaced by the neutral *fuwuyuan* (server). Yet it's still not uncommon for females to address waitresses and young women in public as *xiaojie*, on the assumption it's only inappropriate for men to use the term, while males tend to address young women as *guniang* ("young lady"). Ironically, another popular term of address for young women, *meinu* ("beauty"), is also falling into disfavor for its implicit sexism, and *xiaojie* may sound like a more neutral alternative to some ears. Due to this confusion, address terms are increasingly avoided in favor of a simple *nihao* ("Hello"). This return to a gender-neutral term of address brings us back full circle to the old term of *tongzhi* ("comrade"), used for both sexes in the 1950s-70s.

nese we call "fate."

The minute we separated, I had a strange and inexpressible feeling in my heart. Perhaps through my job as a *xiaojie*, it was the first time I had contact with a foreign friend, that is you, Mr. Isham. These days when it's very quiet at midnight, why do I toss and turn in bed? It is because I hold your small name card in my hand and can't stop reading it, remembering our beautiful time together, "Like fish in water."

I have so much to say but let's keep it short. I will come to Beijing to see you if I have time, and I hope you write back.

Yours sincerely,

Wang

This touching letter from a sex worker, full of simple friendliness, sparks in me a wild chain of thoughts and a modest proposal: to radically level the playing field by making all sex remunerative. That's right, every act of sexual intercourse should be paid for. The price would be determined strictly by the market, by supply and demand, or by whatever price one person is willing to pay and the other accept. Since males tend to have a greater need for spontaneous sex with a variety of bodies, they would continue to serve the main role of customers, while attractive men could sell their services to gay men and older women, and why not younger women as well? As expected, some females could command a higher price than others based on their youth, appearance or other assets (education, fame), though sexual value would stabilize according to these market forces, and everyone would know what to expect over a general price range. A woman's price would nonetheless be elastic and negotiable; she could raise it and lower it at will, rising with wealthier or unattractive men and falling with men she found more to her liking. Once a new generation grew up and adjusted to this new arrangement, upon reaching legal age girls would proudly announce their price in their online profiles and whenever meeting new friends—and potential customers (teenagers of age could operate in their own closed sexual economy).

Married men would not be exempt. Wives could command a price in line with their sexual worth, namely what any man would be willing to pay, and a husband would have to shell out for each session in bed. This would make clear economic sense for housewives, who deserve to receive a stipulated wage for their work, which they are routinely denied even in developed countries. For married women who work full-time outside the home, their sexual fees would be welcome compensation for the extra housework they almost invariably perform on top of their day job. In the event the husband loses his job or both come under financial hardship, their marital economics would adjust to make her price more affordable.

In general, though, there would be no sex on the house. All women would benefit from their increased revenue from domestic sex, rectifying the gender income imbalance across the board. It would also, paradoxically, improve the quality of sex among couples who have wearied of each other. Each payment would inject the woman with a rush of joy, and her excitement would be contagious for the man. He would put out more as well, to make sure he got his money's worth.

In this new sexual ethic, with a quantitative value put on the sex act, the concept of sex for free would invert to something undesirable, even unthinkable. An exception would be volunteers devoted to providing gratis services to people unable to provide for themselves—the indigent, the disabled—just as some people currently take on volunteer jobs to help the disadvantaged or the poor. Outside this sphere, unpaid-for sex would be treated as an eccentric form of altruism.

The comprehensive monetizing of all sexual relations would have a number of salutary results. Putting a price tag on sex would restore value to it, not just in the abstract but more importantly in each particular instance. You'd feel you were getting what you paid for. You could still be ripped off, as we are in any case with cheap or shoddy goods, but this would be the exception among wiser shoppers. With all sexually active adult women participating, the economics of scarcity that enables sex work and its exploitation would disappear. With sex fully sanctioned and brought out into the open, the culture of shame would likewise vanish, sexual education in the schools would flourish, and STDs and unwanted pregnancy would plummet. Prostitution as we know it would cease to exist or to be more precise, there would be no more need for pejorative terms to describe the selling of sex. Sexual negotiation and exchange would lighten up and become a friendly affair, given the greater degree of transparency now involved and the ease with which everyone could shop around with their dignity and morals intact.

10

TRANSGRESSIONS:
FROM PORN TO POLYAMORY

There is not a single individual who does not bear the elements
of fascist feeling and thinking in his structure.
Wilhelm Reich, *The Mass Psychology of Fascism*

The fascism in us all, in our heads and in our everyday behavior,
the fascism that causes us to love power, to desire the very thing
that dominates and exploits us.
Michel Foucault, *Madness and Civilization*

We are using the policeman's eye when we can't see a sex worker
as anything but his or her work, as an object to control.
Melissa Gira Grant, *Playing the Whore*

PORNOGRAPHY

IF YOUR SUPEREGO is repressing the import of *Giving Godhead*,
the title of a poetry collection by Dylan Krieger, it is indeed a pun.

Puns spill out of her book like a punctured bladder, afterbirth from a womb, or whatever metaphors splatter out of her writhing word swamps where religious and sexual symbols freely copulate, as in these opening lines from her poem "swaddling plot":

> every sabbath eve in my rape dreams I swaddle christ's body in spray-on glitter & kitty litter as in, literal pedigree: we bred a savior from king David and a rainstorm spitting brain matter simultaneously baby, rave zombie, and crane-lifted detonator, watch how he weeps for the seepage to fall down—after all, that was what the forty days were all about: god's very first constipation blackout, when fountains of garden/flood penance blood stopped him up, and all he could muster was bad manna & flames the size of a mustard seed.

The surrealist poets also worked with primeval material, often to witty effect, but their singsong word collages seem contrived by comparison, as if the point is to throw words and phrases together in clever combinations from cut-ups: "...clean out your cockpit of intoxicated spiders / Tear the sexual leaves of grief from your heart / Pluck the feathers of nostalgia from your nipples / Push the slow-moving masochistic mudslide / of contralto voices / from your afternoon skull of anxiety" (Jayne Cortez, in *Arsenal*). Too often the surrealists seem interchangeable, a pranksters' poetry drawing its inspiration from the same set of clown suits in the costume shop. At first glance, Krieger might appear to be engaging in similar antics, but there's more going on in the collective unconscious she taps into, something deeper and scarier than anything Carl Jung cooked up. Hers is also a poet's voice conscious of itself as a musical vehicle, an oral art meant to be read aloud. But even Sylvia Plath's incantations of violence, unmoored in her madness from the strictures of suburban America though she was, seem tame next to Krieger's serpentine cadences (from the remainder of "swaddling plot"):

but don't nitpick this ardently faulty arithmetic for the Old
Testicles always give rise to the New—the gospel of *it's-all-*
true, so are you saved or screwed? bathed or bruised? he became just like a regular jew, except w/ more pinpoints to
prove, like perfection according to whom? the narrative arc
of this covenant is askew so no more dumping the bodies of
godheads I once blew: I'll wrap them up in exfoliant seaweed
and roll them like snow into forts. I can never remember the
ending right through—something about cyborg nuns running a whorehouse and a sex act in which I am swallowed
whole and then vomited off into satellite orbit

The other 43 poems in the volume are equally unrelenting, outrageous, and if you are religious, blasphemous. They are indeed
abstruse, but there's an advantage to that: they read afresh each
time, and their music is richly dissonant. For the benefit of the
perplexed, the volume concludes on a more conventional note
with a "Sacreligion Manifesto" (all caps are Krieger's):

TODAY SOMEBODY ASKED ME IF I HAD ANY 'INTER-
EST' IN WRITING ABOUT THINGS OTHER THAN GOD-
DAMN! AND SEXUALITY....PLEASE. SO MAYBE THIS IS
ME: THREE PARTS PUNISHMENT JUNKIE AND SEVEN
TENTACLES SAD MONSTER-BAITING JUST TO MAKE
YOU STARE AWHILE. BUT SERIOUSLY: LANGUAGE IS
MY FUCKTOY.

An effusive *New York Times* review called *Giving Godhead*
"easily among the most inventive and successfully performative
works to appear in living memory" and "the best collection of poetry to appear in English in 2017" (Simmons). I ordered the book
and wasn't disappointed, but the poems were a bit much for me
to get through all at once. I savored a few at a time, grew dis-
turbed, and set the book aside—not to discard but to mull over
it—and finished it a year later. The photogenic headshot of

Krieger on the back page got me curious, and I looked her up. Besides promoting her books and poetry readings (recorded on vinyl) on her Facebook and Twitter feeds, she poses provocatively and has an OnlyFans page (onlyfans.com/fullserpent), where she performs a live striptease. Dubbing herself a "Poet. Sex Worker. Hedonism Guru," as well as a "left-wing anarchist," Krieger, who was brought up and homeschooled in a Christian fundamentalist family in Indiana before earning degrees at Notre Dame and Louisiana State University, is up-front and articulate about her sex work. Whenever people who know her as a poet express shock or dismay upon discovering her pornography credentials, her response is laconic: "I am equally shocked that they're shocked! This has always been a part of my personality and my literary identity." And while she herself avows being immune to shame, "I feel sympathy for other people's shame. I think that's a huge part of sex work: Helping people work through shame":

> I've always put my sexuality front and center in my work, not just because sex sells, but because I am just as fascinated by it as my audience....I see both poetry and sex work as maximizing the pleasure of their audience while also urging them to face tough truths. Just like everyone else, people who hire sex workers often have sexual hang-ups and insecurities; and facing those things can be difficult. It is the poet's job, as well as the sex worker's job, to make that confrontation as memorably pleasurable and insightful as possible. (Interview with Jason Arment)

Dylan Krieger epitomizes the fusion of art and the erotic in several aspects. On its own terms, her poetry is unabashedly sexually explicit, without this in the least diminishing its interest. This is not to confuse it with "erotic poetry," that banal genre that purports and often fails to arouse. Lewdness is in the eye of the beholder, and the problem is not its pornographic content but our pejorative definitions of pornography. It's poetry, rather, that affirms the intellectual kinship of radical art and porn. The graphic arts have long aspired to and converged on sexuality; a trip through the Vatican Museum reveals this in all its schizo-phrenic splendor. Krieger lives this fusion in her work and career. She's not just creating poetry of disarming sexual frankness as a radical act; she's expanding and recasting her audience through her sex work. It is neither therefore a question of whether por-nography is good enough to qualify as "erotic," nor of artists stooping to the pornographic; it's not a question of whether sexu-al explicitness dignifies or diminishes art as if it were merely a matter of style and taste. I would like to flip the terms here to consider the possibility that *any* form of sexual representation is, by its very nature, artistic. There is no contradiction, no valid distinction between the erotic and the pornographic, no line of demarcation separating them except arbitrarily drawn. If not all porn qualifies as art, it is perhaps because it is not pornographic enough.

A notorious case of pornographic art—and art of the highest caliber—is famed Swiss artist H. R. Giger's gorgeous painting *Work 219: Landscape XX* (aka. *Penis Landscape*), which shows an interlocking series of erect penises penetrating finely ren-dered splayed vaginas. When the punk rock band Dead Kennedys included the painting as poster inserts in their 1985 *Franken-christ* album, they were charged under the California penal code with distributing harmful material to minors, and the album was removed from record stores across the U.S. As with the Robert Mapplethorpe and Andres Serrano (of "Piss Christ" fame) contro-versies of the same decade, it's telling that pornography was still politically relevant, and its more accomplished specimens able to elicit the kind of inflammatory public reactions that the fine arts are no longer capable of since Modernism's heyday a century ago. But now three decades on, amidst the deluge of commercial porn on the internet, pornography's shock value is no longer a matter of aesthetics. As the state reasserts its power to legislate sexuali-ty, the terms of the debate have shifted exclusively and ominously to matters of criminality, trafficking, and corruption of minors.

Nothing pleases the state more than to strip porn of any legitimacy. The state aligns public opinion on its side by defining porn as the public tends to define it, in lowbrow, lowest-common-denominator terms. How could cheap X-rated material presume to have the slightest aesthetic value, when the creators of porn themselves would probably dismiss the notion their business had anything to do with art? Regarding the most casual forms of lewd reproduction, people sexting their body parts to each other with their cellphones for instance, it's true that not much effort, much less artistic sensibility, goes into this. Then again, we don't really call that porn. To qualify as "porn," a certain level of professionalism is assumed and required. Even the internet category of "amateur porn" is curated for its quality and survives on the basis of merit born out through audience ratings. Some porn is better than other porn and some is actually very good. The best commercial porn has high production values. It may not be to everyone's taste, obviously. Though good porn can be exquisite, I myself admittedly find most porn lacking in interest. But even the bad acting, silicone breasts, and repetitive choreography of run-of-the-mill porn works for many people and is not an argument against the aesthetic value of porn. I suppose many porn producers do consider themselves artists. They could be said to stand in the same relationship to "art," conventionally understood, as graphic designers do; the best among them are highly sought after and paid.

What all porn has in common is a fascination with the naked body in its primal state of desire. Porn captures the beauty of the body in its entirety, crevices included, and the beauty of its coupling with other bodies. There is an intensity to the sexual moment, and representing this is to enhance and enshrine it. Sexual activity is replicable enough, yet there can never be enough. That's why there is so much porn, always has been, going back thousands of years in sexually explicit artifacts discovered all over the world, and always will be.

People are sexually pulled in different directions. What is it that's singular about porn? What draws performers to it, rather than to other transgressive sexualities like prostitution or bondage? Before tackling this question, I return to a point repeated throughout this book. We must divest ourselves of the lie, fashionable of late, that sex work is inherently degrading, and all people who engage in it are victims of "trafficking." Antipornography and anti-prostitution activists alike are notoriously, comically indifferent toward, and ignorant of, the very people they describe as "victims." The more strident among them are sexual fascists, and like all fascists seek out contentious, hot-button causes to raise their profile with the goal of obtaining political power for draconian ends. If my way of characterizing these activists seems extreme, it's because *they* are extreme. It's one thing to be outraged by genuine trafficking, namely the moving of people across borders to render them more exploitable, sometimes to the point of outright slavery—Bangladeshi men, for instance, locked in foreign construction sites under harsh conditions, or Philippine maids confined to the homes of wealthy Middle-Eastern families for round-the-clock work, no pay, and sexual abuse. It's quite another to equate every instance of sex for money, whether it involves downloading porn, visiting a strip club or being erotically massaged, as "trafficking," the person providing the sexual content or service as a "victim," and all other parties in the transaction including the customer or consumer as "traffickers." The lonely nerd with his digital collection of AV idols is thus equated with major operatives in the human slave trade. This absurd, mendacious rhetoric and willful distortion of language bears little relation to reality and is insulting to those who proudly choose sexual employment as well as those who would engage them as customers. The disturbing reality lies rather with these activists, who have gained inordinate power and constitute a serious legal threat and danger.

Urges are manifold and mysterious. We are almost powerless to alter the path our sexuality thrusts us upon. I will be returning to this point below in discussing prostitution and polyamory. But to give one example of the epic force of sexual compulsion, I became involved with a Chinese female graduate student years ago in Beijing who simply could not get aroused unless spanked, and spanked long and hard, sustained spanking to the point of bruising. This created problems as I not only had little inclination to satisfy her in this way, but I lacked the strength and technique to carry it out. I tried to more than once, but spanking, whipping, and other S/M activities require a surprising amount of skill. In the meantime, she was applying to Ph.D. programs in music history in the UK and accepted an offer at one school. I pointed her to the alt.com website, and she was able to hook up with a man of a similar bent who invited her to live with him for free in exchange for housework and serving as his slave. She was quite happy with the arrangement after getting settled in England, she later told me, and I was happy for her. When people fail to actualize their sexuality, they turn into a shell of themselves in their sexual depression. When, on the other hand, urges find their outlet, it is striking how they enliven and animate people; they become one's raison d'être. That is why sexual proclivities are so intractable and irrepressible.

The predominant urge driving people into commercial porn, according to its many practitioners, is exhibitionism. Author and porn activist Jiz Lee invited 55 fellow performers, some quite famous in the porn world, to submit their accounts of "coming out" to their families and communities and compiled them into an edifying volume, *Coming Out Like a Porn Star*. Sheer sexual freedom and publicly sharing and celebrating this freedom—the ultimate expression of exhibitionism—is a common theme. As one contributor, Phoenix Askani, remarks,

> It was so incredibly freeing to be naked in front of a crew and do something that felt so exhilarating and natural to me while knowing it would later be distributed and on the Internet, available to even more eyeballs....My friends were

mostly supportive and knew how in-tune with my sexuality I was and had heard me speak of my desire to express it on a grander scale.

Likewise, contributor Verta:

> What I loved so much about the idea of doing porn is there is no typical porn star. They're all humans, from different backgrounds, whose common denominator is exhibitionism. To me, having sex for money was not at the top of my list of reasons for going into this industry. All I wanted was to enter a community of people who Get It.

One point of contention among pro-porn activists is the sameness and crassness of so much commercial porn in a male-dominated industry. As entrepreneur Cindy Gallop (cited in Lee) describes it, "when total freedom of access to hardcore porn online meets our society's equally total reluctance to talk openly and honestly about sex," porn becomes "by default, the sex education of today. In not a good way." To counter the lowbrow norm with something more authentic and creative, to capture "what goes on in the real world, in all its funny, messy, wonderful, ridiculous, beautiful humanness," Gallop launched her own forum for viewers to upload their homemade porn (makelovenotporn.tv), only requiring the contributors to adhere to the curators' criteria of "the sex you have in your everyday life naturally and spontaneously, without performing for the camera."

Porn is inescapably a fraught subject in the internet age. Enthusiasts along with free-speech advocates contend that no matter how outrageous or extreme, porn is safely contained behind the veil of representation. Others claim that porn is anything but harmless; they refer to the assault of porn's intense, visceral imagery on young people, allegedly shaping, constricting, and distorting their sexuality. Anecdotal evidence suggests that many, if not most men do seem to prefer women with the bodies and looks of porn stars, and expect their sex partners to match their facility in bed. But the causal relationship between porn and imitative behavior is nonetheless tentative and dubious. In my mid-teens, I once lined my bedroom walls with *Playboy* and *Penthouse* center-folds, but the cheesy, air-brushed models soon palled and I out-grew this phase after a year or two. I knew that they were only that, models, while real women's bodies were infinitely varied. I preferred older, experienced women in my youth, and always women with natural bodies in all their glorious permutations, ever enjoying the prospect of a unique and different woman, in both mind and body, from what I'd experienced before. I have my physical tastes, but there is no ideal body type. Ultimately what matters most is the erotic personality, which can make the most physically unappealing person deliriously seductive.

I cannot speak for others, and the mass media are admittedly potent in their effects. But instead of condemning the deleterious impact of porn on impressionable youth, we ought to get our pri-orities straight and confront the more insidious impact of brute violence in the media, and ask why a constant stream of ma-chinegun fire and explosions must serve as the predominant at-tention-grabbing visual motifs in American TV, film, and video games. Most people, I believe, are bound by the reality principle, and a steady diet of porn or Hollywood violence doesn't cause them to act out in their life what they see on film. Or if it in fact does, then let's start with rolling back media violence as by far the greater of the two evils.

The issue of porn and free speech, and that of sexual expres-sion and rights more generally, leads us to another area of con-tention. That is the question of limits and extreme taboos. There is a nether region of sexuality that civil society understandably condemns and criminalizes: sexual harassment and violence, adult seduction and abuse of minors, and other perversions such as bestiality, necrophilia, and incest (though incest among con-senting adult siblings is arguably benign). Outlier individuals whose urges drive them down these alleys there are indeed, and

all that can be said for them is tough luck. Obviously, not all urges are defensible. Advocates of sexual liberation must draw the
line and pull back from the abyss. One abyss causing intensive
concern in the porn world today is the Dark Web, with its obscure lairs where pedophiles and child-porn collectors congregate.
Media reports from law enforcement suggest that the Dark Web
is churning, exploding with child porn. I am ignorant of the true
extent of this problem and cannot comment about it, as I have
never visited the Dark Web nor am I acquainted with anyone
who has, at least for this nefarious purpose.

At the same time, we must bear in mind that in the name of
fighting crime, the government is fond of hyping dangers to extend its disciplinary hold over the population. It also has a penchant for stretching the definition of pornography well beyond
any dictionary sense. For instance, Texas Governor Gregg Abbott
threatened to prosecute "to the fullest extent of the law" those
responsible for distributing to minors the allegedly pornographic
memoirs *Genderqueer* by Maia Kobabe and *In the Dream House*
by Carmen Maria Machado, both freely available on Amazon (the
former a bestseller and the latter an "Editors' pick"), merely because they involve gay and lesbian relationships (B. Brooks,
"Texas"). And of course child sex scares, particularly in the U.S.,
have a way of blowing up into gigantic proportions which are
then politicized by groups such as QAnon, an atavistic fascist
cult whose adherents believe the Democratic Party annually ab-
ducts hundreds of thousands of children for ritual sexual abuse
and blood sacrifice, which calls to mind the persecutions of alleged baby-eating witches in Renaissance Europe (Lavin). I am
thus suspicious of law enforcement's penchant for exaggerating
the child porn threat as an excuse to justify cracking down on the
entire porn business, exactly as it exaggerates the "trafficking"
threat in order to crack down on prostitution.

PROSTITUTION

Early on in George Eliot's novel *Middlemarch*, Will Ladislaw's German companion Adolf Naumann runs up to him in a corridor of the Vatican Museum to announce the entrancing object he has just espied, not a masterpiece of painting or sculpture but of nature itself. Gesturing from the Sleeping Ariadne sculpture, a famous copy of a Roman original, to his newly discovered object of desire, Naumann exclaims: "'There lies antique beauty, not corpse-like even in death, but arrested in the complete contentment of its sensuous perfection: and here stands beauty in its breathing life,'" that is to say, as the narrator elaborates,

> a breathing blooming girl, whose form, not shamed by the Ariadne, was clad in Quakerish gray drapery; her long cloak, fastened at the neck, was thrown backward from her arms, and one beautiful ungloved hand pillowed her cheek, pushing somewhat backward the white beaver bonnet which made a sort of halo to her face around the simply braided dark-brown hair. She was not looking at the sculpture, probably not thinking of it: her large eyes were fixed dreamily on a streak of sunlight which fell across the floor.

Thus did Eliot cleverly introduce the novel's heroine, Dorothea Brooke, as strangers might see her. But I have elsewhere dubbed this the "museum paradox," which holds that the most renowned masterpieces in the greatest museums pale next to the intrusion of an attractive fellow visitor.[21] Caress it for all it's worth, the lushness of that painted or sculpted flesh is forever trapped beneath the skin of representation (the same wall of torment separating the viewer of porn from the performer). In their shared contemplation, however, our two viewers are brought into intimate proximity. When the intruder happens to

---

[21] Isham Cook, *Lust & Philosophy*, a novel (Magic Theater Books, 2012).

be hot, the sheen, the fragrance of this new creature standing by your side overwhelms and obscures the dead object in front of you. No matter how ideally rendered, the image of beauty simply can't compete with reality.

Aggressive males of a more cultured stamp haunt the palaces of the unacquainted to take advantage of these fleeting moments of spontaneous intimacy and work their charm upon the solitary museumgoer. But unless you act fast and have a way with words, and the attraction is mutual and the scene propitious, that lovely presence standing next to you is also out of reach. In fact, just about every attractive person you see around you as you go about your day is out of reach. There are too many obstacles standing in the way. You have to contend with ingrained habits of social propriety and etiquette and people's natural shyness and fear of public interaction, not to mention blind devotion to their significant other and corresponding indifference to strangers. In the rare instance when feelings are reciprocated, you then have to contend with the convoluted and usually hopeless procedure of wooing the already attached, the success of which stands in inverse proportion to their attractiveness.

Prostitution cuts through all of this like a knife. It delivers the living, breathing object to you instantly. This is at once its purpose and its fascination. The fascination is mutual, and this explains the peculiar allure of this form of sex work for its practitioners. Prostitutes who enjoy their work find the immediacy of the sexual encounter every bit as exciting and arousing as do their customers. Bars and parties can't compete, where it turns out to be about as difficult to score a hot person as in a museum. The porn and tech worlds can't compete. There are indeed big plans for digital sex—people copulating with holographic images, body sensors allowing couples to "feel" each other at a distance, massage by mechanical hands operated remotely, and in the pipeline, affordable sexbots of astounding complexity, or the hyped-up "metaverse," which can be expected to offer all manner of virtual orgies. I'm sure all these toys will be fun, but no, they will never, ever replace having a real person in your arms.

On the subject of technology, another paradox might be called the "Bill Gates paradox," not to single out this particular icon but to make a general observation about really smart people, the entrepreneurs and the gurus of the tech world, so idolized and lionized in our time to the exclusion of almost everyone else, so that we all feel like second-class citizens and rather stupid next to them. And yet, when it comes to their sex lives, they are often the most ordinary, bumbling oafs, bound to the most blinkered notions, conservative without knowing why, at the utter mercy of their impotent fantasies and possibly emotionally retarded as well, with all their intelligence concentrated in one half of their brain while they crawl uncomprehendingly through their relationships with their reptilian other half.

A word on terminology. Many prostitutes now eschew the term in favor of "escort," "sex worker," "contact sex worker," "in-person sex worker," "full-service sex worker," even "somatic therapist." But to reject the term, I believe, only serves to reinforce its negativity—and the unfortunate, widespread assumption that prostitution is bad and wrong. I reject the negative associations of the term, not the term itself. I would like to see restored its positivity, specificity, and distinctiveness, something along the lines of the courtesan, a term also fallen out of favor. Another reason for retaining the old term is that "sex worker" is too broad; it includes people in the porn, striptease, bondage, and massage businesses, as well as prostitutes. To avoid ambiguity, I employ a perfectly adequate and recognized word of historical coinage, the prostitute, whose literal meaning from the Latin original—"to place in front" (as in goods for sale)—contains nothing pejorative.

When people comment on the profession, they tend to decry it in such emotional language as "pathetic," "demeaning," "degrading," and so forth. I suspect they don't really know why they object to it, other than to parrot what everyone else says. Yet however much I rack my brain, I cannot find any rationale, ethically or otherwise, as to why people should not be able to exchange sex

for money and to do so freely and legally. Fear, I suggest, underlies much of the hostility toward prostitution. For if the profession were decriminalized, normalized, valued, and celebrated, I'd
guess that a lot of women, a frightening number of women, wom-
en you know and could never imagine would take it up (and men
as well; I'm sticking to females here since that's where the fear
lies). And they would have good reason to, given their lousy
treatment under patriarchy from time immemorial right up
through the present, with their thousands of hours of unpaid labor at home and the gender pay gap in the workplace, not to
mention the myriad forms of sexual discrimination they face on a
daily basis. Nothing restores power and autonomy to women
more than the full control over their bodies that sex work affords,
provided of course they are free agents. But we must not forget
that the bourgeois family is already a form of prostitution, and
that of the worst kind, where the husband in his dual role as customer and pimp has a lifelong claim over his prostitute and de-
clines to remunerate her financially for her sexual and household
labor.

As one sex worker has noted, the profession with the most
natural affinity to the prostitute is the psychologist: "What a
good sex worker and a good therapist share is the gift of their
professional attention to something most of us do intuitively. If
they're any good at what they do, they can set themselves aside
to focus on you, the client" (Davina). I'd expand this to include
women in academia and the arts. The intellectual courtesan, the
artistic courtesan, has a storied tradition not just in Asia which
perhaps first comes to mind but in Europe as well. The European
prostitute—whether called "courtesan" or "whore" (the latter was
regarded affectionately and the terms often interchangeable)—
was highly valued for her culture and society. "The libertine
whore," as Kathryn Norberg remarks on her apex in seventeenth
and eighteenth-century France, "is well read and sophisticated....The warrior, the lawyer, the financier and especially the
philosopher share their wisdom with the whore. A student of

pleasure, the prostitute is also a student of philosophy, in particular of the Enlightenment materialism that colors so much of
this libertine literature."

This tradition of the prostitute as radical thinker and philosopher needs resurrecting, and intellectual women are best poised
to do this—and set an example for all women. Prostitution is
more than an exercise in freedom, drawing people together for
sexual and philosophical communion and enabling and easing
this through money. The discovery of it, the decision to venture
upon it, in the process peeling off layers of ideological conditioning to reveal the stultifying creed of monogamism at its core, is a
profoundly intellectual act. The intricate challenge of meshing
sex work with one's existing career, whether professor, therapist
or housewife, of coming out openly to friends and marketing oneself on social media or discreetly through word of mouth, are all
vital choices requiring a revolution of the mind.

A fuller understanding of paid sexuality cannot, of course,
ignore the question of violence, above all in the U.S. with its
stringent anti-trafficking laws, whose effect is only to reinforce
violence against sex workers. As noted above, mainstream discourse on sex work is presently dominated by the strident anti-
prostitution camp, who've drowned out more reasoned voices. As
they characterize it, wherever she exists in the world the sex
worker is inexorably enslaved and brutalized. The rhetorical tac-
tic regularly adopted, designed to elicit maximum moral outrage,
is to ignore what sex workers themselves have to say and to
cherry-pick the most abject, mute examples of female exploitation, typically in impoverished countries, holding them up as representative of all sex workers.[22] As one sex worker describes this
rhetoric:

---

[22] Catharine MacKinnon's "Trafficking, prostitution, and inequality"
exemplifies this rhetoric. She's very thorough when describing the terrible conditions of her prime exemplars, child sex slaves in India, but otherwise forecloses all debate: "Everywhere, prostituted people are over-
whelmingly poor, indeed normally destitute. There is no disagreement on

The sex work debate, no matter how sedate and sympathetic its interlocutors claim it to be, is a spectacle. It attracts an audience with the lure of a crisis—prostitution sweeping the nation!—and a promise of doing good by feeling terrible. Sad stories about sex work are offered like sequins, displayed to be admired and then swept off the stage when the number is done. As a treat, the organizers may even decide to invite a token whore to perform. (Grant)

To shore up their argument that the prostitute is a perpetual victim of violence, stereotypically at the hands of the pimp who relieves her of her daily earnings and smacks her back into obedience if she dares protest, requires the anti-sex work crowd to posit that the sex worker is by definition "trafficked," held captive, and enslaved. When the evidence shows, on the contrary, that sex workers enter into the work of their own accord it is countered that they delude themselves into believing they are free agents, whereas in fact they are compelled into the trade out of economic necessity, forced into the only job that pays enough to enable them to stay financially afloat. Yes this specious, tired

---

this fact. Urgent financial need is the most frequent reason mentioned by people in prostitution for being in the sex trade. Having gotten in because of poverty, almost no one gets out of poverty through prostituting. They are lucky to get out with their lives, given the mortality figures." Instead of engaging articulate sex workers in this controversy, she cites a predictably hostile government representative, French Social Affairs Minister Roselyne Bachelot: 'There is no such thing as prostitution which is freely chosen and consenting....The sale of sexual acts means that women's bodies are made available, for men, independently of the wishes of those women.'" On the contrary, the state itself serves as a pimp profiting off sex work when, for example, convicted prostitutes and their clients are forced to enroll in anti-trafficking rehabilitation programs at their own expense, such as the "Law Enforcement Assisted Diversion (LEAD)" in Seattle, "while sex buyers are funneled into a similar diversion program called the Men's Accountability Program through Seattle Against Slavery. To take part in this program costs anywhere from $400 to $1,200 per sex buyer" (LeMoon). For more background on the trafficking controversy, see Grant; Halperin; Lancaster.

argument begs the question of why so many people live paycheck to paycheck and are often drowning in debt yet manage to refrain from going into sex work. Women have the power to refuse to engage in anything against their will; to be truly forced into prostitution, they would have to be kidnapped and shackled. There are indeed abusive pimps in the lower echelons of the trade. But the norm is to work either as a free agent or for a boss or madam in a mutually beneficial arrangement. Many sex workers actually enjoy their work and wouldn't do anything else.

Singling out the cartoonish figure of the pimp as an explanatory bogeyman in fact serves to obscure and hence reinforce the sway of real violence over the sex worker. If it were *merely* the violence of the pimp, of certain pimps, the pitfalls of prostitution might be ameliorated; the prostitute would only have to step out of her harmful relationship. The larger problem, however, is that those who should be protecting them, the police, and those who should be enjoying them, their customers, are quite as capable of violence as the pimp, and their violence, particularly that of customers, is more pervasive and unpredictable. With her decades of experience as a sex worker in the U.S., Lola Davina spends the first chapter of *Thriving in Sex Work*, her popular manual on the profession, giving the rundown on minimizing violence at the hands of both "clients" (a term favored by escorts over "customers") and the police, though "most cops," she notes, "don't want to arrest sex workers," having more important things to do; many cops *are* their clients.

Law enforcement has long had an ambivalent relationship with prostitution. Outright physical assault and harassment of streetwalkers and masseuses (of the shadier sort of parlor) by the police varies from locale to locale, and their personalities. The police are human and can be brutal towards sex workers for the same reasons customers can: they can't control themselves; they calculate they can get away with it toward those engaged in illegal activity; or they may really believe the prostitute deserves it. The cops' hostility and mistreatment can also take passive-aggressive forms, as when they decline to come to the aid of a prostitute in distress.

Online platforms provide a measure of protection for in-person sex work but are a double-edged sword. Though Twitter prohibits ads for prostitution, escorts skirt around this by providing their private contact information. America's most liberal major social media site is in fact useful as a tool for weeding out bad customers. Sex workers have a way of getting around; they tend to all know and look out for each other, wherever they hail from. Trolls who harass their Twitter feeds, would-be customers who are rude, and the odd client from hell who slips through their screening process, soon find themselves blacklisted as their screenshots and identities go viral in the adult Twittersphere. But if you've ever wondered why escort services are allowed to advertise at all when prostitution is supposed to be illegal, the police depend upon these ads to gain information about sex workers and surveil them.

In *Playing the Whore: The Work of Sex Work*, sex-worker activist Melissa Gira Grant's theory of "acceptable violence" is a useful way of framing the issue of sex work's fraught relationship with the law. Prostitutes are tolerated, even necessitated or "produced," for the benefit of society so that they can be punished as negative exemplars of dissipation and harm, and law-abiding citizens made fearful and attentive to the moral imperatives of the state:

> The stigma and violence faced by sex workers are far greater harms than sex work itself....Prostitution marks out the far reach of what's acceptable for women and men, where rights end and violence is justice. This is accepted as the cost of protecting those most deserving of protection. Opponents of sex work decry prostitution as a violent institution, yet concede that violence is also useful to keep people from it....To truly confront this type of violence would require us to admit that we permit some violence against women to be commit-

ted in order to protect the social and sexual value of other women.

The more violent the society, the more sex workers bear the brunt of this violence. It's above all a problem in the most violent of developed nations, the United States. Not only, of course, sex workers. There is the endemic problem of male violence against women generally, and not just that inflicted by psychopaths but more pervasively, intimate-partner violence. If men find it so easy to beat up their wife or girlfriend, how much easier it must be to beat up a prostitute. Then there are all the normal, well-adjusted gentlemen who don't beat their partners, who know how to compartmentalize their rage and let off a bit of steam by channeling it away from the domestic hearth and onto the prostitute. We may forgive these men for they know not what they do (all the easier if hatred of the prostitute has our unconditional support), but I'm going to have to complicate things here. The problem is not just that of misogyny. Violence toward the prostitute is a function of fascism.

The fascist state is at its optimum when it has enough popular support to delegate its dirty work to ordinary folk. In Nazi Germany, ordinary folk were given brown uniforms and swastika armbands and called Brownshirts. In Trump's America, they are given red MAGA caps and form armed Christian militias (Villarreal). But they don't actually need uniforms and operate more effectively behind the scenes when you don't know who they are. They themselves don't have to know who they are, or that they are being employed by the state to do its bidding (all the better if they don't know, as they can be relied on to work for free). Fascism has evolved over the past century into subtler forms; it no longer crudely trumpets itself a la Nazi Germany or Imperial Japan, parading the entire nation by the nose. When it isn't outsourcing its violence to other countries in overt or covert warfare, it offloads its rage onto the disadvantaged at home—racial and ethnic minorities and sexual deviants (historically the two often

get conflated). Sexually independent women, perhaps the greatest symbolic and potentially real threat to fascism, are smacked
down through socially tolerated harassment and violence. As tolerance for such violence shrinks in the #MeToo era, other outlets
must be found. Sex workers fit the bill and are still fair game for
assault. Echoing what the Jews received at the hands of good
Germans: they've only brought it onto themselves. It's not the
police who are primarily responsible for this; this work is dele-
gated to customers. But even as the customer doesn't know why
he does it, his coiled fist released against the prostitute is not
haphazard or random but draws its thrust and power from the
state; he is himself the fist of the state.

POLYAMORY

Nothing is more logical than polyamory. Consider, for starters,
the reasons why the extended family—vertically encompassing
three generations—is superior to the nuclear family. A nuclear
family is an isolated unit, with the burden of household labor and
childrearing falling heavily on two people, the parents. The extended family adds two, three or four retired people with time on
their hands to take on these responsibilities, freeing up the parents to devote themselves to their day jobs. Grandparents are
well poised to educate children with their life experience and
wisdom; in return, surrounded by loved ones, they are less lonely,
and assistance in the event of accidents or infirmity is close at
hand. The common objections to the extended family—
intergenerational friction and the lack of privacy—do not invali-
date the extended family; it's a commentary on our distorted expectations of privacy in modern times. The generations have a
responsibility to get along with each other. Finally, by pooling
resources, the family saves money. This can cut both ways. In the
U.S., retirement pensions seem to be on the way out as more and
more people are confined to jobs in the gig economy, and paltry

Social Security payments can force the retired to depend on their children financially. However, this is not always so; many grandparents may be in a better position to help out their children than the other way around. In any case, the U.S. is not representative of most countries, which tend to have better social safety nets.

Polyamory reaps the benefits of the extended family by extending it horizontally, joining two families into one. Or more than two families, the only constraints being the size of the kitchen and the number of bedrooms and bathrooms, and the degree of complexity members are willing to take on in managing a many-parented family. The same advantages of the vertically extended family apply to the horizontally extended, or polyamorous family, and more: the conviviality of a big dinner table and the relish of food prepared by different hands; the costs saved from the pooling of resources, along with the pooling of skills, trades, and backgrounds; greater opportunity for social and sexual interaction for those often denied these, the elderly and the severely disabled; the benefits to children of a multiparent household[23]; and the checks and balances of differing adult viewpoints and outlooks, seeding a wider array of ideas and safeguarding against tyrannical parenting and neurotic behaviors hidden away in the isolated nuclear family.

I would add that my characterization of the insular nuclear family as potentially harmful to its members could be seen as an understatement. Wilhelm Reich called the nuclear family a "factory" or "incubator" of fascism, a point starkly elaborated by Shiri Eisner:

> Most violence perpetrated against women, as well as children, happens within heteronormative families. Intimate violence, sexual violence, spousal rape, spousal murder, incest,

---

[23] Attested by a fifteen-year longitudinal study by the sociologist Elisabeth Sheff.

violence against children, and economic violence are only some of the horrors that marriage is designed to contain....Marriage is also used as an instrument of control by the state and government. Dividing its subjects into minimal units keeps people as separate from one another as possible. Minimizing communities in this way makes it harder for people to oppose the state or government, keeping it safe from civil uprisings. In addition, heteronormative families serve as convenient production units, manufacturing productive citizens, workers for the capitalist system, and soldiers for the military. Most people learn to love and serve their governments first and foremost within their families, through "educational values" such as patriotism, nationalism, militarism, and capitalism.

The many-parented family household is not immune to these same influences and may be susceptible to something even worse—intentional group coercion and cult formation. However, people who are consciously polyamorous usually carry within them democratic principles and a healthy sense of communitarianism as a check against this.

Now, polyamory may stop here, contenting itself with the communal meshing and mingling of several families and their children in the daytime, while each nuclear unit retreats to its private sphere at night. Or it may go further. If two couples (I'll keep things simple) willingly go to the length of merging their daily lives and perhaps their finances as well, if mutual fondness and compatibility have brought them this far, it's not such a stretch to imagine them popping open another bottle of wine and interacting on a more intimate level—romantically and sexually. Indeed, to become "nesting partners" may have been the purpose all along and the reason why they sought each other out in the first place. Many practitioners hold that polyamory by definition requires some degree of intercouple sexual engagement; a looser definition recognizes a level of required intimacy in the mere sharing of daily lives.

Nothing is more logical than polyamory, and nothing is more radical than polyamory. Polyamory is fluid, and this is terrifying to monogamy, which is rigid. Polyamory is negotiable and allows for sexual interaction or not as the parties are so inclined; monogamy is non-negotiable. What's radical isn't so much the more daring forms of polyamory, such as the sexually communal household, "whose members," for example, "have decided that in the event of pregnancy, all the men will have parenting duties," and "the woman will get a paternity test to determine the biological father," as polyamorists Veaux and Rickert note. What's even more radical is the fluidity and elasticity of the concept itself. However carried out in practice, the very idea of polyamory is existentially threatening to monogamy; it seems to threaten love itself. This is perhaps what many people find the hardest thing to grasp about polyamory: how the burning intensity of love kindled by two people can survive the intrusion of a third person without being dispersed or snuffed out. But if we can imagine a couple as kindling a wick, we can imagine three, or four people together kindling an even brighter wick.

There is no requirement that those in poly relationships, whether involving three, four or more people, live communally; they may all live separately. A poly relationship may be as simple as a "V," with one half of a couple, the "pivot," involved with a third person or "metamour," and there is no contact between the latter and the pivot's other half. What is required and what differentiates such a triad from a traditional love triangle, or from cheating, is that all three are aware of the arrangement and approve of it. Or two poly couples may engage erotically only on occasion without it altering their normal lives, as among the polyamorous in conservative communities who are wary of coming out. This more sporadic version of polyamory might seem indistinguishable from swinging; the difference is that poly couples tend to work harder at cultivating each other on more than just the sexual plane.

There is no agreed-upon set of rules or requirements for polyamory, only the principle that human relationships can be more
fulfilling and enlivening when three or more people engage in the
same ways as monogamous couples do. Polyamory includes monogamy in that it accommodates couples who consider themselves monogamous but are polycurious and experimental
enough to loosen the shackles of sexual exclusivity. But to arrive
at this insight nonetheless constitutes a momentous, radical conceptual breakthrough: the realization that monogamy is no longer needed.

The millennia-old regime of conjugal psychological terror
known as monogamy is at long last, we hope, embarking on its
historical endgame and the opening phase of its collapse. The
best way to understand monogamy is to see it for what it is: a
faith, a dogma, a religion—the religion of monogamism. Monogamism has such a grip on society because it underlies all patriarchal religions. It even ensnares atheists. It's the Ur-religion,
molding itself from an early age to your very conception of reality
so that you are enjoined to follow its dictates without ever realiz-
ing it. You believe in exclusive happiness with one lifelong partner and only one lifelong partner for no other reason than you've
always believed it, and your parents believed it. Yet it's a belief
as illusory, arbitrary, and contrary to nature and reason as belief
in any of the garden-variety deities proffered by organized religion, distinguishable only by the different styles of rags worn by
their prophets.

Granted, many monogamous couples may be truly sufficient
unto themselves and would find the notion of tinkering experi-
mentally with their domesticity simply redundant. More power to
the lucky few who find their soulmate and stay together out of
sheer love. Nor should we discount the many who have difficulty
making it through the day, for whom life is complex enough as it
is and who would find the prospect of venturing beyond monogamy exhausting. But polyamory is an option, not an imposition.
Monogamism, by contrast, is equivalent to dictating that for ob-

scure ethical or cultural reasons, once you choose your major in college you must accept a lifelong career in the same and can only get out of it in a court of law, or that to preserve a neighborhood's pride in its long-standing residents, you may never move out of your first purchased home, or that for the sake of shielding the citizenry from corrupt foreign influences you aren't allowed to travel abroad. In any other context, this would be regarded as totalitarianism, or something akin to old-school communism. Yet you would embrace totalitarianism in marriage as common sense and blithely count yourself among the faithful.

The most potent antidote to monogamism is bisexuality, which lies at the core of polyamory. Bisexuality implies the love of a third person. One cannot be bisexual without violating traditional monogamy. When a couple brings a third person into their life in a shared sexual capacity and one is of different sex or gender, two of them are being bi. Poly relationships build on the idea of bisexuality, if not always carry it out in practice. There is a well-known conundrum in the poly movement that females are more likely to be bi than males. When a couple takes on a woman, she typically has sex with them both, but if it's a man, the two males can hardly bring themselves to get physical with each other even if their female partner desires it. I suppose there's comfort in their willingness to go this far and get naked in close proximity, but it's not an ideal state of affairs when male heterosexual anxiety straightjackets the polyamorous "throuple" from fully engaging. Then there are, of course, exclusively gay poly relationships, and gay sexuality has its own role to play in the undoing of monogamism, but I concur with Shiri Eisner that the gay rights movement's endorsement of gay marriage, as its main ticket to social respectability, is reactionary and backward: not because we would want to deny gays the same rights and benefits as the legally married, but because it further entrenches monogamy's ideology and grip over society.

Bisexuality is progressive and vital because it implies and initiates conceptual momentum. People *become* bi, not the other way around; people don't become straight after their eyes are opened. People do settle down in heterosexual marriage after experimenting with bi encounters, but they never lose the idea or the longing. In this respect polyamory is a kind of advanced bisexuality, opening up its potential, transmuting it further into something so elaborate that monogamy fades into irrelevance. But because they catalyze change, bisexuality and polyamory alike usher in uncertainty. That can be a good thing, as it makes participants work harder at their relationships rather than take them for granted. Sometimes people move on. The two couples who move in together and share each other may end up switching partners. People who embark on polyamory understand the inherent instability of multiple and simultaneous relationships. Many thrive on this shifting territory, seeking out change and personal growth through close involvement with new people and benefiting from their influence. Veaux and Rickert call this the "game-changer":

> When we open our hearts to multiple relationships, every now and then someone comes along who changes everything....They upset existing arrangements. People confronted with a game-changing relationship will not be likely to remain happy with old rules and agreements for long; the definition of a game-changing relationship is that it reshuffles priorities.

One game-changer is the portentous arrival of the exceptionally attractive person, possibly sexually and intellectually charismatic to boot, enthralling everyone. The experienced polyamorous pride themselves on their ability to manage jealousy and keep this destructive force under tight leash. Indeed, they can even take pleasure in a partner's new lover, a novel emotion dubbed "compersion." But the entrance of a hot person onto the scene inevitably stirs up fear and envy among everyone since she commands choice; she can take her pick of anyone and she knows it (I take the female as my example but it could equally apply to the male). Even when she devotes herself to one "polycule," her commitment is provisional; she has nothing to lose and everything to gain by moving on to ever more interesting people. Her privilege may make her impatient, preventing her from reciprocating intimacy and inadvertently sparking tension among the rest.

This is where sex work has a role to play in polyamory. By offering her body for a fee, the hot female can apportion her intimacy more evenly among everyone. This would tamp down jealousy and competitiveness as she would be limiting and regulating her multiple ties in a transparent way. It would also solve the problem of the "unicorn," polyamory's ironic term for the virtually unattainable, and hence mythical, hot female willing to satisfy hetero couples' common fantasy for their perfect bi plaything— unattainable because no one wants to be used in this way. Unless, that is, for a little tip.

I suspect that many polyamorists would be aghast at this suggestion, just as they would squirm at being yoked to an essay on pornography and prostitution. Isn't the whole purpose of polyamory to open up sexual possibilities beyond the confines of monogamy in an organic way? Wouldn't this laudable goal be contaminated and poisoned by money? But the objection to sex work is predicated on nothing other than the tautological reason that it is objectionable. With a bit of imagination, we are free to reject the presupposition, the prejudice that sex work is bad, and view it instead not as a problem but as a solution to a problem.

Sex work and polyamory are not incompatible. They are both logical solutions to the intractable problem of monogamy. They add two indispensable battalions to the forces of sexual transgression in its war against conventional propriety and the sexual fascism at the heart of convention. It's a culture war, but with real casualties. In the trenches in their harlequin uniforms of golden hair, silver lipstick, and sequined miniskirts are the most emboldened of the sexual radicals, trans women prostitutes, especially Black trans women, who visibly embody everything that's insulting and frightening to conventional morality—racial antagonism, sexual commerce, gender confusion—which lashes out at these beautiful souls and dumps their bodies in back alleys. Forty-seven cases of murdered transgendered people were reported in the U.S. in 2021, the highest number yet and likely an underestimate (Cohen). As polyamorists Easton and Liszt remark, "many of our dearest friends work in the sex industry, doing essential and positive work healing the wounds inflicted by our sex-negative culture." The transgendered can "tell us a lot about how differently other people treat you when they see you as a man, or as a woman. Perforce, transgendered people become experts at living in a very hostile world. No other sexual minority is more likely to suffer direct physical oppression in the form of queer-bashing."

Perhaps the most liberal country in its attitudes to the transgendered is Thailand, where trans people are often celebrated in the media, and violence against them is comparatively rare. The problems that do exist are poignant and reminiscent of the accounts of people in the porn industry (cited in Lee above), in their often sad stories of coming out to shocked family and friends, particularly those hailing from the conservative countryside. On the other hand, it's a measure of social progress when the ramifications of choosing a stigmatized sexual orientation result not in violence but a family squabble. The parents typically come round anyway and end up accepting them (Aldous & Sereemongkonpol).

Sexual transgression is routinely condemned and punished by society, all the more severely the healthier and more liberatory its forms of expression are. Hiatuses of relative sexual freedom are always contingent and ready to backslide as the forces of reaction gain the upper hand. Gay rights have made dramatic advances not only in the developed West but in many countries over the past half-century. It's easy to forget how atrociously gays had been treated in the U.S. and the UK prior to that when the revelation a person was homosexual was utterly scandalous and dev-astating to their career. Recall for one the great Englishman Alan Turing's (possibly suicidal) death from chemical castration in 1954, whose code-breaking genius helped turn the tide against the Nazis in World War Two, due to another brand of fascism, the sexual fascism of the British Government. Sexual liberation, including the freedom to practice polyamory, has followed not so much from the "free love" culture of the sixties as from Stonewall 1969 and the arduous political fight for these rights spearheaded by gays and the transgendered. Everyone who regards sexual freedom as important—you don't have to be gay to appreciate this—owes the gay rights movement ongoing gratitude for their courage and sacrifices, which we all benefit from. I would add that those fond of ridiculing free love as a hippie cliché should beware of ventriloquizing the voice of the state.

Polyamory is still relatively new—the term wasn't coined un-til the 1970s—so new that many non-English-speaking countries don't even have a word for it, and their poly people have been able to slip under the radar. But it has existed as an unspoken phenomenon surely since time immemorial. In Imperial Chi-na, *zhao fu yang fu*, or "enlisting one husband to support the oth-er husband," euphemistically referred to the practice of an im-poverished couple inviting a better-off single male to move in with them and share the wife's bed in exchange for his economic help or labor. Typically the arrangement was only for mutual convenience, but as Matthew Sommer documents in *Polyandry and Wife-Selling in Qing Dynasty China*, in many instances the wife was sexually fulfilled, transforming the relationship from a polyandrous to a "polyamorous" one; things could take a violent turn if she transferred her affection to the new partner. While the government forbade polyandry and punished it harshly, local authorities and communities tended to look the other way. Today in China, since the "Professor Ma" scandal of 2012 (referring to a man nabbed for recruiting people online for sex parties), under the "group licentiousness" law it's illegal for more than two people to have sex together and those caught can expect several years in prison. Polyamory in China is thus banned without being named, the authorities clearly preferring that the practice remain unnamable and unthinkable, although I have heard the apt term *duo ai*, or "many loves," used colloquially.

Over the past decade or two, polyamory has gotten increasing exposure in the mainstream American media. Online poly organizations have proliferated on Facebook and Twitter. The echo chamber of like-minded enthusiasts can nonetheless be misleading, and whether this trend will gain more traction or hit a wall is too early to say. My impression on the ground is that most people, and I mean educated liberals I know who in other respects are openminded in their outlook, find the idea of polyamory bizarre and off-putting if they've heard of it at all. I have to be very careful how to even broach the topic without seeming to recruit them or otherwise spooking them.

It's also for this reason, I believe, that no major, incisive, politically informed publication on polyamory has yet come out that I am aware of. Instead, the books that have come out have been calibrated to narrow readerships of the already converted. Dossie Easton and Catherine A. Liszt's *The Ethical Slut: A Guide to Infinite Sexual Possibilities*, published in 1997, was the first book to embrace the topic and reach a receptive audience (Liszt scrapped her pseudonym for her real name, Janet W. Hardy, in their 2017 edition). Written in a breezy feel-good style suited to sex-positive New Age feminists, the book remains fresh and startling in its frank advocacy of no-holds-barred multi-partner sexual experimentation, but without much to say about real-world polyamory's traps and minefields. Franklin Veaux and Eve Rickert stepped in to fill this gap with *More Than Two: A Practical Guide to Ethical Polyamory*, downplaying the erotics to focus on the emotional complexities of juggling simultaneous relationships. At once exhaustive and exhausting, their tome covers every possible chemical reaction from resentment to rage which three or four people can be guaranteed to cook up with the lowering of territorial barriers, and the best advice the authors can muster in response with their decades of experience.

Both books have had a tricky balancing act in appealing to the more adventurous among average readers while not alienating too many with polyamory's stark implications, which candidly put, invite you to overturn your familiar reality and join the sexual avant-garde in weakening or dissolving altogether the obligatory ties of matrimony. Consequently, they are at pains to avoid situating polyamory alongside other radical sexualities with which it has more in common than it acknowledges. What aligns all of these movements is the difficult but inevitable process of coming out—and defending oneself from the potentially damaging results of coming out. It's quite revealing to see how key texts in practices as varied as bisexuality and transsexuality (Aldous & Sereemongkonpol; Eisner), the lesbian BDSM and leather scenes (Rubin), prostitution (Davina; Grant), pornography (Lee), and polyamory (Easton & Liszt; Veaux & Rickert), to name just a few of the many titles in publication, address this duty in such similar ways. As Eisner puts it in *Bi: Notes for a Bisexual Revolution*:

> Oppression of any one group doesn't happen in isolation, but parallels, draws from, and intersects with that of others....The bisexual community is also shared by transgender and gender-queer people; nonmonogamous, polyamorous, slutty or promiscuous people; sex workers; BDSM practitioners; drug users; HIV+ people, disabled, chronically ill and mentally disabled people; working-class people, migrants, illegal immigrants, refugees, racialized people, and many, many more.

If polyamorists have long sought to sneak into mainstream respectability by presenting themselves as reassuringly ordinary white-picket-fence neighbors, what they really need to do is join up in political action with other sexual radicals to shout down and combat institutionalized monogamy's power to destroy lives. I'll give the last word to Easton and Liszt on the precarious situation of polyamory in the very country where it has made the most headway:

> There absolutely are costs to being out. Polyamory is not a protected status; people can lose their housing or their jobs if they have a hostile landlord or boss. If you are divorced and not on good terms with your ex, custody of your children may be at stake....Children also complicate whether to be out publicly. Depending on where you live, you and your kids may experience stigma, and you may even face legal threats. Particularly in some conservative areas of the United States, polyamory can be and is used as a powerful weapon in custody battles.

BIBLIOGRAPHY

Agren, David. "Mexico sues US gunmakers in unprecedented bid to stop weapons crossing border." *The Guardian*, 4 Aug. 2021.

Aldous, Susan, and Pornchai Sereemongkonpol. *Ladyboys: The Secret World of Thailand's Third Gender*. Maverick House, 2008.

Anguiano, Dani, and Johana Bhuiyan. "Video shows police dog severely mauls Uber driver who missed car payments." *The Guardian*, 5 Jan. 2022.

Arment, Jason. "Poetry and sex work: An interview with Dylan Krieger," *The Big Smoke*, 19 May 2021. https://thebigsmoke.com/2021/05/19/poetry-and-sex-work-an-interview-with-dylan-krieger/

Arsenal: Surrealist Subversion. Edited by Franklin Rosemont. Black Swan Press, 1989.

Baker, Katie J. M. "More than 180 women have reported sexual assaults at Massage Envy." *Buzzfeed News*, 26 Nov. 2017.

Baker, Sinéad. "Chinese city orders all indoor pets belonging to COVID-19 patients in one neighborhood to be killed." *Business Insider*, 30 March 2022.

Banco, Erin. "'It is embarrassing': CDC struggles to track Covid cases as Omicron looms." *Politico*, 19 Dec. 2021.

Bandoim, Lana. "Study: Almost half of new cancer patients lose their entire life savings." *Insider*, 24 Oct. 2018.

Banks, Gabrielle. "Many surprised at sentence for ex-Baylor doctor who raped a Houston hospital patient." *Houston Chronicle*, 17 Aug. 2018.

Banks, Russell. *Lost Memory of Skin*. Ecco, 2011.

Barcan, Ruth. "Dirty spaces separation, concealment, and shame in the public toilet." *Toilet: Public Restrooms and the Politics of Sharing*, edited by Harvey Molotch and Laura Norén. New York U Press, 2010.

Bauer, Shane. *American Prison: A Reporter's Undercover Jour-*

ney into the Business of Punishment. Penguin, 2018.

Baum, Vicki. *Love and Death in Bali.* Tuttle, 1937.

Benjamin, Medea. "The U.S. drops an average of 46 bombs a day: Why should the world see us as a force for peace?" *Salon*, 11 Jan. 2022.

"Berlin's new toilets: Would you use a women's urinal?" *BBC News*, 11 Aug. 2017.

Bernstein, Elizabeth. *Brokered Subjects: Sex, Trafficking, and the Politics of Freedom.* U of Chicago, 2019.

Bhardwaj, Naina. "A prisoner was 'covered in filth and barking like a dog' after 600 days of solitary confinement in a Virginia jail." *Business Insider*, 17 Apr. 2021.

Bosque, Melissa del. "Checkpoint nation: Border agents are expanding their reach into the country's interior." *Harper's Magazine*, Oct. 2018.

Botella, Elena. "I worked at Capital One for five years. This is how we justified piling debt on poor customers." *The New Republic*, 2 Oct. 2019.

Brakke, Paul. *The Costly U.S. Prison System: Too Costly in Dollars, National Prestige and Lives.* American Leadership Books, 2017.

Brooks, Brad. "Ohio sheriff's deputy charged with murder for shooting Black man in the back." *Reuters*, 2 Dec. 2021.

Brooks, Brad. "Texas governor calls for investigation into 'pornography' in school libraries." *Reuters*, 10 Nov. 2021.

Brooks, Kim. "Motherhood in the age of fear." *The New York Times*, 27 July 2018.

Bryan, Nicola. "TikTok school abuse: Teachers quitting over paedophile slurs." *BBC News*, 23 Nov. 2021.

Burke, Minyvonne. "Deaf Colorado man arrested for not complying with police that he couldn't understand, suit says." *NBC News*, 29 Sept. 2021.

Carter, Tom. "Unsavory elements." *Unsavory Elements: Stories of Foreigners on the Loose in China*, edited by Tom Carter. Earnshaw Books, 2013.

Case, Mary Anne. "Why not abolish laws of urinary segregation?" *Toilet: Public Restrooms and the Politics of Sharing*, edited by Harvey Molotch and Laura Norén. New York U Press, 2010.

Cochrane, Joe. "Indonesia approves castration for sex offenders who prey on children." *The New York Times*, 25 May 2016.

Cohen, Li. "2021 marks deadliest year yet for transgender people in the U.S." *CBS News*, 20 Nov. 2021.

Conway, Sarah. Twitter thread reporting hunger strike at Logan Correctional Center, 12 June 2021 (@sarahanneconway).

Cook, Isham. *Massage and the Writer: Essays on Asian Massage*. Magic Theater Books, 2014.

"Coronavirus pandemic prompts global mental health crisis as millions feel alone, anxious and depressed," *Democracy Now!*, 14 May 2020.

"Coronavirus: Zambia sex workers praised for contact tracing," *BBC News*, 10 May 2020.

Cramer, Maria. "At 18, he had consensual gay sex. Montana wants him to stay a registered offender." *The New York Times*, 15 May 2021.

"Crime rate in the United States in 2020, by type of crime." Statista, 2021. https://www.statista.com/statistics/202703/crime-rate-in-the-usa-by-type-of-crime/

Darling, Diana. *The Painted Alphabet*. Editions Didier Millet, 1992.

Dastagir, Alia E. "What the public keeps getting wrong about pedophilia." *USA Today*, 11 Jan. 2022.

Davies, Robert H. *Prisoner 13498: A True Story of Love, Drugs and Jail in Modern China*. Mainstream Publishing, 2002.

Davina, Lola. *Thriving in Sex Work: Heartfelt Advice for Staying Sane in the Sex Industry*. Erotic as Power Press, 2017.

"Detention of migrant children." National Conference of State Legislatures, 24 Nov. 2020. https://www.ncsl.org/research/immigration/detention-of-migrant-children.aspx

Dewan, Shaila. "Probation may sound light, but punishments can land hard." *The New York Times*, 2 Aug. 2015.

Easton, Dossie, and Liszt, Catherine A. *The Ethical Slut: A Guide to Infinite Sexual Possibilities*. Greenery Press, 1997.

"The Economics of Incarceration," Prison Policy Initiative (https://www.prisonpolicy.org/research/economics_of_incarcer ation).

Eisen, Lauren-Brooke. "Charging inmates perpetuates mass in-carceration." Brennan Center for Justice, 2015. https://www.brennancenter.org/sites/default/files/blog/Chargi ng_Inmates_Mass_Incarceration.pdf

Eisner, Shiri. *Bi: Notes for a Bisexual Revolution*. Seal Press, 2013.

Eliot, George. Middlemarch. Penguin Books, 2015 (orig. pub. 1871-72).

Engels, Friedrich. *The Origin of the Family, Private Property and the State*. International Publishers Co., 1972 (orig. pub. 1884).

Fadulu, Lola. "As hunger spreads with pandemic, government takes timid steps." *The New York Times*, 13 May 2020.

Faraj, Jabril. "Former sex offenders left out in the cold by city residency restrictions." *Urban Milwaukee*, 15 Dec. 2015.

Farley, Lara Geer. "The Adam Walsh Act: The scarlet letter of the 21st century." *Washburn Law Journal*. Winter, 2008.

Fausto-Sterling, Anne. "The Five Sexes: Why male and female are not enough." *The Sciences*, March/April 1993.

Ferner, Matt. "The full cost of incarceration in the U.S. is over $1 trillion, study finds." *Huffington Post*, 13 Sept. 2016.

Firestone, Shulamith. *The Dialectic of Sex: The Case for Femi-nist Revolution*. William Morrow & Company, 1970.

Flowers, Garin. "Report: U.S. gun injuries result in at least $1B in health care costs per year." *Yahoo News*, 15 July 2021.

Foster, Caitlin. "9 times Trump or his top officials threatened to attack or nuke other countries in 2018." *Business Insider Australia*, 19 Dec. 2018.

Francis, Marquise. "Rikers Island, one of America's most notorious jails, is now one of its deadliest." *Yahoo! News*, 6 Nov. 2021.

Fransdottir, Edda, and Jeffrey A. Butts "Who pays for gun violence? You do," John Jay College of Criminal Justice Research and Evaluation Center, 11 May 2020 https://johnjayrec.nyc/2020/05/11/whopays/

Gan, Nectar. "China is installing surveillance cameras outside people's front doors and sometimes inside their homes," *CNN*, 28 Apr. 2020.

Germain, Atahabih. "A 4-foot-8 Black woman was accosted by group of boys, minutes later a Louisiana deputy was flinging her by her hair in shocking video; investigation launched." *Atlanta Black Star*, 21 Oct. 2021.

Gershenson, Olga. "The restroom revolution: Unisex toilets and campus politics." *Toilet: Public Restrooms and the Politics of Sharing*, edited by Harvey Molotch and Laura Norén. New York U Press, 2010.

Gibson, Carrie. *El Norte: The Epic and Forgotten Story of Hispanic North America*. Atlantic Monthly Press, 2019.

Gibson, James W. *The Perfect War: Technowar in Vietnam*. Atlantic Monthly Press, 1986.

Gilbert, Elizabeth. *Eat, Pray, Love: One Woman's Search for Everything Across Italy, India and Indonesia*. Penguin, 2006.

Gleeson, Scott. "A Texas man took COVID-19 tests at an emergency room. Then, he got a bill for $54,000." *USA Today*, 30 Sept. 2021.

Gold, Hal. *Japan's Infamous Unit 731: Firsthand Accounts of Japan's Wartime Human Experimentation Program*. Tuttle, 1996.

Gopnik, Adam. "The caging of America: Why do we lock up so many people?" *The New Yorker*, 30 Jan. 2012.

Gounder, Celine. "The death toll says it all." *The Atlantic*, 17 Dec. 2021.

Graeber, David. *Debt: The First 5,000 Years*. Melville House,

2011.

Grant, Melissa Gira. *Playing the Whore: The Work of Sex Work.* Verso, 2014.

Halperin, David M. "Introduction: The war on sex." *The War on Sex*, edited by David M. Halperin and Trevor Hoppe. Duke UP, 2017.

Harmsen, Peter. *Nanjing 1937: Battle for a Doomed City.* Casemate, 2015.

Harmsen, Peter. *Shanghai 1937: Stalingrad on the Yangtze.* Casemate, 2015.

"Health authorities explain how choir practice caused the 'superspread' of 52 coronavirus cases in US town." *ABC*, 13 May 2020.

Hess, Corrinne. "Communities continue to rethink sex offender residency rules." *Wisconsin Public Radio*, 28 Jan. 2019.

Hinton, Elizabeth. *America on Fire: The Untold History of Political Violence and Black Rebellion Since the 1960s.* Liveright Publishing, 2021.

Horesh, Theo. *The Fascism This Time and the Global Future of Democracy.* Cosmopolis Press, 2020.

"ICE detains man driving pregnant wife to deliver baby, says he is wanted for homicide in Mexico." *CBS News*, 18 Aug. 2018.

"Incarceration in Norway." Wikipedia.
    https://en.wikipedia.org/wiki/Incarceration_in_Norway

Kaba, Mariame. *We Do This 'Til We Free Us: Abolitionist Organizing and Transforming Justice.* Haymarket Books, 2021.

Karakatsanis, Alec. *Usual Cruelty: The Complicity of Lawyers in the Criminal Injustice System.* The New Press, 2019.

Keshner, Andrew. "Texas abortion law: $10,000 penalty could incentivize 'bounty hunters' to make 'tens of thousands of dollars.'" *MarketWatch*, 3 Sept. 2021.

Kim, Nemo. "South Korea struggles to contain new outbreak amid anti-gay backlash." *The Guardian*, 11 May 2020.

Kira, Alexander. *The Bathroom.* Rev. ed., Viking, 1976.

Kliff, Sarah. "Covid killed his father. Then came $1 million in medical bills." *The New York Times*, 21 May 2021.

Kliff, Sarah, and Margot Sanger-Katz. "For surprise medical bills, it's the beginning of the end." *The New York Times*, 1 July 2021.

Korecki, Natasha. "Illinois governor profits off ICE detention center contracts." *Politico*, 9 July 2018.

Korn, Melissa, and Andrea Fuller. "'Financially hobbled for life': The elite master's degrees that don't pay off." *The Wall Street Journal*, 8 July 2021.

Krieger, Dylan. *Giving Godhead.* Delete Press, 2017.

Lal, Vinay. *The Fury of COVID-19: The Politics, Histories, and Unrequited Love of the Coronavirus.* Pan Macmillan, 2020.

Lam, Elene. "Anti-racism: Asian massage and sex workers should not be left behind." *Ricochet*, 28 Mar. 2021.

Lancaster, Roger N. *Sex Panic and the Punitive State.* U California Press, 2011.

Lantry, Lauren, and Cheyenne Haslett. "Texas woman faces jail time after being convicted of voting illegally while on supervised release in 2016." *ABC News*, 19 June 2021.

Lavin, Talia. "QAnon, blood libel, and the Satanic panic." *The New Republic*, 29 Sept. 2020.

Lee, Jiz (ed.). *Coming Out Like a Porn Star: Essays on Pornography, Protection, and Privacy.* Three L Media, 2015.

LeMoon, Laura. "Opinion: Prostitution and the city—Seattle's 'End Demand' problem." *South Seattle Emerald*, 18 Nov. 2021. https://southseattleemerald.com/2021/11/18/opinion-prostitution-and-the-city-seattles-end-demand-problem/?amp

Levine, Judith. "Sympathy for the devil: Why progressives haven't helped the sex offender, why they should, and how they can." *The War on Sex*, edited by David M. Halperin and Trevor Hoppe. Duke UP, 2017.

Levine, Judith, and Erica R. Meiners. *The Feminist and the Sex Offender: Confronting Sexual Harm, Ending State Violence.* Verso Books, 2020.

Levine, Sam. "Texas man who waited seven hours at polls is

charged with voting illegally." *The Guardian*, 9 July 2021.

Levitan, Corey, and Bettmann/Corbis, "You might be a sex offender and not even know it!" *Men's Health*, 19 May 2015.

Lewis, Nicole, and Beatrix Lockwood. "The hidden cost of incarceration." The Marshall Project, 17 Dec. 2019
https://www.themarshallproject.org/2019/12/17/the-hidden-
cost-of-incarceration

Littlewood, Ian. *Sultry Climates: Travel and Sex*. J. Murray,
2001.

MacKinnon, Catharine. "Trafficking, prostitution, and inequality." *Harvard Civil Rights-Civil Liberties Law Review,
46* (2011).

Macmillan, Douglas, and Abha Bhattarai. "Police crackdowns on
illicit massage businesses pose harms to the women they aim
to help." *The Washington Post*, 3 Apr. 2021.

Madani, Doha. "Breastfeeding mother says officials took her baby
at immigrant detention center." *Huffington Post*, 13 June
2018.

Manson, Joshua. "How many people are in solitary confinement
today?" *Solitary Watch*, 4 Jan. 2019
https://solitarywatch.org/2019/01/04/how-many-people-are-in-
solitary-today/

Marcus, Josh. "'I'm speechless': Video of Atlanta police kicking
handcuffed woman in face leaves family 'horrified.'" *The Independent,* 28 July 2021.

Mayer, Arno J. *Why Did the Heavens Not Darken? The "Final
Solution" in History*. Pantheon, 1988.

Mays, Jeff. "New York City collects record $1.9 billion in fines
and fees." *DNA Info*, 24 Mar. 2016.

McDade, Aaron. "Author says outcry over book on preventing sex
abuse partly linked to their trans identity." *Newsweek*, 24
Nov. 2021.

McKay, Michael. "How many kids are on the sex offender registry?" National Association for Rational Sex Offense Laws, 12
June 2018. https://narsol.org/2018/06/how-many-kids-are-on-

the-sex-offender-registry/

McPhee, Colin. *A House in Bali*. Pickle Partners, 1946.

Melville, Herman. *Typee: A Peep at Polynesian Life*. Penguin Books, 1996 (orig. pub. 1846).

Meursault, Arthur. *Party Members*. Camphor Press, 2016.

Molotch, Harvey. "On not making history: What NYU did with the toilet and what it means for the world." *Toilet: Public Restrooms and the Politics of Sharing*, edited by Harvey Molotch and Laura Norén, New York U Press, 2010.

"More than 9,000 anti-Asian incidents have been reported since the pandemic began." *The Associated Press*, 12 Aug. 2021.

Morris, Nathaniel P. "Detention without data: Public tracking of civil commitment." *Psychiatry Online*, 22 May 2020. https://ps.psychiatryonline.org/doi/10.1176/appi.ps.202000212

Mozur, Paul, and Aaron Krolik. "A surveillance net blankets China's cities, giving police vast powers." *The New York Times*, 17 Dec. 2019.

Niemeyer, Kenneth. "Chicago police officers raiding the wrong house pointed guns at two young girls, then tried to cover it up, lawsuit alleges." *Insider*, 5 Aug. 2021.

Nir, Sarah Maslin. "Inside fentanyl's mounting death toll: 'This is poison.'" *The New York Times*, 20 Nov. 2021.

Nir, Sarah Maslin. "A 7-year-old was accused of rape. Is arresting him the answer?" *The New York Times*, 3 June 2021.

No easy answers: Sex offender laws in the U.S. Human Rights Watch, Sept. 2007. http://hrw.org/reports/2007/us0907/us0907web.pdf

Norberg, Kathryn. "The libertine whore: Prostitution in French pornography from Margot to Juliette." *The Invention of Pornography: Obscenity and the Origins of Modernity, 1500-1800*, edited by Lynn Hunt. Zone Books, 1996.

Nunca Mas: The Report of the Argentine National Commission on the Disappeared, English and Spanish edition. Farrar Straus & Giroux, 1986.

Ockerman, Emma. "She tried to steal $15 pants as a teen. The fines devastated her family." *Vice*, 18 June 2021.

Oladipo, Gloria. "More than half of US police killings are mislabeled or not reported, study finds." *The Guardian*, 1 Oct. 2021.

Oudekerk, Barbara, and Danielle Kaeble. "Probation and parole in the United States, 2019." U.S. Department of Justice, July 2021
https://bjs.ojp.gov/sites/g/files/xyckuh236/files/media/docume nt/ppus19.pdf

Paxton, Robert O. *The Anatomy of Fascism*. Vintage, 2004.

"The Peequal: Will the new women's urinal spell the end of queues for the ladies'?" *The Guardian*, 7 June 2021.

Phippen, J. Weston. "Kill every buffalo you can! Every buffalo dead is an Indian gone." *The Atlantic*, 14 May 2016.

Press, Eyal. "A fight to expose the hidden human costs of incarceration." *The New Yorker*, 16 Aug. 2021.

Przybylski, Roger. "Recidivism of Adult Sexual Offenders." U.S. Department of Justice, July 2015.
https://smart.ojp.gov/sites/g/files/xyckuh231/files/media/docu ment/recidivismofadultsexualoffenders.pdf

Quintana, Chris. "We found two dozen massage schools tied to prostitution or fraud. Here's what to know." *USA Today*, 12 July 2021.

Rabuy, Bernadette, and Daniel Kopf. "Detaining the poor: How money bail perpetuates an endless cycle of poverty and jail time." Prison Policy Initiative, 10 May 2016.
https://www.prisonpolicy.org/reports/incomejails.html

Reich, Wilhelm. *The Mass Psychology of Fascism*, translated by Mary Boyd Higgins. Farrar, Straus and Giroux, 2013 (orig. pub. 1933).

Reid, Daniel P. *Shots from the Hip, Vol. 1: Sex, Drugs and the Tao*. Lamplight Books, 2019.

Reid, Daniel P. *The Tao of Health, Sex, and Longevity: A Modern Practical Guide to the Ancient Way*. Revised edition, Atria Books, 2011 (orig. pub. 1988).

Rhodes, Richard. *Masters of Death: The SS-Einsatzgruppen and the Invention of the Holocaust.* Knopf, 2002.

Rogers, Tom. "My own pupils targeted me in the TikTok paedophile craze—now I can't go back to our school." *The Telegraph*, 23 Nov. 2021.

Rubin, Gayle S. *Deviations: A Gayle Rubin Reader.* Duke UP, 2011.

Samuel, Geoffrey. *The Origins of Yoga and Tantra: Indic Religions to the Thirteenth Century.* Cambridge UP, 2008.

Sandoval, Edgar, and Tim Arango. "Complaints against Texas' juvenile prisons include violence and sex abuse." *The New York Times*, 15 Oct. 2021.

Santana, Rebecca, et al. "316 people are shot every day in America. Here are 5 stories." *The Associated Press*, 24 July 2021.

Sawa, Dale Berning. "Ballaké Sissoko: Picking up the pieces after US customs broke his kora." *The Guardian*, 7 Apr. 2021.

Sawyer, Wendy, and Peter Wagner. "Mass Incarceration: The Whole Pie 2020." Prison Policy Initiative, 24 Mar. 2020. https://www.prisonpolicy.org/reports/pie2020.html

Schick, Irvin C. *The Erotic Margin: Sexuality and Spatiality in Alterist Discourse.* Verso, 1999.

Sedaris, David. "David Sedaris: Chicken toenails, anyone?" *The Guardian*, 15 July 2011.

Sharaf, Myron. *Fury on Earth: A Biography of Wilhelm Reich.* St. Martin's, 1983.

Sharlet, Jeff. "'He's the Chosen One to run America': Inside the cult of Trump, his rallies are church and he is the Gospel." *Vanity Fair*, 18 June 2020.

Sheff, Elisabeth. *The Polyamorists Next Door: Inside Multiple-Partner Relationships and Families.* Rowman & Littlefield, 2013.

Shirer, William L. *The Rise and Fall of the Third Reich: A History of Nazi Germany.* Simon & Schuster, 1960.

"Should I be worried by indecent exposure and public urination crimes?" Gravel & Associates. Michigan Sex Crimes Lawyers.

https://www.michigan-sex-offense.com/public-urination.html

Simmons, Thomas. "A poetry collection born of fury, sex and trauma." *The New York Times*, 3 Aug. 2017.

Snedeker, Rick. *Holy Smoke: How Christianity Smothered the American Dream*. Station Square, 2020.

Sommer, Matthew H. *Polyandry and Wife-Selling in Qing Dynasty China: Survival Strategies and Judicial Interventions*. U California Press, 2015.

"South Korea to use facial recognition to track COVID-19 patients." *Al Jazeera*, 13 Dec. 2021.

Span, Paula, "Looking to tackle prescription overload." *The New York Times*, 7 June 2021.

Spitz, Vivien. *Doctors from Hell: The Horrific Account of Nazi Experiments on Humans*. Sentient, 2005.

Stanley, Jason. *How Fascism Works: The Politics of Us and Them*. Random House, 2018.

Stargardt, Nicholas. *The German War: A Nation Under Arms, 1939-1945*. Basic Books, 2015.

Stillman, Sarah. "Get out of jail, Inc. Does the alternatives-to-incarceration industry profit from injustice?" *The New Yorker,* 23 June 2014.

Stillman, Sarah. "The List. When juveniles are found guilty of sexual misconduct, the sex-offender registry can be a life sentence." *The New Yorker*, 14 Mar. 2016.

Sullivan, Eileen. "'It should not have happened': Asylum officers detail migrants' accounts of abuse." *The New York Times*, 21 Oct. 2021.

Sun, Lena H. "50 hospitals charge uninsured more than 10 times cost of care, study finds." *The Washington Post*, June 8, 2015.

Sverdlov, Leon. "Benjamin Netanyahu suggests microchipping kids, slammed by experts," *Jerusalem Post*, 8 May 2020.

Sweetman, David. *Gauguin: A Life*. Simon & Schuster, 1995.

Szekely, Peter, and Nathan Layne. "Police 'executed' black man in North Carolina shooting, lawyers say." *Reuters*, 26 Apr. 2021.

"Teacher acquitted of having sex with student finds work as a waitress." *Inside Edition*, 28 Sept. 2018.

Terry, Jermont. "University of Chicago graduate who was shot and killed in robbery is identified as Dennis Shaoxiong Zheng; Vigil held at site of his murder." *CBS Chicago*, 10 Nov. 2021.

"Thai temple to build separate toilets for non-Chinese visitors after complaints: Report." *Straights Times*, 28 Feb. 2015.

Tomso, Gregory. "HIV monsters: Gay men, criminal law, and the new political economy of HIV." *The War on Sex*, edited by David M. Halperin and Trevor Hoppe. Duke UP, 2017.

"Traffic tickets are big business." National Motorists Association Blog, 12 Oct. 2007. https://ww2.motorists.org/blog/traffic-tickets-are-big-business/

United States. Bureau of Prisons. Inmate statistics. 27 Nov. 2021. https://www.bop.gov/about/statistics/statistics_inmate_race.jsp

Veaux, Franklin, and Eve Rickert. *More Than Two: A Practical Guide to Ethical Polyamory*. Thorntree Press, 2014.

Vickers, Adrian. *Bali: A Paradise Created*. Tuttle, 2012.

Villarreal, Daniel. "'Buy firearms and form Christian militias': Far Right reacts to Rittenhouse verdict." *Newsweek*, 19 Nov. 2021.

Walter, Barbara F. *How Civil Wars Start: And How to Stop Them*. Crown, 2022.

Wang, Jackie. *Carceral Capitalism*. Semiotext(e), 2018.

Weber, Christopher. "'I think she's out,' deputy says after violent arrest." *The Associated Press*, 18 Aug. 2021.

Weixel, Nathaniel. "Trump sought to 'undermine' COVID-19 response, says panel." *The Hill*, 17 Dec. 2021.

Wheeler, Cat. *Bali Daze: Freefall Off the Tourist Trail*. Tokay Press, 2013.

Wheeler, Cat. *Retired, Rewired: Living Without Adult Supervision in Bali*. CV. Bayu Graphic, 2016.

Whitehead, John W. *Battlefield America: The War on the Ameri-*

can People. SelectBooks, 2015.

Winerip, Michael. "Convicted of sex crimes, but with no victims." *The New York Times*, 26 Aug. 2020.

Yeung, Jessie, and Isaac Yee. "Tens of thousands of Singapore's migrant workers are infected. The rest are stuck in their dorms as the country opens up." *CNN*, 14 May 2020.

Yuko, Elizabeth. "The glamorous, sexist history of the women's restroom lounge." *Bloomberg CityLab*, 3 Dec. 2018.

Zitser, Joshua. "Distressing footage shows police officers dragging a man with paraplegia by his hair and throwing him to the ground during a traffic stop." *Insider*, 9 Oct. 2021.

ALSO BY ISHAM COOK

Have foreigners shaped China's history to a greater extent than has previously been acknowledged, reaching back possibly millennia? Was Confucius' most famous book, the Analects, inspired by entheogenic medicines imported from abroad, possession of which in the 1930s brought one before the firing squad in the name of Confucius? In these book review essays by Isham Cook, foreign devils, old China Hands, eccentric expatriates, and a few Chinese tell an offbeat history of China's last two centuries, with a backward glance at ancient China as told by Western mummies.

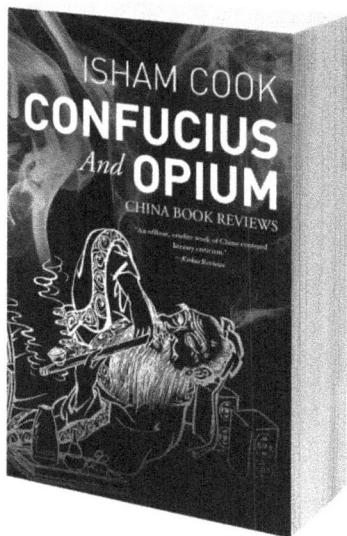

"The book slapped me awake and made me wonder about fresh ways to observe and write about a culture as intriguing, complex and so radically different from our own as China. " — David Leffman, author of *The Mercenary Mandarin*

"Confucius and Opium is an unmitigated delight...[It] reads like a better, more interesting version of [Jonathan Spence's] The Chan's Great Continent and leaves the reader eager to follow the trail of references that garnish every review. " — Arthur Meursault, author of *Party Members*

"Isham Cook's erudite, snarky, and very funny meander through books by and about Western expatriates in China serves up culture clashes that rarely see print. " — Hill Gates, author of *China's Motor: A Thousand Years of Petty Capitalism*

"Candid, edgy, fearless, and unsparing, Isham Cook writes as though with a sword in this oddly titled compendium of book reviews. Books and China are clearly life passions for him--Cook is embedded in both--making him ideally placed to comment on other writers grappling to understand and provide insight into the country, its culture, and its people. " — Graeme Sheppard, author of *A Death in Peking*